Drafting Contracts in Legal English

ASPEN COURSEBOOK SERIES

Drafting Contracts in Legal English

Cross-Border Agreements Governed by U.S. Law

CYNTHIA M. ADAMS
Clinical Professor of Law
Indiana University Robert H. McKinney School of Law

PETER K. CRAMER
Assistant Dean for Graduate Programs
Washington University School of Law in St. Louis

Wolters Kluwer
Law & Business

Published by Wolters Kluwer Law & Business in New York.

Wolters Kluwer Law & Business serves customers worldwide with CCH, Aspen Publishers, and Kluwer Law International products. (www.wolterskluwerlb.com)

To contact Customer Service, e-mail customer.service@wolterskluwer.com, call 1-800-234-1660, fax 1-800-901-9075, or mail correspondence to:

Wolters Kluwer Law & Business
Attn: Order Department
PO Box 990
Frederick, MD 21705

Printed in the United States of America.

3 4 5 6 7 8 9 0

ISBN 978-1-4548-0546-5

Library of Congress Cataloging-in-Publication Data

Adams, Cynthia M. (Cynthia Matson)
    Drafting contracts in legal English : cross-border agreements governed by U.S. law / Cynthia Matson Adams, Clinical Professor of Law, Indiana University Robert H. McKinney School of Law; Peter K. Cramer, Assistant Dean for Graduate Programs, Washington University School of Law in St. Louis.
        pages cm.—(Aspen coursebook series)
    Includes bibliographical references and index.
    ISBN 978-1-4548-0546-5 (alk. paper)
    1. Contracts—Language. 2. International business enterprises—Law and legislation. 3. Legal composition. 4. English language—Textbooks for foreign speakers. 5. Contracts—United States—Language. 6. International business enterprises—Law and legislation. I. Cramer, Peter K. II. Title.
    K840.A925 2013
    808.06'6346—dc23

                                                                        2013003015

About Wolters Kluwer Law & Business

Wolters Kluwer Law & Business is a leading global provider of intelligent information and digital solutions for legal and business professionals in key specialty areas, and respected educational resources for professors and law students. Wolters Kluwer Law & Business connects legal and business professionals as well as those in the education market with timely, specialized authoritative content and information-enabled solutions to support success through productivity, accuracy and mobility.

Serving customers worldwide, Wolters Kluwer Law & Business products include those under the Aspen Publishers, CCH, Kluwer Law International, Loislaw, Best Case, ftwilliam. com and MediRegs family of products.

CCH products have been a trusted resource since 1913, and are highly regarded resources for legal, securities, antitrust and trade regulation, government contracting, banking, pension, payroll, employment and labor, and healthcare reimbursement and compliance professionals.

Aspen Publishers products provide essential information to attorneys, business professionals and law students. Written by preeminent authorities, the product line offers analytical and practical information in a range of specialty practice areas from securities law and intellectual property to mergers and acquisitions and pension/benefits. Aspen's trusted legal education resources provide professors and students with high-quality, up-to-date and effective resources for successful instruction and study in all areas of the law.

Kluwer Law International products provide the global business community with reliable international legal information in English. Legal practitioners, corporate counsel and business executives around the world rely on Kluwer Law journals, looseleafs, books, and electronic products for comprehensive information in many areas of international legal practice.

Loislaw is a comprehensive online legal research product providing legal content to law firm practitioners of various specializations. Loislaw provides attorneys with the ability to quickly and efficiently find the necessary legal information they need, when and where they need it, by facilitating access to primary law as well as state-specific law, records, forms and treatises.

Best Case Solutions is the leading bankruptcy software product to the bankruptcy industry. It provides software and workflow tools to flawlessly streamline petition preparation and the electronic filing process, while timely incorporating ever-changing court requirements.

ftwilliam.com offers employee benefits professionals the highest quality plan documents (retirement, welfare and non-qualified) and government forms (5500/PBGC, 1099 and IRS) software at highly competitive prices.

MediRegs products provide integrated health care compliance content and software solutions for professionals in healthcare, higher education and life sciences, including professionals in accounting, law and consulting.

Wolters Kluwer Law & Business, a division of Wolters Kluwer, is headquartered in New York. Wolters Kluwer is a market-leading global information services company focused on professionals.

For my most precious treasures—Mer, Zach, and Forrest.

CMA

For Cathy, Ferb, Lena, and my parents.

DKC

Summary of Contents

Table of Contents

Chapter 11 *Exit Provisions*   237

Preface

In the summer of 2009 we sat in a coffeehouse having a friendly chat. As always, our conversation quickly turned to a shared professional passion, teaching law students whose native language is not English. For many years, we had taught legal drafting, analysis, and communication to nonnative English-speaking (NNES) law students, both in the United States and abroad. We had also made numerous presentations nationally and internationally on the pedagogy of teaching NNES students. Over cups of coffee, we lamented the fact that no drafting book on contracts addressed the linguistic and cultural challenges of the NNES student. We began discussing what the ideal book might include. At some point in the conversation we decided to combine our knowledge of linguistics, law, contract drafting and years of teaching experience to write a book to fill the gap.

As a result of this unique collaboration, we were able to create a drafting guide that not only shows **the process** for drafting contracts but also helps in understanding **how to phrase** contract provisions in correct and concise English. The text—which includes annotations explaining language, business, and legal terminology along with extensive end-of-chapter exercises—is aimed at developing a better understanding of language, drafting strategies, and U.S. contract law. Additionally, the exercises referencing contracts available on the companion website (www.aspenlawschool.com/books/Adams) will help build additional skills so important to corporate law practice: critically reviewing and revising precedent contracts. While this book was written primarily for NNES students, native English-speaking students will find the information and exercises in this book just as instructive. Therefore, to all of our readers, think of this book as your "mentor" for understanding how to draft contracts in legal English, available for consultation in and beyond the classroom, twenty-four hours a day, seven days a week.

Peter K. Cramer & Cynthia M. Adams
February 2013

Acknowledgements

Writing this book was a collaborative effort, but this book was not merely the creative product of two people. From formulating ideas for this book to its final draft, the authors relied on the wisdom and support of many people.

Cynthia is grateful to Indiana University Robert H. McKinney School of Law and Dean Gary R. Roberts for their support in this endeavor. Also, thanks to Paul N. Cox who as Vice Dean recognized the value of contract drafting courses, supported Cynthia's efforts to create new courses and corporate externships and, when the popularity of the basic drafting course grew, supported her endeavor to create additional sections of the course so that today four to five sections of contract drafting, filled with J.D. and LL.M. students, are taught every semester. She also wishes to thank her professional colleagues in the law trenches everyday, who have shared openly their experiences and wisdom gleaned from many years of corporate law practice and who are key supporters of the law school's transactional skills program: Michael Ray Smith, Norman R. Newman, Hannah K. Joseph, Ricky Pate, Michael J. Muller, and Joseph H. Marxer. Also, thank you to Richard K. Neumann, Jr., for his willingness to listen to Cynthia's early brainstorming for this book. And, warm wishes to Tina Stark, whose professional generosity and encouragement to write this book will not be forgotten. Thanks, also, to the faculty of Kenya Law School whose wonderfully candid discussions led Cynthia to key insights in writing this book, especially with regard to using legalese.

Peter would like to thank his colleagues at Washington University School of Law in St. Louis who have given him input on the book at various stages of the project, namely Mary Perry and Michael Peil. The idea for writing a book on contract drafting to NNES developed over many years and through the influence of many people. Peter would also like to thank Mark Wojcik who started his interest in the field with his book *Introduction to Legal English*. Peter also thanks his European colleagues from EULETA (The European Legal English Teachers Association) who kept his horizon open for the influence of other laws than just U.S. law. Peter would like to thank Matt Firth for his great insights on creating textbook exercises and Jim Faulkner for exposing him to the principles of contract drafting at one of his presentations in Germany. Peter would also like to thank his colleague Craig Hoffman from Georgetown Law for his insights and advice as a linguist lawyer. Last but not least, Peter would like to thank all his friends at the IEP (Intensive English Program) at Indiana University where he was able to hone his skills of teaching non-native speakers of English—ironically being a non-native speaker himself.

The authors extend a huge thank you to Juli Campagna and Helene Whalen-Bridges, as well as the anonymous reviewers, for reading drafts of this book and providing so many thoughtful, brilliant suggestions. Words cannot express how much the authors appreciated your input. Also, thank you to those at Aspen: Carol McGeehan for sharing the authors' vision; Dana Wilson for her understanding and gentle but firm guidance in keeping the authors on task when they were flagging and feeling overwhelmed; and Julie Nahil who read the manuscript with "beady eyes" and an uncanny attention to detail.

A note of appreciation also goes to the Legal Writing Institute and its many members who have given the authors so much in sharing their wealth of teaching experience and deep friendships. Their appreciation also goes to Mark Wojcik and his Global Legal Skills Conferences. Attended by legal educators and lawyers worldwide, these international conferences provided invaluable forums for the authors' research and writing.

Last, but certainly not least, the authors thank their students over the years, both at home and abroad. Without you, this book simply could not have been written.

About the Authors

Cynthia M. Adams is a Clinical Professor of Law at Indiana University Robert H. McKinney School of Law. She practiced corporate law before joining the law faculty full time. For over twenty years Professor Adams has taught various theory and skills courses, including integrated contracts, basic contract drafting, and advanced transactional drafting. Professor Adams specializes in working with nonnative English-speaking (NNES) law students and has taught theory and skills courses to NNES lawyers and students both in the United States and abroad. In addition to this book, Professor Adams coauthored *The International Lawyer's Guide to Legal Analysis and Communication in the United States* (Aspen 2008), which teaches lawyering communication skills to NNES law students.

    Peter K. Cramer, Ph.D., MA.TESOL, and LL.M., is Assistant Dean for Graduate Programs at Washington University School of Law in St. Louis. Dr. Cramer is an internationally renowned specialist on Legal English, who has taught at Georgetown University, Harvard University, and Washington University. He combines his expertise and training in common and civil law systems with his experience as a linguist and teacher of English as a Second Language.

Drafting Contracts in Legal English

Introduction

1.1 Overview

Clear. Concise. Precise. These are the hallmarks of a well-drafted contract and are at the heart of the drafting principles discussed in this book. Our goal is to give you a practical guide to drafting contracts in plain English with an emphasis on cross-border agreements and U.S. contract law. English is the working language of international business. Thus, many cross-border contracts are drafted in English, including those between non-native speakers. It wouldn't be unusual, for instance, for a Russian party and an Italian party to enter into a contract drafted in English. Because this book primarily focuses on the mechanics of drafting, the drafting principles found in these pages can apply to drafting contracts in English throughout the world. Sections 1.2 through 1.7 summarize what you can expect from this book.

> **Draft**: As used in transaction work, either (1) a noun meaning either (i) a suggested version of a document, or (ii) a written order by one party instructing another party to pay money from an account to a third party; or (2) a verb meaning to write a suggested version of a document.
>
> **Drafter** is a person who writes a suggested version of a document.

1.2 Learning to draft from scratch and from precedents

In their busy day-to-day practice, lawyers are compelled to produce a quality work product in the most time-efficient, cost-effective way possible. Thus, when faced with drafting a contract—for example, a construction loan agreement—a lawyer will likely use as a starting point a model form or a construction loan agreement from a previous business deal rather than creating an entirely new contract. Using a model form or a prior contract (often referred to as **precedent**) as the basis for drafting another contract is a reality of transactional law practice. Creating an entirely new contract without using precedents will likely take more time and cost the

> **Deal**, as used in transactional work, means an agreement between two or more parties, to transact business for their mutual benefit.

client more money. Drafting provisions without the aid of precedents is called **zero-based drafting** or *drafting from scratch*. Although lawyers will often use precedents in drafting a contract, no two business deals—or, using the earlier example, no two construction loan agreements—are identical. Inevitably, some provisions in the precedent and some provisions in the new contract will be unique to that business deal. Therefore, even when relying on precedent, lawyers will often draft some provisions from scratch.

The unique opportunity offered in this book is access to precedents in the form of a collection of 120 authentic contracts, many involving international business deals.[1] Just as a person learns a language more quickly and more thoroughly by visiting a foreign culture, you will immerse yourself in the native culture of contract drafting by visiting a large community of contract drafters. On the companion website to this book (www.aspenlawschool. com/books/Adams), you can access hundreds of pages of contracts, written by real lawyers. Keep in mind, though, there is no such thing as a perfect contract. We do not intend for provisions in these contracts to serve as models for "cutting and pasting" into your contracts. But when you work through these provisions, you will learn to think critically (an invaluable skill when reviewing contracts) and gain confidence in identifying issues in precedent and making revisions. You will gather ideas from these precedents, deleting, adding, or modifying language, as needed, with the drafting principles in this book.

Still, we also designed many exercises that ask you to draft contract provisions without using precedents because practicing zero-based drafting will quickly improve your drafting skills. Comparing precedents in many guided activities will give you the confidence to engage in zero-based drafting. Applying the drafting principles discussed in this book, you will be drafting provisions with a clarity and conciseness not found in most contracts and model forms.

1.3 Learning how to critically review contract provisions to create your own provision

Using the precedents compiled on the companion website, you will be able to evaluate the similarities and differences of related provisions across the precedents. You can work on your own or with your peers inside and outside

---

1. These contracts, along with thousands of others, can be accessed on a U.S. government-supported website called *EDGAR*. The acronym stands for Electronic Data Gathering, Analysis, and Retrieval system, and is an electronic collection of information and documents filed by companies, as required by law, with the U.S. Securities and Exchange Commission (SEC). For more information about EDGAR and to access documents on EDGAR, go to www.sec.gov/edgar.shtml.

the classroom on drafting and fine-tuning provisions based on these precedents.

These exercises will help you avoid common mistakes made by inexperienced contract drafters or non-native English speakers. Inexperienced drafters or non-native speakers of the language often rely on a "cut and paste" approach to contract drafting: The drafter finds a provision from precedent that appears ideal for his or her purpose and, without appropriate critical reflection, wholly integrates it into the new contract.

The following example shows the problem of cutting and pasting without adequate reflection and demonstrates how a critical comparison of similar provisions can aid in drafting a clear and concise provision. Note that at the end of each clause there is a citation to "DA#" "CA#," or "APA#" followed by a numeral. These citations will be used throughout this book to refer to the collection of contracts on the companion website.[2] The letter combination *DA* stands for *Distribution Agreements*; the letter combination *CA* stands for *Consulting Agreements*; and the letter combination *APA* stands for *Asset Purchase Agreements*.

> *Clause* is often used to refer to a particular type of contract provision (e.g., severability clause, non-compete clause).

The drafter chose as the basis for his adaptation two "entire agreement" clauses.[3]

Two "Entire Agreement" Precedents

This Agreement constitutes the entire understanding of the Parties hereto and supersede all previous agreements between the Parties with respect to the matters contained herein. No modifications of this Agreement shall be binding upon either Party unless approved in writing by an authorized representative of each of the Parties. [DA#24]

This Agreement supersedes all proposals, oral or written, all negotiations, conversations or discussions between or among parties relating to the subject matter of this Agreement and all past dealing or industry custom. [DA#25]

---

2. The three collections can be found in the "Contract Database" file on the companion website: www.aspenlawschool.com/books/Adams.

3. *Entire agreement* clauses are also commonly referred to as *merger* clauses or *integration* clauses.

Being able to compare several provisions can definitely facilitate drafting, but it also carries the danger of copying mistakes from the original precedents, as can be seen in the following example.

Entire Agreement Clause from Cutting and Pasting

This Agreement constitutes the entire understanding of the Parties hereto and supersede [DA#24] all proposals, oral or written, all negotiations, conversations or discussions between or among parties of this Agreement [C#25] and all past dealing or industry custom [DA#25]

In this cut and paste version of the entire agreement clause, the drafter copied the verb *supersede,* which was used incorrectly in DA#24. The correct form should be *supersedes* because a singular subject ("This Agreement") needs a verb that is in the singular form. The same grammar issue turns up when the drafter copied "all past dealing or industry custom," a phrase that lacks the plural version of the words *dealing* and possibly also *custom.* Furthermore, the drafter copied the word *Parties* from one version, where the word is capitalized because it is a defined term,[4] and then used a non-capitalized form of *parties* from another provision, creating an inconsistency and possible confusion in the use of one term.[5]

Fortunately, this book offers enough activities and guidelines to train you in the critical analysis of precedents.

1.4 Learning the language of contracts through commonly occurring word combinations

Words frequently appear in predictable groups and combinations referred to as *collocations.* For example, think of everyday English word combinations such as "take a picture" or "pay attention" (not "make a picture" or "provide attention"). As fixed expressions, these phrases often have very specific meanings. Similarly, in a contract it is much more common to see the combination "commercially reasonable" than the combination "commercially sensible."[6] Even though *sensible* is a synonym for *reasonable,* the phrase

---

4. See Chapter 4 for a discussion of defined terms.

5. The effect of misrepresenting legal requirements in a "cut and paste" provision is discussed in detail in Chapter 2.

6. There are 50 instances of the use of *commercially* in the 40 sample distribution agreements on the companion website. Forty-three times, *commercially* appears together with *reasonable* as *commercially reasonable.* There is no single instance of the use of *commercially sensible.* The combination *commercially reasonable efforts* is used 28 times.

"commercially sensible" would not likely be used in a contract. If it were, it probably would have a different meaning and possibly change the legal effect of the provision. Thus, your approach to drafting a contract provision should not be that of translating word-for-word from your native language and randomly choosing a word from a list of synonyms.

Let's look at an example of word-by-word translation into English from German. The German contract heading *Vertragsgebiet* consists of a combination of the word *Vertrag*, which means *contract*, and *Gebiet*, which means *territory*. If you look up the corresponding English words in a dictionary, you might find *agreement* or *contract* for *Vertrag*, and *region, territory*, or *area* for *Gebiet*. An untrained drafter, unfamiliar with the proper English translation of *territory* may choose the combination *area of agreement*, an expression that is somehow misleading. It might imply the terms that the parties agree on.

This book provides a convenient way for you to discover how words and even sentences typically combine in contract provisions. If you want to find out, for example, how the noun *subject* appears together with other words in a contract, simply use the FIND function in your word processing program and search for the word in the collection of contracts provided on the companion website. (For detailed instructions on how to use this function, read the document "Introduction to the Use of the Contract Database" in the Chapter 1 materials section of the companion website at www.aspenlawschool.com/books/Adams.) In your search results, you will see that the combination *subject to* is much more often used than the combination *subject of* and that these two phrases have different meanings. *Subject to* is frequently used to express a condition.

> ***Example 1:***
> All orders for the Products by Distributor will be *subject to* acceptance by Supplier.
>
> ***Example 2:***
> Distributor's shipping instructions are *subject to* change upon written notice from Distributor.

Subject of is often used to mean *center* or *focus*:

> ***Example 1:***
> The results of these negotiations will be the *subject of* a separate agreement.
>
> ***Example 2:***
> If the Products, or any part of the Products, are the *subject of* any claim or lawsuit. . . .

The advantage of looking up words or phrases in the precedents on the companion website is that you can compile a list of commonly occurring words and combinations, and you can set up your own individual vocabulary list. It is easier to remember new words from their context. To help with memorization, you should enter new vocabulary together with examples of its use in context in a vocabulary list that you periodically update or modify. You can also add questions and notes and mark commonly occurring word combinations. When applicable, comment on the legal effects of the wording.

The following table is an example of a vocabulary list entry.

Contrary

Contrary to:	
Nothing contained herein shall be construed to require the commission of any act **contrary** to law. [DA#7]	Translation into the drafter's native language: German: Im Gegensatz zu/ widersprechend French: contrairement à Chinese: weifan 违反
If the Distributor or its general manager receives a payment of the Distributors portion of the Distributors Share **contrary to** the provisions of this paragraph, the Distributor and/or the general manager shall be required to timely return such sums received to the Company; [DA#20]	Notes: *Contrary to* seems to appear together with words such as provision/ law Synonyms: counter to, in contrast to, in opposition to, opposed to, opposing
If any provision or provisions of this International Distribution Agreement, including these Standard Terms and Conditions, shall be held by a court of competent jurisdiction to be **contrary to** law, such provision or provisions shall be deemed to be null and void . . . [DA#30]	Question: Can all synonyms be used equally in this context? I need to find samples in the contracts.
Supplier will be under no obligation to accept the return of nonconforming Product **contrary to** this provision, or to accept return of Product that conforms to the applicable specifications for such Product. [DA#34]	

Continued

Contrary to:

As described in the License Agreement, if Distributor distributes Products in member states of the European Union (EU), right or obligations created or imposed by this Agreement may not be exercised or enforced in a manner **contrary to** Community Law [DA#29]

To the contrary:

Notwithstanding anything else in this Agreement **to the contrary**, the parties agree that Sections 1, 2, 3, 4, 8, 9, 11, 19 and 20 shall survive the termination or expiration of this Agreement, [DA#8]	Translation into the drafter's native language

Notes: combination verb + to the contrary
To indicate something to the contrary
To notify someone to the contrary |
(c) Any provision of this Agreement **to the contrary** notwithstanding, the Company shall have the right to terminate this Agreement, if . . . [DA#13]	Ask professor what "notwithstanding to the contrary" means
Upon the expiration of the Term, at Supplier's sole discretion, this Agreement may be renewed for an additional period of one year, and will be considered so renewed unless Supplier indicates in writing its desire **to the contrary** more than thirty (30) days before the end of the Term. [DA#12]	
Any Materials submitted to Supplier shall be deemed approved unless Supplier notifies Distributor **to the contrary** within ten (10) days after receipt of such Materials [DA#21]	
As to the terms defined and used herein, the singular shall be understood to include the plural and vice-versa, unless the context clearly indicates **to the contrary**. [DA#24]	

Continued

Contrary (adjective):

Each Purchase Order shall be deemed to be an offer by Distributor to purchase the Products pursuant to the terms of this Agreement, and, if accepted by the Company shall give rise to a contract on the terms set forth herein to the exclusion of any additional or **contrary** terms set forth in the Purchase Order. [DA#27]

Translation into the drafter's native language

Notes: I need to look for synonyms

Question: What is the legal rule in the U.S. regarding contrary terms in a purchase order?

1.5 Learning to build on your existing knowledge

Having a database of comparable contract provisions can help you learn about the style and phrasing of a specific contract provision. Yet, relying too heavily on precedents can also cause you to omit words, phrases, or provisions that better reflect the parties' intent in the contract you are drafting.

Thus, you should start drafting a contract provision from your own wording, if possible, integrating the specific agreed points of the current business deal. Your first version may sound awkward and not like contract language at all, and you may not even know all the words in English. Just write down as much as you can, and if you don't know the English word, write down the word in your native language. Once you have made a serious first effort to draft from your existing knowledge base, you can always refer to the precedents on the companion website (www.aspenlawschool.com/books/Adams) to further polish your draft. Comparing a large selection of contracts does increase the chance that you will learn to discern between wording that is commonly chosen for certain provisions and wording that shows individual choices or even indicates mistakes.

Let's assume your native language is French, but you are drafting a contract in English between your client, a French company, and a U.S. corporation. The parties have agreed that California law will govern the contract. You are unsure about the correct phrasing or even the appropriate English words to use in choice of law and forum selection clauses for a contract governed by U.S. law, so you initially draft the following (using French words as a temporary place marker for the English words that you need to look up):

> This Contract shall be ruled by the laws of the state of California. Any **disputes [French word spelled the same way as the English word]** resulting from the Contract shall be brought to **un tribunal compétent** in the State of California.

Checking your draft against a number of existing choice of law and forum selection clauses in the precedents on the companion website, you gradually modify your own version. The following is what your final result might look like after comparing several choice of law and forum selection clauses in the precedents as well as consulting the drafting guidelines in this book:

> This agreement is governed by the laws of the state of California, and any actions for the resolution of **disputes** arising under this agreement will be brought in a **court of competent jurisdiction** in California.

Your initial draft started with the phrase *this contract*, a reasonable assumption since *contract* is the word commonly used to refer to an agreement where rights and obligations are created. You will see, however, that the word *contract* is less likely used to refer to the document creating the contract. Rather, the word *agreement* is the preferred choice. Next, let's look at the word *brought*. From looking up the use of the word *brought* in several provisions, you can see that the common combination/collocation is not *brought to* a court, but is *brought in* or *brought before* a court. Word combinations that contain a preposition are extremely difficult for a non-native speaker to learn since there are no fixed rules and since the preposition used in the speaker's native language may be different.[7]

In your first draft, you inserted a few French words because you might have been unsure how they translated into English. Once you looked up the French word "dispute" in a dictionary, you might have found the English words *quarrel, fight,* or *dispute* as options. By comparing several *choice of law* provisions in the precedents found on the companion website (www. aspenlawschool.com/books/Adams), you would discover that the legal term used in the context of a choice of law provision is *dispute*. In this case, you have a 1-to-1 match of the English and French word. Don't be fooled by similarities, however. For example, don't translate the French word *tribunal* into the English word *tribunal*. The correct English word is *court*. Finally, you also chose the expression *shall be ruled* in your first draft because you might have seen or heard this expression used. As you will see in Chapter 7, the expression *shall* in American contracts should be used to express the obligation of a party to the contract such as "Distributor shall deliver. . . ." Thus, "This Agreement shall be ruled by the laws of . . ." is grammatically possible, but the expression "This Agreement is ruled by the laws of . . ." would be the preferred version.

---

7. A prime example is the combination *depend on* in English, which has very similar counterparts in French, Spanish, and other Romance languages—for example, *dépendre de, depender de,* and so on. The literal translation of the preposition *de* would be *of* in English and often leads non-native speaker to say *depend of* in English.

For many aspiring drafters, it is often a rewarding experience when they can see that their ultimate version of a provision is actually more precise than the version that was written by a seasoned drafter.

1.6 Final words of caution

Remember, there is no such thing as the perfect contract. Thus, none of the 120 authentic contracts on the companion website should be viewed as perfect. Model provisions that we, the authors, provide in this book, are marked. These model provisions have been carefully crafted and reviewed, and reflect many of the elements of good drafting the book proposes. Still, you should never thoughtlessly copy and paste examples from this book—even those promoted as examples of good drafting—into your draft without considering appropriate modifications.

Exercises

The following exercises give you a chance to familiarize yourself with the kind of activities you will find throughout the book. Before starting any of the exercises in the book, read the document "Introduction to the Use of the Contract Database" in the Chapter 1 materials section of the companion website (www.aspenlawschool.com/books/Adams). The files referred to in the following exercises are available on the companion website.

▶ **Exercise 1-1 Finding words in a contract I**
Write down a few examples of how you would use the word *incur* in a sentence. If you don't know the word, use the FIND function in your word processing program to look it up in the "Distribution Agreements" file on the companion website. What words does it commonly appear with? If you still do not know the meaning of the word *incur*, look it up in a legal dictionary.
Does it appear in one particular provision more than in others?

▶ **Exercise 1-2 Finding words in a contract II**
Using the FIND function in your word processing program, look for the word *mutual* in the same file. What words does it commonly combine with?

▶ **Exercise 1-3 Finding headings in a contract**
Using the FIND function in your word processing program, you can look for headings to search for similar provisions across contracts.[8] In the

---

8. As described in the document "Introduction to the Use of the Contract Database" on the companion website (www.aspenlawschool.com/books/Adams).

"Distribution Agreements" file on the companion website, find three provisions in three different contracts that have the provision heading *Governing Law*.

▶ **Exercise 1-4   Drafting a provision**

Imagine that you are drafting an agreement where a professional golfer will be consulting with a golf club manufacturer on the design of a new line of golf clubs. The parties agree on an initial term of three years for the contract. The parties want the right to extend the contract for another three years in writing. How will this be expressed in the agreement? Draft a brief provision stating the initial term of the agreement and how the parties will extend the agreement for another three years. Use words from your native language if you cannot come up with any of the English words. When you are done, use the FIND function of your word processing program and look for the use of the word *extend* in the "Consulting Agreements" file on the companion website. This will probably lead you to contract provisions that address contract extension. Compare your version with several other versions from the database. Is there a common heading you can find for passages that contain the word *extend*?

▶ **Exercise 1-5   Pegasus/Azteca deal—phone call with Cynthia Adler**

Listen to the phone conversation between Cynthia Adler, partner in Whitney & Adler, and Peter Craven, senior associate, about a meeting Cynthia had with James Sordano, President of Pegasus Snowboards Inc. regarding a proposed contract with Deportes Azteca, Ltda., a distributor from Chile. Assume that you are Peter and take notes and compose an email to Cynthia summarizing the content of this phone conversation. The audio recording and transcript can be found in the materials section of Chapter 1 on the companion website.

Preliminary Drafting Concerns

When parties decide to enter into a contract, they must determine who will create the first draft of the document. Hopefully, for reasons discussed below, you will be the author of that draft. But even before creating the first draft, the parties can expend much time and effort in discussing proposals and settling issues. The extent of your role, as legal counsel to your client, in this pre-drafting process will vary from deal to deal. Your client, and sometimes even you on behalf of your client, will be negotiating issues with the other party.[1] A basic understanding of the business purpose underlying the deal and knowledge of the law governing the contract are crucial to effectively advising your client during negotiations.

This book focuses on the technical skill of drafting, but creating a clear, concise, and precise contract cannot be accomplished without (1) understanding the underlying business deal, (2) knowing the governing law, and (3) recognizing the audience. The first two of these three concerns play a crucial role from the moment the parties begin deliberations. But, even if you are not involved in the negotiation stage of the deal, you must still understand the business side of the deal and know the governing law before you can create a draft of the contract or review someone else's draft. Another important drafting concern is recognizing the contract's audience, those who will be reading, implementing, or enforcing the provisions. The importance of understanding the business deal, knowing the governing law, and recognizing the audience will be often repeated throughout this book.

Still another preliminary drafting concern is whether you will draft a provision from scratch or whether you will use precedent to assist you in drafting. If you use precedent, you must be careful to critically review it

---

1. There are many excellent books on negotiation strategy, including James R. Silkenat, Jeffrey M. Aresty & Jacqueline Klosek, eds., *The ABA Guide to International Business Negotiations: A Comparison of Cross-Cultural Issues and Successful Approaches* (3d ed., ABA 2009); Deepak Malhotra & Max H. Bazerman, *Negotiation Genius* (Bantam Books 2007); Roger Fisher & William L. Ury, *Getting to Yes: Negotiating Agreement without Giving In* (Bruce Patton, ed., 2d ed., Penguin 1991).

and, if necessary, revise it to clearly express the parties' intent, adequately protect your client's interests, and comply with governing law.

2.1 Authoring the draft and ethical drafting

The American Bar Association, the professional organization for U.S. lawyers, has adopted Model Rules of Professional Conduct (Model R. Prof. Conduct), which serve as a basis for rules of lawyer conduct in most states. See footnote 2 in this chapter for cites to some relevant rules. The MRPC addresses, among other things, representing clients, advising clients, and misconduct. For more information on states that have adopted a version of the MRPC and for a link to the text of the MRPC, go to http:// www.americanbar.org/groups/ professional_responsibility/ publications/model_rules_of_ professional_conduct.html.

The party responsible for drafting the contract might be predetermined by the nature of the business transaction. For example, lenders typically create loan documents for their borrowers and landlords typically create leases for their tenants. But in transactions where the drafter is not predetermined, you should always insist on authoring the first draft. Your client may have to pay a little more for the time spent creating the draft, but the benefits gained by your client will outweigh the cost. Savvy business clients understand this. For less experienced clients, you may have to explain the benefits to them.

The first draft sets the tone for revisions and further negotiations. As the original author of the draft, you will carefully decide on words, sentence structure, and placement of the provisions, all to ensure that the parties' intent is clearly expressed and your client's interests are adequately protected. While the other party will have an opportunity to review your draft and make suggestions or changes, you, as creator of the draft, will be intimately familiar with every line of the document and how the various provisions relate to each other. Certainly, all is not lost if another party creates the first draft. By methodically and critically reviewing someone else's draft, you will be able to grasp the details and identify issues of concern. And you can still advocate on behalf of your client to make important revisions, but you might never become as familiar with a contract as when you are the original author. Furthermore, you might find that another person's draft lacks in quality and content; if this happens, you might spend extensive time negotiating and making revisions to it. For these reasons, always offer to create the first draft if given the opportunity to do so.

Whether you are the original drafter or revising someone else's draft, you must create provisions that fairly and accurately state the parties' negotiated terms of agreement. While you want to ensure that your client's interests are adequately protected, never change terms already agreed upon by the parties and never draft provisions on important issues that still need to be settled. In both instances, you must discuss these matters with your client, and if required by good business and legal ethics, you must discuss these matters with the other party. If you foresee problems for your client on any points already agreed upon or anticipate problems with issues that have yet to be settled between the parties, contact your client to discuss these problems and decide on an honest, open, and fair way to resolve them.

Drafting a document that does not accurately reflect the parties' agreed terms or purposely creates ambiguities can lead to serious problems. Here are some examples of what could happen: First, you risk upsetting your client. Second, the other party could lose trust in your client and in you. Third, working on revisions and negotiating other unsettled issues could take longer and become unnecessarily difficult. Fourth, communication between the parties might entirely break down and the deal could be killed. Fifth, even if the parties sign the document with defective provisions, disputes could arise later, leading to costly proceedings to resolve them and perhaps ultimately result in unenforceable provisions. Sixth, your professional and personal reputation could be called into question. A damaged reputation is extremely difficult to repair. And last, but equally important, in serious cases you could lose your license to practice law.

While working on the exercises and drafting assignments in this book, conduct yourself as if you were actually engaged in a real business deal. Practicing ethical behavior now will reinforce right action in the future. Along the way, issues will undoubtedly arise and you will have questions as to how to properly resolve them. Your professor will discuss with you common professional ethics issues that arise in transactional practice and work with you on resolutions.[2] Be mindful of applicable rules of professional conduct and follow them. Beyond this, always conduct yourself in a reputable and fair manner. By doing so, you will be respected by your peers, your clients, and other parties. It can open the door to other opportunities.

2.2 Understanding the business deal

In order to draft the contract, you will need to understand the parties' agreed deal and, in particular, the agreed terms. You may gather this information

---

2. The American Bar Association's Model Rules of Professional Conduct relevant to representing and advising clients in transactional work include the following: Rule 1.1 (Lawyer Competence); Rule 1.2(d) (Engaging in Criminal, Fraudulent, or Prohibited Transactions); Rule 1.3 (Exercising Reasonable Diligence); Rule 1.4 (Communicating with the Client); Rule 1.5 (Fees); Rule 1.6 (Revealing Confidential Information); Rules 1.7, 1.8, 1.9, and 1.10 (Conflict of Interest in Representing Different Clients); Rule 13 (Representing an Organization as a Client); Rule 1.15 (Safekeeping Property of Others); Rule 1.16 (Declining or Terminating Representation); Rule 2.1 (Acting as Advisor to a Client); Rule 4.1(Making Truthful Statements to Others); Rule 4.2 (Communicating with Persons Represented by Legal Counsel); Rule 4.3 (Dealing with Persons Not Represented by Legal Counsel); Rule 5.1 (Responsibilities of a Partner or Supervising Attorney); Rule 5.2 (Responsibilities of a Subordinate Lawyer); Rule 5.5 (Unauthorized Practice of Law and Multijurisdictional Practice of Law); and Rule 8.4 (Misconduct).

from the client through a telephone call, a face-to-face meeting, or by written communication.[3] If you are a subordinate attorney in your law firm, you may receive this information through your supervising attorney via notes, memos, files, or conversation. In the case of a telephone conversation or a personal meeting with the client or supervising attorney, prepare ahead of time, if possible, a checklist or list of questions to ask the client or supervising attorney about the deal. Sometimes your employer may have already prepared a checklist or list of questions for more common transactions. For example, if your office routinely works on mergers and acquisitions, it may have a checklist of questions to ask the client, a list of documents to prepare, a process for completing due diligence, and a proposed timeline for completing pre-closing[4] tasks and for completing tasks post-closing. Practice manuals and published articles, especially those related to the subject matter of the transaction on which you are working, can offer helpful checklists or lists of questions.

*In transactional work, **due diligence** means conducting an investigation of the target company, property, or security to evaluate it for purposes of whether to move forward with the acquisition.*

While it might be unnecessary to understand every detail of the business underlying the transaction, you should strive to have a basic understanding of the business aspects of the deal in order to identify issues or spot gaps in the parties' agreement. For example, if your party wants to buy land on which to build a shopping center, you will want to be familiar with the zoning for that land to ensure it permits this type of improvement or, if the land is not zoned for this type of use, you will need to know the process for rezoning the property and the likelihood of success. In the event the land is not zoned for this type of use, you will want to include in the purchase agreement a condition that closing on the transaction is conditioned on successful rezoning of the property to permit the building of a shopping center.

In your research, consider reviewing precedent for transactions similar to the current deal. Research any relevant documents previously prepared for this client. For example, if your office has handled a number of hospital acquisitions for this client, you will want to review those files and note any issues or features that might be relevant to the current deal. Talk with colleagues who have experience in drafting these transactions.

Based on your research, add to the list of questions and items that you have already compiled. As you draft the contract, you may discover additional questions need to be answered. Make a list of questions to ask your client or supervising attorney the next time you communicate with them.

---

3. If you are working with a new client, consider practice tips for interviewing a client discussed in the following article: Clay Abbott & Charles Bubaney, "The Anatomy of a Client Interview (with Resources and Sample Questions)," 8 Prac. Law. 61 (1996).

4. For a definition of *closing*, see the discussion in Chapter 3, section 3.1.2(a).

Finally, when the contract has been signed and the transaction completed, save your compiled checklists and questions for future projects. Over time you will refine these checklists and questions, thus making the drafting process for future projects go more smoothly and quickly.

2.3 The contract's audience

When drafting a contract, you must also anticipate who will be the audience for the contract. Naturally, the immediate audience is the contracting parties. Therefore, you will draft provisions that effectively carry out the intent and goals of the contracting parties.

Also, though, you should consider those who will be responsible for implementing the contract provisions. These persons are often not those who negotiated the deal or signed the contract. People responsible for implementing the contract might be employees of the contracting parties, such as bookkeepers, accountants, salespersons, marketing personnel, and financial officers. Therefore, you will want to draft provisions that not only give adequate direction to personnel but also ensure that the performance requirements are compatible with the day-to-day operation of the business. For example, if a provision requires a company to pay royalties to a party based on product sales in the previous year, it would be unrealistic to require the company to pay the royalty on the first business day of the new year. The provision should allow for reasonable time before payment is made in order to settle accounts, verify records, and otherwise process the disbursement.

Third parties, those who are not the contracting parties, or employees or agents of the contracting parties, also may have an interest in the contract. For example, if a contracting party is purchasing assets of a business with borrowed money, the lender of that money will want to review the purchase agreement along with any other important documents connected with the sale to ensure its interest in the purchased assets is protected.

Finally, in the event a dispute later arises between the parties in the performance of the contract, arbitral judges or court judges may be called on to interpret the contract. You will want to draft provisions that protect your client's interest and express the parties' agreement as clearly, concisely, and precisely as possible. By doing so, you will reduce the likelihood that a costly dispute will arise. But even if a dispute does arise and it is submitted to a judge for resolution, your well-drafted provisions will hopefully bring about a quick resolution to the dispute that best protects your client.

2.4 The importance of governing law

A contract creates a private set of obligations and rights between the contracting parties. Even so, sometimes disputes occur because the contract fails to address a situation that later arises when the parties are performing the contract, or the parties disagree about the application of or performance required by a contract provision. In these instances, applicable law will (1) fill gaps in the contract with default rules, (2) provide standards for interpreting contract provisions, and (3) in some instances, override provisions that are found to be unreasonable. You must be familiar with the governing law in order to provide your client with accurate advice during the contracting process. If you are not familiar with the governing law, then you may want to research the law or obtain the services of legal counsel who is familiar with the law. Be aware that rules prohibit lawyers from practicing law in jurisdictions where they are not authorized to practice, which includes offering legal service or advice.[5]

2.4.1 Contract law in the United States

In the United States, contract law is mostly a matter of state law.[6] Each state has its own body of law for contracts. In each state, some contract laws are found in the state's codified statutes, and others are found in the state's common law.[7] Many states base their contract laws on model rules. All fifty states have enacted versions of the Uniform Commercial Code (UCC).[8] The UCC is a series of rules, drafted by lawyers and legal scholars, governing different types of business transactions. Article 2 of the UCC, for example, focuses on rules for transactions involving the sale of goods. Also, because the United States is a signatory to the Convention on Contracts for the International Sale of Goods (CISG),[9] the CISG is law in all fifty states[10] and, except in certain limited circumstances, will supersede any state-adopted UCC rules when a transaction involves the international sale of goods. A series of contract rules that are not binding on any court but can be used by a court as a basis for making common law is the ***Restatement of the Law of Contracts***. There are two series of these Restatements, the first treatise was published in 1929, and a second edition, called the *Restatement (Second) of the Law of Contracts* (R2d)[11], was published in 1979. Both

---

5. *See, e.g.,* ABA Model R. Prof. Conduct 5.5.

6. **Federal law**, meaning national law, relating to contracts is largely limited to situations of national interest, such as regulating interstate commerce or contracts where the federal government is a party.

7. **Common law** is a body of rules and principles created by the state courts to respond to legal issues not addressed by statute.

8. For links to the text of the UCC, see http://www.law.cornell.edu/ucc.

9. For links to the text of the CISG, see http://www.uncitral.org/uncitral/en/uncitral_texts/sale_goods/1980CISG.html.

10. As mandated by the Supremacy Clause of the U.S. Constitution. *See* U.S. Const. art. VI, § 2.

11. For links to the text of R2d, see http://www.lexinter.net/LOTWVers4/restatement_(second)_of_contracts.htm.

Restatements were prepared by the American Law Institute, an organization of lawyers, law professors, and judges. The rules are intended to provide general principles of contract law, which state courts widely use to create common law.

Courses on U.S. contract law use the UCC, CISG, and R2d to teach general concepts in U.S. contract law, rather than addressing the specific laws of each of the fifty states. This book will do the same whenever generally referencing U.S. contract law. Nevertheless, remember that although states share similar contract laws (by codifying a version of the UCC, enforcing the CISG, and adopting rules based on R2d), there can also be some significant differences in contract law from state to state. An example of this is demonstrated in the severability clause problem in section 2.5.

2.4.2 Canons of contract interpretation

When interpreting a contract provision in dispute, a court may use a variety of canons of interpretation to help determine the provision's meaning. These canons do not take the place of statutes or common law. They are merely persuasive guidelines or principles that courts may use to help them interpret the meaning of ambiguous language in a contract. There are many different canons of construction, some of which contradict each other. To further complicate matters, you can never be certain which canons a court will use to help resolve a dispute. Each contract and each dispute raises a unique set of circumstances. Sometimes the contracting parties will include preferred canons of interpretation in the contract to give the court some guidance on the parties' intent and to encourage the court to apply the canons if a dispute arises. Even so, only the court has the power to decide whether to use a canon of interpretation.

> *Language is **ambiguous** when it is capable of two or more reasonable but contradictory meanings.*

The following is a sampling of commonly used canons of construction.

(1) Ambiguous words or phrases are construed against the drafter (also referred to as *contra proferentem*).[12] Based on this canon, you might conclude that being the author of a contract provision is not so beneficial after all, if a court applies this canon and interprets a provision against you. But you can sidestep this problem by writing a clear and concise provision.

(2) Words are given their ordinary and common meaning, unless otherwise specifically defined in the contract. For example, *product*

---

12. Here, "it is incumbent on the dominant party to make terms clear." *Penn Mut. Life Ins. Co. v. Oglesby*, 695 A.2d 1146, 1150 (Del. 1997), *quoted in* Michelle E. Boardman, "Contra Proferentem: The Allure of Ambiguous Boilerplate," 104 Mich. L. Rev. 1105, 1121 (2006).

can refer to all types of goods produced by various businesses. But within the context of a contract the meaning of *product* might be explicitly limited to specific goods produced by one of the contracting parties.

(3) Contract provisions should be read so that their meaning is consistent with other provisions in the contract. Thus, if a contract provision stated, "The term of this agreement is for two years," and another provision in the contract provided, "Either party may terminate this contract at any time in the event of the other party's failure to perform as promised," then the provision stating the term would be interpreted to mean that the duration of the contract is two years, unless terminated earlier because of a failure of one of the parties to perform as promised.

(4) General words following specifically listed words include only those items similar in nature to the listed words (also referred to as *ejusdem generis*). If a contract provision referenced the distribution of corn, melon, beans, and peas, then *produce* would not include eggs because this is produced by an animal, not a plant.

(5) The meaning of a word or phrase may be known from the words surrounding it (also referred to as *noscitur a sociis*). In a lease for office space, for example, if the landlord promised to keep all floors, stairs and hallways free of obstruction, then a floor used exclusively for storage is not included because stairs and hallways refer to passageways.

2.4.3 Governing law provisions

Because the law plays such an important role in contract enforcement and interpretation, the parties should decide on the law that they want to govern the contract before they begin negotiations. In the contract, state the law that should be applied to resolve any disputes. Nevertheless, including a governing law provision in the contract does not necessarily mean that a court will enforce it. For example, a court may decide not to enforce the provision if the law chosen by the parties bears no relationship to the transaction.[13] Considerations for drafting this provision are discussed in Chapter 13.

2.5 Using precedent

Ideally, you will draft a contract from scratch without relying on precedents. Nevertheless, as mentioned in Chapter 1, using a precedent as a beginning point for your draft can save time that would otherwise be spent creating a

---

13. *See* Tina L. Stark, ed., *Negotiating and Drafting Contract Boilerplate* 109-128 (ALM Publg. 2003) for a detailed discussion of drafting governing law provisions.

completely new contract. Reviewing precedents can also help you spot possible issues or important points or provisions that the parties might want to address in their ongoing negotiations. You might also review precedents to identify provisions that are essential or beneficial to use in specific types of transactions. This is especially helpful if you have had no previous experience drafting a particular type of contract, such as, for example, an asset purchase agreement. Reviewing precedents for deals similar to your current deal can jump-start the drafting process, saving you time and, consequently, saving your client money. Nevertheless, precedents should be used cautiously.

Form precedents covering a wide range of transactions are available on the Internet (including the EDGAR database) as well as in books. Some are offered for purchase while others are available at no cost. The quality of these forms, whether purchased or free, varies widely. Another resource for precedents might be found in contracts from previous business deals drafted by colleagues in your office.[14] No matter if you use a form precedent or a precedent from a previous deal, they are both limited in their usefulness. A precedent often includes provisions that are unique to that business deal. Also, a precedent might have been drafted in favor of one party over another. For instance, if you are drafting an asset purchase agreement, you may use as a starting point a contract drafted by a colleague for another asset purchase. Perhaps in that previous deal your colleague represented the buyer, so the provisions favored the buyer. If you are representing the seller in the current deal, you will not use provisions from the precedent that unnecessarily favor the buyer. Or, perhaps that precedent included a provision that is inapplicable to your business deal, such as a provision stating the parties will comply with state law that requires notice to seller's creditors of the purchase.[15] If that law was recently repealed so that notice is no longer necessary, or if your client's transaction takes place in another state where there is no such law, you will need to omit that compliance provision from your draft. Even if the precedent includes provisions appropriate for the present deal, you should still use the precedent cautiously. Provisions in the precedent could be poorly written. By applying the drafting guidelines provided in this book, you can create contract provisions that are more clear, concise, and precise than those found in most precedents. Therefore, whenever using precedent, be prepared to make deletions, additions, and revisions to adequately address the unique circumstances of the present business deal and to adequately protect your client's interests.

By far the best resource for precedent is a collection of contracts that you have drafted. As the author, you will be intimately familiar with the

---

14. Be careful, however, in using contracts drafted for use in other business deals.

15. This law is commonly referred to as the *law on bulk sales*, addressed in Article 6 of the UCC.

precedent. You will have organized the provisions and carefully chosen words and structured sentences so that they are clear and concise. You will know which provisions were specially drafted to reflect the parties' agreement in that deal and why some provisions, which in other deals might be included, were omitted. Thus, consider collecting contracts that you have drafted to create your own collection of precedent for future deals.

In section 1.3 of Chapter 1, you were cautioned against merely "cutting and pasting" precedent into your draft without adequate reflection. The example used earlier highlighted grammar problems that can arise, but problems with cutting and pasting can also create more substantive issues. One of the biggest mistakes made by drafters is using words, passages, or formatting from a precedent without thinking about how governing law will affect the current contract's interpretation. The following scenario demonstrates this, but it also shows how you can critically compare similar provisions across precedents to create a provision that adequately protects the interests of the parties in your draft.

The three severability clauses in the box below were taken from different precedents on the companion website (www.aspenlawschool.com/books/Adams).

In case any one or more provisions contained in this Agreement or any application thereof shall be invalid, illegal or unenforceable in any respect, the validity, legality and enforceability of the remaining provisions contained herein and other applications thereof shall not be in any way affected or impaired. [DA#1]

Whenever possible, each provision of this Agreement and all related documents shall be interpreted in such a manner as to be valid under applicable law, but if any such provision is invalid or prohibited under said applicable law, such provision shall be in effect up to the extent of such invalidity or prohibition without invalidating the remainder of such provision or the remaining provisions of this Agreement. [DA#6]

To the extent any provision or term of this Agreement is or becomes unenforceable or invalid by operation of Law, such unenforceability or invalidity shall not affect the remaining provisions of this Agreement. The Parties agree to renegotiate in good faith a substitute provision that to the extent possible accomplishes the original business purpose of the provision held to be unenforceable. [DA#25]

All three examples state that if a provision in the contract is found unenforceable, the other provisions of the contract will remain in force between the parties. The severability clauses make clear the parties' intent that the entire contract should not be declared unenforceable merely because of an unenforceable provision.

A closer look at DA#1's provision, however, reveals that it differs from the other two severability clauses. Unlike the clauses in DA#6 and DA#25, the DA#1 provision does not address what happens to the matter covered by the unenforceable provision. As previously mentioned, when a contract is silent, the governing law of the contract will step in to fill the gap. In the United States, each state has its own law for contracts. Although states may have similar laws, there also can be some significant differences. The situation raised by DA#1's severability provision is a case on point. To illustrate, let's say an executive working for a company promises in an employment agreement not to compete with the company's business in the United States during the term of the contract and for three years after the contract ends. A dispute later arises between the parties over whether the non-competition clause is unreasonable because it covers far more territory than where the company actually does business. The court deciding the dispute finds that the geographical area is unreasonable. If DA#1's severability clause was used in that contract, the question of whether the non-competition clause survives in some form depends on the state law governing the contract. Here are three possible alternative resolutions depending on the law of the applicable state:

1. Despite the severability clause, the court will refuse to enforce the entire non-competition clause.[16] The company will find this outcome unsatisfactory, especially if the unenforceable provision was an essential part of the contract. Undoubtedly, the company would consider the non-competition clause an essential part of the contract.

2. The court will delete the unreasonable words if grammatically separable from the rest of the clause and enforce the remaining words in the clause (commonly referred to as **the blue pencil doctrine**). In this instance, whether a part of the original non-competition clause can be enforced depends on the wording of the geographical restriction in the original non-competition clause. If the geographical restriction in the non-competition clause of the employment agreement had stated "anywhere in the United States," striking this phrase would result in no geographical area at all; thus, the entire non-compete could not be enforced.[17] But if the geographical restriction listed

---

16. *See, e.g.*, Wis. Stat. § 103.465 (2002) (mandating no enforcement of unreasonable non-compete clause); *Bendinger v. Marshalltown Trowell Co.*, 994 S.W.2d 468 (Ark. 1999). Some states simply will not enforce a non-competition clause in an employment agreement, even if it is reasonable, because it is considered an unreasonable restraint of trade. *See, e.g.*, Calif. Bus. & Prof. Code § 16600 (West 1997); N.D. Cent. Code § 9-08-06 (WL current through 2011 Reg. & Spec. Sess.).

17. *See, e.g.*, *Fearnow v. Ridenour, Swenson, Cleere & Evans, P.C.*, 138 P.3d 723 (Ariz. 2006); *Dicen v. New Sesco, Inc.*, 839 N.E.2d 684 (Ind. 2005).

each of the 50 states, then the court could strike those states where the company did not conduct business and enforce the non-compete for the remaining states.[18] Therefore, in states following the blue pencil doctrine, you must be extremely careful how you word the clause.

3. The court might strike the unenforceable parts of the clause and rewrite it to make it reasonable under the circumstances and enforce the provision as reformed.[19] Here, the court—not the parties—has the power to reform the provision.

The company would not be satisfied with resolutions 1 or 2. And either or both parties might not be satisfied with the court reforming the non-competition clause under resolution 3. Using the non-competition clause in DA#6 does not increase the likelihood of a satisfactory outcome. The clause in this contract states that the unenforceable provision will be given "effect up to the extent of such invalidity or prohibition." Despite the parties' intent to direct the court to enforce the non-competition clause to the broadest extent possible, the court's ability to enforce the provision is still limited by the governing law. In application, the general added language in DA#6's clause has probably not changed the outcome from that under DA#1's clause.

The provision in DA#25 appears to be the most satisfactory of the three. Here, the parties will conduct good faith negotiations for a replacement provision that will "to the extent possible accomplish[ ] the original business purpose of the provision held to be unenforceable." Thus the parties, not the court, determine the replacement provision. While DA#25 may be the most preferable, substantively, of the three precedents, you will want to edit the words so that they match those used in your contract. Also, because you want as clear and concise a provision as possible, you will further edit the provision so that it is expressed in plain English according to the principles discussed in this book. The following is an edited version of DA#25 stated in plain English. Note that the provision in DA#1 was not dismissed entirely! The drafter borrowed some of the wording from DA#1 for the clause stating that provisions, excepting the unenforceable provision, remain enforceable.

> If any provision in this agreement is held unenforceable or invalid, the validity and enforceability of the remaining provisions will not be affected or impaired in any way. Additionally, the parties shall negotiate in good faith a substitute provision that to the extent possible is (1) valid and enforceable and (2) accomplishes the original business purpose, as intended by the parties, of the unenforceable or invalid provision.

---

18. *See, e.g., Coates v. Heat Wagons, Inc.*, 942 N.E.2d 905 (Ind. App. 2011).

19. *See, e.g., Brignull v. Albert*, 666 A.2d 82 (Me. 1995); *Cobb v. Kayne Publ'g Group, Inc.*, 322 S.W.3d 780 (Tex. App.–Fort Worth 2010).

Therefore, when reviewing precedent to gather ideas for your draft, consider looking at several different sources. Note similarities and distinctions between the precedents. Ensure that any precedent used in your draft is revised to (1) clearly express the parties' intent, (2) adequately protect your client's interests, and (3) comply with governing law. Many of the exercises in this book will help you gain confidence and skill to critically review precedents and make important revisions to accomplish these goals.

Exercises

▶ **Exercise 2-1   Drafting provisions that comply with the law**

Review the following sections from a state statute requiring that disclaimers of implied warranties must appear conspicuously in the contract. Then read the contract provision following it. The governing law for the contract is the law of this state.

State Code § 216:

> (2) To exclude or modify the implied warranty of merchantability or any part of it, the exclusion must mention "merchantability" and, in case of a writing, must be conspicuous.
>
> (3) To exclude or modify any implied warranty of fitness the exclusion must be by a writing and conspicuous. Language to exclude all implied warranties of fitness is sufficient if it states, for example, "There are no warranties that extend beyond the description on the face of this document."

State Code § 201:

> (10) "Conspicuous" means written, displayed, or presented so that a reasonable person against whom it is to operate ought to have noticed it. Conspicuous terms include the following:
>
> (A) a heading in capitals equal to or greater in size than the surrounding text, or in contrasting type, font, or color to the surrounding text of the same or lesser size; and
>
> (B) language in the body in larger type than the surrounding text, or in contrasting type, font, or color to the surrounding text of the same size, or set off from surrounding text of the same size by symbols or other marks that call attention to the language.

Contract provision:

> PRODUCT WARRANTY. MANUFACTURER warrants to DISTRIBU-
> TOR that the Products sold to DISTRIBUTOR (i) are fit for the
> purpose of use as an intraoral camera system by trained personnel
> and (ii) shall be free from defects in materials and workmanship for
> a period of one (1) year from the date the Products are received by
> the actual end user thereof, provided however, that this warranty
> shall in no event extend beyond the close of the eighteenth (18th)
> full calendar month following the date of shipment by MANUFAC-
> TURER. EXCEPT AS JUST PROVIDED, MANUFACTURER GIVES
> NO WARRANTY AS TO MERCHANTIBILITY, FITNESS FOR
> PARTICULAR PURPOSE, OR ANY OTHER WARRANTY, EXPRESS
> OR IMPLIED, CONCERNING THE PRODUCTS. DISTRIBUTOR
> shall not make any other warranty, guarantee, or representation
> with respect to the Products or their use except at its own risk
> and expense. If DISTRIBUTOR or its customers are made parties
> to any claim or action involving the Products, including claims
> relating to the manufacture or use of the Products, DISTRIBUTOR
> shall immediately notify MANUFACTURER in writing. This
> paragraph (ii) sets forth the sole and entire warranty obligation of
> MANUFACTURER with respect to Products. [DA#6]

Did the drafter satisfy the law? Explain the reason for your answer by noting the relevant statutory requirements and how each has been satisfied by
the language.

▶ Exercise 2-2   Pegasus/Azteca deal—second phone call with Cynthia Adler

Listen to another phone conversation between Cynthia A. from Whitney &
Adler and Peter C., senior associate at the same firm, about a follow-up meeting Cynthia had with James Sordano, President of Pegasus Snowboards Inc.,
regarding a proposed contract with Deportes Azteca, Ltda. Assume that you
are Peter and take notes and compose an email to Cynthia summarizing the
content of this phone conversation. The audio recording and transcript can
be found in the materials section of Chapter 2 on the companion website
(www.aspenlawschool.com/books/Adams).

▶ Exercise 2-3   Pegasus/Azteca deal—making a list of questions

Now that you have a list of notes that you turned into emails from Exercise
1-5 in Chapter 1 and Exercise 2-2 in this chapter, make a list of questions that
you would want to ask Pegasus or Azteca.

Example:

Cynthia: So they, I mean Pegasus, is thinking of granting Azteca the exclusive right to distribute, market, and sell the snowboard products produced by Pegasus. The distribution territory covered by the agreement will be Chile, at least for the next four years.

Question: How big is their competition in Chile? Are there bigger distributors out there than Azteca?

Question: Is there a chance to get into other South American markets?

Contract Structure

Before discussing the details of a contract in the following chapters, we begin here with an overview of contract structure. This chapter introduces you to the basic parts of a contract, contract provision headings, and numbering formats.

3.1 Basic parts of a contract

A formal written contract, like a story, has a beginning, a middle, and an end. Each of these basic parts of a contract serves a particular purpose and includes distinct components:

- ◆ **Beginning of the contract**
  - Title of the document
  - Introductory statement
  - Recitals (optional)
  - Transitional clause (optional)

- ◆ **Middle of the contract**
  - Core provisions
  - Exit provisions
  - Alternative dispute resolution provisions, if any
  - Miscellaneous provisions

- ◆ **End of the contract**
  - Concluding statement (optional)
  - Signature blocks
  - Attachments (exhibits or schedules), if any

3.1.1 The beginning of a contract

> *The legal definition of a joint venture varies from state to state in the United States. Generally, though, a **joint venture** is a for-profit business enterprise conducted by a group of people, entities, or both. Unlike a partnership, a joint venture is of limited duration and is created for a specific purpose.*

The beginning of a contract introduces the reader to the nature of the agreement and identifies the contracting parties. See Figure 3-1 for an example of the beginning of a joint venture agreement. This part of a contract opens with the *title of the document*. Typically, an *introductory statement* follows. The **introductory statement** is a paragraph identifying the contracting parties. The introductory statement might also provide the date of the contract. Sometimes the beginning of a contract also includes **recitals**, which are statements about background history or the contract's purpose. These statements are not substantive provisions, such as those creating obligations, rights, or conditions, which are found in the middle part of the contract. Finally, a *transitional clause*, while unnecessary, is often included in a formal written agreement. If included, the **transitional clause** merely serves to signal to the reader a shift from the contract's beginning to the middle part of the contract. Chapter 5 discusses suggestions for drafting the beginning of the contract.

Joint Venture Agreement — Title

This agreement, dated May 1, 20XX, is between Go-Go Bike Company, Inc., a United States corporation incorporated under Illinois law (**"Go-Go"**), and Tong Corp., a Taiwanese corporation (**"Tong"**). — Introductory statement

Go-Go engages in the business of developing, manufacturing, and marketing bicycles (the **"Product"**).

Tong is a leading manufacturer of lightweight solar rechargeable batteries and has access to distribution markets throughout in the Republic of China, South Korea, Japan, Singapore, Philippines, Malaysia, Indonesia, Brunei, Thailand, Vietnam, Laos, and Cambodia (the **"Territory"**). — Recitals

The parties desire to enter into this joint venture for the purpose of developing, manufacturing, and distributing solar-powered electric bicycles for sale in the Territory.

Therefore, the parties agree as follows: — Transitional clause

Figure 3-1 Example of the beginning of a joint venture contract

3.1.2 The middle of a contract

The middle part of a contract contains the provisions governing the parties' rights and obligations. This part of the contract can be further arranged into subgroups: (1) the *core provisions*; (2) the *exit provisions*; (3) the *alternative dispute resolution provisions*, if any; and (4) the *miscellaneous provisions*. You might also consider including a *definitions section* in this part of the contract, especially if

> An **obligation** *in a contract is a promise made by a party "to do or to not do something."* Black's Law Dictionary, *1179 (Bryan A. Garner ed., 9th ed. West 2009).*

many defined terms are used in the contract. Chapter 4 discusses suggestions for drafting definitions and when to include a definitions section.

a. Core provisions

Core provisions state the details of the parties' association with each other. The middle part of the contract typically begins with core provisions that establish the nature of the contract by stating the primary performance or obligations. Any other details of the parties' association that do not belong in the exit provisions, dispute resolution provisions, or miscellaneous provisions are included in the core provisions subgroup. This includes the term of the contract and any options to renew or continue the contract. Rights or obligations related to payment of monies are also included in the core provisions. See Figure 3-2 for examples of these types of core provisions for the joint venture agreement between Go-Go Bike Company, Inc. ("Go-Go") and Tong Corp. ("Tong"), introduced in Figure 3-1.

---

1. Creation of Joint Venture. By signing this agreement, the parties create a joint venture to develop, manufacture, and distribute solar-powered electric bicycles in the Territory as provided under the terms of this agreement (the "**Joint Venture**"). The Joint Venture will be conducted under the name of Solar Bikes in Taipei, Taiwan, according to the business plan attached as **Schedule A**. Each party will have one-half interest in the Joint Venture and will share equally in the profits or losses of the Joint Venture.

2. Contract Term. The effective date of this agreement is the date stated in the introductory paragraph to this agreement. Unless sooner terminated under the provisions of this agreement, the term of this agreement will continue from the effective date until April 30, 20XX.

3. Capital Contribution. Upon signing this agreement, each party shall make an initial capital contribution to the Joint Venture in the amount of One Million USD.

Figure 3-2 Example of core provisions for a joint venture contract

Additional core provisions depend on the nature of the parties' agreement. Using the joint venture example, the agreement between Go-Go and Tong might include provisions for making additional capital contributions to the joint venture; managing the joint venture and its property; calculating profits; computing losses; maintaining business records; stating representations; prohibiting competition with each other or the joint venture; and keeping some types of information confidential.

> **Representation** *provisions in a contract are declarations of fact (past or present) made by a contracting party to induce the other party to enter into the contract.*

Sometimes a business deal will also involve a closing. If so, then the core provisions will also include provisions stating the place, date, and time of the closing, as well as provisions listing documents and other items each party will bring to the closing. The joint venture agreement between Go-Go and Tong does not have a closing, so no closing provisions are included in that agreement.

> *A* **closing** *is a meeting where the parties sign documents and, if relevant, the business deal is funded. If the deal involves a sale of property, the seller will transfer ownership of the property to the buyer in exchange for the buyer's payment of the purchase price.*

Suggestions for drafting a variety of core provisions are more specifically discussed in Chapter 10.

b. Exit provisions

Exit provisions state events that will bring a premature end to a contract, such as a party's failure to perform an obligation as promised (often referred to as a *breach*) or a party's misrepresentation of a fact. An exit provision might also address circumstances when a defaulting party will be given time to correct a breach or other problem. Other exit provisions might identify the rights or obligations of the respective parties after the ending of the contract.

> **Exit provision** *is a colloquial term often used in conversation or informal communications to describe a provision that addresses the ending of a contract. Another colloquial term used to describe this type of provision is endgame provision.*

The following are exit provisions included in the joint venture agreement between Go-Go and Tong.

> **12. Termination by Mutual Consent.** This agreement will terminate immediately and at any time upon the mutual written consent of Go-Go and Tong.
>
> **13. Termination for Breach or Misrepresentation.** Either party may terminate this agreement upon written notice to the other party if the other party breaches any material obligation of this agreement and fails to cure the breach within thirty days of its receipt of written notice of the breach. Notwithstanding the previous sentence, this Agreement can be terminated by the non-defaulting

Continued

party immediately upon written notice to the defaulting party in the event of an irremediable breach by the defaulting party or a misrepresentation of fact.

14. Automatic Termination. Either party may immediately terminate this agreement upon giving written notice to the other party in the event that party makes (i) an assignment for the benefit of creditors, or (ii) petitions, applies for, or permits, with or without its consent, the appointment of a custodian, receiver, trustee in bankruptcy, or similar officer for all or substantially all of its business or assets.

15. Dissolution of Joint Venture. Upon termination of this agreement for any cause whatever, the joint venture will be wound up and dissolved according to the laws of the Republic of China.

Figure 3-3 Example of exit provisions for a joint venture contract

Chapter 11 discusses suggestions for drafting exit provisions.

c. Alternative dispute resolution provisions

Alternative dispute resolution provisions, such as informal negotiations, mediation, and arbitration, provide means to resolve disputes other than through formal litigation in the courts. These alternative dispute mechanisms offer greater privacy. And, in some instances, save time and reduce cost as opposed to litigating in the courts. Therefore, including alternative dispute resolution provisions in a contract has become quite common. Figure 3-4 provides the arbitration clause appearing in the joint venture agreement between Go-Go and Tong.

16. Arbitration. The parties shall submit disputes arising under or related to this agreement for settlement by binding arbitration under the International Chamber of Commerce rules. Disputes will be heard and settled by a panel of three arbitrators, each of whom must speak fluent English and will be appointed according to the International Chamber of Commerce rules. Arbitration will be held in Oak Park, Illinois, in the United States, and will be conducted in the English language.

The fees and expenses of the arbitrators will be split evenly between the parties, and each party will bear its own costs in any arbitration proceeding.

Figure 3-4 Example of alternative dispute resolution provisions for a joint venture contract

Chapter 12 provides guidelines for drafting these provisions.

d. Miscellaneous provisions

Miscellaneous provisions are placed after the core, exit, and dispute resolution provisions. These provisions cover matters not addressed elsewhere in the contract. Miscellaneous provisions typically cover matters such as interpreting the contract, assigning parties' rights or delegating parties' obligations, amending the contract, waiving obligations, or enforcing the contract.

> *Miscellaneous provisions are also commonly referred to as* general provisions. *Colloquial terms sometimes used in conversation or informal communications to describe these types of provisions are* housekeeping provisions *or* boilerplate provisions.

Because these miscellaneous provisions often look similar across various contracts, you might be tempted to take a provision found in one contract and simply cut and paste it into another contract without considering the wording of the provision or how it might affect the contracting parties' respective interests. Care in drafting miscellaneous provisions is just as important as in drafting other provisions. Therefore, you should give attention to the language contained in these provisions to ensure that the parties' intent and respective interests are adequately protected. Figure 3-5 shows a sampling of miscellaneous provisions included in the joint venture agreement.

---

17. Notice. Any notice required or permitted under this Agreement will be in writing, delivered either by overnight mail and be addressed as follows:

If to Go-Go:
Go-Go Bike Company, Inc.
1024 West Boulevard
Oak Park, Illinois 60301 USA
Attention: Legal Department

If to Tong:
Tong Corp.
10th Floor, 108
Ming Sheng West Road
Taipei, Taiwan
Attention: Legal Department

Any notice given will be deemed effectively given and received on the date of delivery.

18. Contract Language. English is the governing language of this Agreement and of any arbitration proceeding.

19. Governing Law. Illinois law governs all matters arising under or related to this agreement.

Figure 3-5 Example of miscellaneous provisions for a joint venture contract

Common miscellaneous provisions and considerations for these provisions are discussed in Chapter 13.

3.1.3 The end of a contract

The end of the contract includes the contracting parties' signature blocks and any attachments (such as exhibits or schedules) to the contract. This part of the contract also might include a **concluding statement**, which signals to the reader the formal end to the body of the contract.

A concluding statement and signature blocks signal the end of a contract. If there are any attachments, these will be affixed to the back of the contract. Figure 3-6 shows the concluding statement and signature blocks for the joint venture agreement between Go-Go and Tong. You might recall paragraph 1 of the joint venture agreement, shown in Figure 3-2, references a business plan attached as "Schedule A." This schedule would be attached to the back of the joint venture agreement.

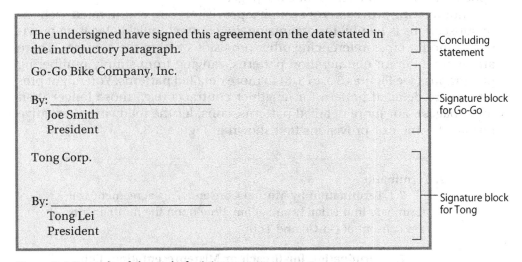

The undersigned have signed this agreement on the date stated in the introductory paragraph. — Concluding statement

Go-Go Bike Company, Inc.

By: _____

    Joe Smith
    President — Signature block for Go-Go

Tong Corp.

By: _____

    Tong Lei
    President — Signature block for Tong

Figure 3-6 Example of the end of a joint venture contract

Tips for drafting the end of the contract are discussed in Chapter 14.

3.2 Headings

Contract provisions appearing in the middle of the contract are often organized under headings for ease of the reader's reference. Because they are used for organizational purposes, headings are not considered a substantive part of the contract, though a judge might consider a heading to help interpret an ambiguous provision. Headings signal to the reader the general content of the provisions

Avoid using colloquial terms in headings, even though parties and lawyers may use these words in spoken conversation or informal communications. For example, do not use "exit provisions" or "endgame provisions" in a heading; instead, consider using "termination" or other related words. Also, do not use "housekeeping provisions" or "boilerplate" in a heading; instead, consider using "Miscellaneous provisions" or "general provisions."

found underneath. Therefore, you will want to review the language of the provisions to decide the theme of those provisions. Express the theme as a heading, but state it as concisely as possible. If a heading is more than four words in length, you should try to shorten it, if possible. To give emphasis, consider typing the heading in bold typeface. For an example of headings, see the provisions in Figures 3-2 to 3-5.

3.3 Numbering formats

For ease of reference and navigation, pages are numbered and contract provisions in the middle part of the contract are enumerated. Every page of a contract, except for the attachments, is numbered. Page numbers typically appear at the bottom center of each page.

Enumerating provisions or grouping provisions into enumerated sections or subsections is helpful for organizing the contract, quickly locating provisions, and for cross-referencing other provisions within the contract. There are many different enumeration patterns, ranging from simply numbering paragraphs (see Figures 3-2 to 3-5) to more detailed patterns. You might prefer a more detailed pattern for lengthier contracts (e.g., those longer than three pages). For more detailed patterns, consider the following alternative formats for the exit provisions first shown in Figure 3-3.

---

7. Termination

7.1 Termination by Mutual Consent. This agreement will terminate immediately and at any time upon the mutual written consent of Go-Go and Tong.

7.2 Termination for Breach or Misrepresentation. Either party may terminate this agreement upon written notice to the other party if the other party breaches any material obligation of this agreement and fails to cure the breach within thirty days of its receipt of written notice of the breach. Notwithstanding the previous sentence, this Agreement can be terminated by the non-defaulting party immediately upon written notice to the defaulting party in the event of an irremediable breach by the defaulting party or a misrepresentation of fact.

7.3 Automatic Termination. Either party may immediately terminate this agreement upon giving written notice to the other party in the event that party makes (i) an assignment for the benefit of creditors, or (ii) petitions, applies for, or permits, with or without its consent, the appointment of a custodian, receiver, trustee in bankruptcy, or similar officer for all or substantially all of its business or assets.

Continued

> **7.4 Dissolution of Joint Venture.** Upon termination of this agreement for any cause whatever, the joint venture will be wound up and dissolved according to the laws of the Republic of China.

Figure 3-7 Sample enumeration format: an intermediate version

> **Article 7 Termination**
>
> **7.1 Termination by Mutual Consent.** This agreement will terminate immediately and at any time upon the mutual written consent of Go-Go and Tong.
>
> **7.2 Termination for Breach or Misrepresentation.** Either party may terminate this agreement upon written notice to the other party if the other party breaches any material obligation of this agreement and fails to cure the breach within thirty days of its receipt of written notice of the breach. Notwithstanding the previous sentence, this Agreement can be terminated by the non-defaulting party immediately upon written notice to the defaulting party in the event of an irremediable breach by the defaulting party or a misrepresentation of fact.
>
> **7.3 Automatic Termination.** Either party may immediately terminate this agreement upon giving written notice to the other party in the event that party makes (i) an assignment for the benefit of creditors, or (ii) petitions, applies for, or permits, with or without its consent, the appointment of a custodian, receiver, trustee in bankruptcy, or similar officer for all or substantially all of its business or assets.
>
> **7.4 Dissolution of Joint Venture.** Upon termination of this agreement for any cause whatever, the joint venture will be wound up and dissolved according to the laws of the Republic of China.

Figure 3-8 Sample enumeration format: a more complex version

Whichever pattern you decide to use, simple numbering or a more detailed pattern, consistently use that format throughout the middle of the contract.

Exercises

▶ **Exercise 3-1   Skim two tables of contents**
Look at the Table of Contents (TOCs) of DA#5, and DA# 8 to get a general overview of the structure of a contract. How much overlap of headings do you detect?

CONTRACT DA# 5	CONTRACT DA# 8
1. APPOINTMENT AS DISTRIBUTOR	1. PRODUCTS AND TERRITORY.
2. MINIMUM PURCHASE COMMITMENT	2. PRICES AND PAYMENT
3. PURCHASES: PRICES, AND TERMS OF PURCHASES	3. OTHER OBLIGATIONS OF DISTRIBUTOR.
4. TERM/TERMINATION	4. MANUFACTURER'S OBLIGATIONS.
5. REPRESENTATIONS, WARRANTIES AND COVENANTS	5. RELATIONSHIP OF THE PARTIES.
6. INTELLECTUAL PROPERTY	6. MINIMUM PURCHASE REQUIREMENTS.
7. WARRANTY AND SERVICE MATTERS	7. REPORTING.
8. INSURANCE	8. TRADEMARKS, SERVICE MARKS AND TRADE NAMES.
9. INDEMNITY	9. COVENANT NOT TO COMPETE.
10. INDEPENDENT CONTRACTOR	10. LIMITED WARRANTY
11. ASSIGNMENT	11. INDEMNIFICATION.
12. MISCELLANEOUS	12. TERMINATION.
12.1 Entire Agreement	13. SELLING OFF OF INVENTORY.
12.2 Modification, Amendment	14. MODIFICATION.
12.3 No Waiver	15. ASSIGNMENT.
12.4 Section Headings	16. NOTICE.
12.5 Severability	17. WAIVER.
12.6 Successors and Assigns	18. VALIDITY.
12.7 Notices, Requests, Approvals	19. CONSTRUCTION OF AGREEMENT AND RESOLUTION OF DISPUTES.
12.8 Counterparts	20. CONFIDENTIALITY MAINTAINED.
12.9 Confidential Information	21. ENTIRE AGREEMENT
13. FORCE MAJEURE	
14. DISPUTE RESOLUTION	

Continued

CONTRACT DA# 5	CONTRACT DA# 8
15. APPLICABLE LAW AND JURISDICTION	22. NO RIGHTS BY IMPLICATION. 23. RESPONSIBILITY FOR TAXES. 24. MODIFICATION OF PRODUCT. 25. FORCE MAJEURE. 26. COMPLIANCE WITH LAWS. 27. SEVERABILITY. 28. COUNTERPARTS. 29. DEFINITION OF AFFILIATES.

Follow-up activity #1: After class, read the full text of DA#5, and DA#8, which can be found in the "Distribution Agreements" file on the companion website (www.aspenlawschool.com/books/Adams), trying to use a dictionary as little as possible. Make margin notes if you see something you find interesting, new, or difficult to understand. This activity will give you a chance to develop a feeling for structure and actual wording of a contract.

Follow-up activity #2: Prepare the TOCs of two consulting and two asset purchase agreements from the companion website by compiling just the headings of the contracts. Then, compare the TOCs. What headings/provisions do they share across the two contract areas, and where are they different?

▶ **Exercise 3-2   Guess the content of a provision**

On your own or with a partner, consider what content you can expect in a Force Majeure[1] provision and write down all the words that come to mind with respect to that provision. Then, go to the heading "Force Majeure" in DA#8 in the "Distribution Agreements" file on the companion website and mark all the words from your list that appear in that provision.

> *Example:*
> After you have brainstormed the words related to indemnity, mark the words in an actual *indemnity* provision.

---

1. French expression commonly used in U.S. contracts, meaning "greater force." Even if you don't know this kind of provision, can you guess how a "greater force" could affect a contract? Can you think of examples of a "greater force"?

Words associated with an indemnity provision: indemnify, responsible, damages, supplier, distributor, harmless, pay, damages, breach, claims, agreement, fault, liability.

Indemnity

Distributor, its parent and subsidiaries (collectively the **"Distributor"**), shall require, in a written statement acceptable to **Supplier**, that its affiliates, sales representatives, agents and sub-distributors (collectively the "Distributor Network") **indemnify**, **defend** and hold **harmless Supplier**, its parent, subsidiaries and affiliates, and its and their officers, directors, shareholders, employees, representatives and agents, from and against any and all **claims**, **liabilities**, suits, proceedings, judgments, orders, fines, penalties, damages, costs, and expenses, including but not limited to reasonable attorney fees and other expenses of litigation, which it or they may hereafter incur, become responsible for or **pay** out as a result of death or bodily injuries to any person, destruction or any **damage** to any property or contamination of or adverse effect on the environment, arising out of or resulting from any **fault** or negligent act or omission of the Distributor Network, including, without limitation, any sale or distribution of solvents by the Distributor Network for use in the Equipment not approved by Supplier, or any material **breach** of this **Agreement** by the Distributor Network, except to the extent that such **claims**, liabilities, suits, proceedings, judgments, orders, fines, penalties, **damages**, costs and expenses are caused by or result from the **fault** or negligent act or failure to act of **Supplier**. [DA#5]

▶ **Exercise 3-3   Find the heading based on a definition**
Look at the following definitions and decide what heading they refer to.

1. The geographic area where a party performs its obligation.

   _____

2. Fact statements inserted in the front part of a contract between the introductory statement and the transitional clause of a contract, providing important historical background that lead to the contract or indicating the reasons or the purpose for the contract.

   _____

3. The duration of the contractual relationship.

   _____

4. The ending of a contract.

   _____

   _____

5. A party agrees to compensate another party for loss or damages arising out of various circumstances like the compensating party's
   breach of an obligation, misrepresentation of fact, or negligent
   action.

   _____

6. Contract provisions covering matters not addressed elsewhere in the
   contract, such as the governing law of the contract, assigning the
   parties' rights or delegating the parties' duties, giving notice to the
   other party, or amending the contract.

   _____

   _____

7. A contract clause providing for the suspension of certain obligations
   under a contract without incurring a penalty upon the occurrence of
   an event outside the control of the contracting parties, e.g., natural
   disasters, fire, war, or embargoes.

   _____

   _____

8. The transfer of a party's legal rights or property to another party.

   _____

9. The transfer of a party's performance obligations to party who was
   not one of the original parties to the contract.

   _____

   _____

10. A contract provision stating whether remaining provisions in a con-
    tract will still be enforced if any provisions in the contract are found
    unreasonable and thus enforceable.

    _____

    _____

Look up several examples of these provisions in your database of contracts
once you have finished this activity.

▶ **Exercise 3-4   Assign headings to various contract provisions**

The headings of the contract provisions 13.1 through 13.7 in the following
sample passage (see box below) have been removed. Try to find the right
heading by underlining key words of the provision.

Example: The answer for the heading of 13.1 is "Governing Law." The key
words/expressions in the passage are "governed by the law."

Article 13 MISCELLANEOUS PROVISIONS
[Taken from contract DA#8]

13.1 [Heading omitted.] This Agreement shall be governed by the laws (key words) of the Commonwealth of Pennsylvania.

Heading : Governing Law

13.2 [Heading omitted.] The existence of this Agreement and its terms, and all communications between the Parties and their representatives relating to the subject matters of this Agreement shall be considered Confidential Information under the existing Confidentiality Agreement between Supplier (or its Affiliate) and Distributor, and shall not be disclosed by either Party except as authorized by the Confidentiality Agreement or required by law. All confidential communications between the Parties pertaining to legal matters shall be conducted subject to a Common Interest Privilege Agreement between the Parties.

Heading 13.2: _____

13.3 [Heading omitted.] Each Party shall, at its sole cost and expense, maintain in full force and effect all necessary licenses, permits, and other authorizations required by law in order to carry out its duties and obligations hereunder.

Heading 13.3 : _____

13.4 [Heading omitted.] This Agreement shall not constitute or give rise to any employer-employee, agency, partnership, or joint venture relationship among or between the Parties, and each Party's performance hereunder is that of a separate, independent entity in pursuit of a common purpose.

Heading 13.4: _____

13.5 [Heading omitted.] None of the terms of this Agreement shall be amended or modified except in writing signed by both Parties.

Heading 13.5 : _____

13.6 [Heading omitted.] This Agreement shall be binding upon and inure to the benefit of Supplier and Distributor and their successors and assigns of all or substantially all of either Party's business or assets. Any change of control of either Party shall not affect either Party's rights or obligations under this Agreement. Except for an assignment to an Affiliate of a Party, neither Party shall assign or transfer any of its rights or obligations under this Agreement without the prior written consent of the other Party, such consent not to be unreasonably withheld. Each Party shall be entitled to assign all or any of its rights or obligations under this Agreement to an Affiliate or to a successor entity by way of merger or acquisition of substantially all of the assets of the assigning Party; provided

Continued

the Affiliate or other successor entity expressly assumes those rights, duties and obligations under this Agreement and the Agreement itself, and the Affiliate or other successor is a financially capable business entity. The assigning Party shall provide the other Party written notice of any such assignment pursuant to this Section as soon as practicable thereafter. Any assignment or transfer in contravention of this Agreement shall be null and void.

Heading 13.6 : _____

13.7 [Heading omitted.] This Agreement constitutes the entire agreement between the Parties respecting the subject matter hereof and supersedes all previous term sheets, correspondence and any and all other writings and understandings.

Heading 13.7 : _____

▶ **Exercise 3-5   Reconstruct a contract**

Your computer crashed, and you are supposed to submit a draft of your contract to the associate by noon. It is 11:30 a.m. and you have a paper copy, but it is just paper slips in no specific order without complete numbering. Put the slips in the correct order so you can scan them in and work on the numbering. Copy the slips (which can be found in the materials section of Chapter 3 on the companion website at www.aspenlawschool.com/books/ Adams) and rearrange them. Mark all key words at the beginning and the end of the paper slip that could indicate how the slips could be rearranged.

Example: The following part of a contract has been cut apart, but from the section headings and the key words in the passage (marked in bold letters), you can see how the parts fit together.

Patent and Trademark

Supplier or its Affiliates shall have the exclusive right to prepare, **file**, prosecute and **maintain** at its or their own expense all **patent and trademark applications** and **patents** and **trademarks** relating to the Product, and shall use reasonable efforts to **file such applications** as may be required to protect the intellectual property associated with the Product in the Territory.

Distributor shall provide reasonable assistance to Supplier to facilitate the **filing** and **maintenance** of all such **patent and trademark**

Continued

> **applications** and **patents and trademarks**, and shall execute all
> documents which Supplier deems necessary or desirable therefor.
> [DA#24]

▶ **Exercise 3-6   Add to your vocabulary list**

Add to your vocabulary list at least ten new words from the "Contract
Database" file on the companion website. Use the model from section 1.4
of Chapter 1 for guidance. Modify your old lists if you have new information
regarding a word.

▶ **Exercise 3-7   Pegasus/Azteca deal—first outline of the contract**

So far in exercises in Chapters 1 and 2, you have written two emails to
Cynthia Adler regarding a proposed contract between Pegasus Snowboards
Inc. and Deportes Azteca, Ltda. Your emails summarized the terms agreed to
by the parties up to today. The parties have much more to negotiate before
the contract is finalized, but using the agreed terms summarized in the
memo, state where these terms will go in the contract (e.g., the title in the
beginning of the contract; the recitals in the beginning part of the contract;
the core provisions in the middle part of the contract). Use the following
chart to help you in this process. Suggest a heading for each agreed term
that you have identified should be placed in the middle part of the contract.
Also add a short description of the agreed term next to the heading.

◆ **Beginning of the contract**
  • Title of the document
  • Introductory statement
  • Recitals (optional)
  • Transitional clause (optional)

◆ **Middle of the contract**
  • Core provisions
  • Exit provisions
  • Alternative dispute resolution provisions, if any
  • Miscellaneous provisions

◆ **End of the contract**
  • Concluding statement (optional)
  • Signature blocks
  • Attachments (exhibits or schedules), if any

Example: Your client has told you that her company wants to have exclusive
rights for the distribution of a product in Spain, Great Britain, and Greece.
In your outline you include a heading and a short description of each agreed
term:

◆ **Middle of the contract**
  • Core provisions
    1. **Right to distribute: exclusive**
    2. **Distribution territory: Spain, Great Britain, and Greece**
  • Exit provisions
  • Alternative dispute resolution provisions, if any
  • Miscellaneous provisions

Defined Terms

Before reading this chapter, work on Exercise 4-1 at the end of the chapter as a warm-up exercise.

Defined terms are commonly used in contracts for clarity, conciseness, and precision. A **defined term** means a word or phrase that is given a unique meaning in a contract. You should create defined terms only when necessary. Needlessly creating too many defined terms can make provisions unnecessarily complex and difficult to understand. In these instances, readers are more likely to lose track of the meaning of defined terms. Their reading is continually disrupted as they hunt again for a definition to refresh their memory. Limit creating defined terms to the following situations:

> *Unlike many civil law systems, the United States does not have an extensive body of statutorily defined contract terms. Therefore, U.S. contracts often include more definitions of terms than might appear in contracts governed by the law of a civil law system.*

- **To resolve an ambiguity when a word or phrase could have more than one reasonable but conflicting meaning.** As an example of an ambiguous word, consider the following provision in a distribution contract between two companies, Samar Corp. and Lieber Gmbh & Co.: "The company will establish pricing for the products." Both parties are companies, so which one establishes pricing?
- **To give special meaning to a word or phrase that has broader meaning in everyday language.** For example, *products* in everyday language can refer to all types of goods produced by various businesses. But within the context of a distribution contract, the meaning might be limited to specific goods produced by one of the contracting parties. In the contract between Samar Corp. and Lieber Gmbh & Co., the distributed goods will be "sandals, belts, watchbands, and sunglasses retainers produced by Samar Corp." Therefore, *products* will be defined in the contract with this limited meaning. Using the defined term *Products* in the contract will always have the meaning given in the definition.

● ***To shorten a phrase that is used repeatedly throughout the
contract.*** In the same distribution contract mentioned in the
previous examples, the products subject to distribution and the parties
will be mentioned repeatedly throughout the contract. Instead of
repeating "sandals, belts, watchbands, and sunglasses retainers
produced by Samar Corp.," these goods in the contract will be defined,
and in the rest of the contract be referred to, as *Products.* Furthermore,
instead of using the parties' complete names each time they are
mentioned, treat each as a defined term. Samar Corp., the supplier of
the products for distribution could be identified as *Samar* or *Supplier.*
Lieber Gmbh & Co., the distributor of the products, could be identified
as *Lieber* or *Distributor.* Note that referring to each party by a defined
term would also resolve the ambiguity presented in the first example
above: "Lieber will establish pricing for the Products."

4.1 Creating defined terms

Capitalize the first letter of every word in a defined term. If *products* is the
defined term for goods supplied by Samar, then capitalize the *p* in *Products*
every time it used as the defined term. Also, to make it easier for the reader to
locate the definition in the contract, consider placing the defined term in
bold typeface when it is defined. Thereafter, use regular typeface but continue capitalizing the defined term.

Samar engages in the business of developing, designing, producing,
packaging, and marketing sandals, belts, watchbands, and sunglasses retainers. Distributor promotes, sells, and distributes merchandise in the European Union, including merchandise similar to
those of the Product.

"**Force Majeure Event**" means war, flood, lightning, drought, earthquake, fire, hurricane, cyclone, tornado, explosion, civil distur-
bance, terrorism, military action, epidemic, government action,
or labor strike.

Neither party is liable for any delay or failure of performance resulting directly from a Force Majeure Event.

When you create a defined term, think of a word or phrase that logically
reflects what is being defined. For conciseness, try to limit the defined term
to three or fewer words. Thus, for Samar Corp., the supplier in the example
distribution contract, a logical defined term would be either *Samar* or *Supplier.* If Samar was called "Samar Sunglass Corp.," it would be less desirable

to use *Sunglass* as the defined term for the party because this could be confused with some of the goods being distributed.

As another example, *product* is a logical word to use for the defined term for goods being distributed. Referring to a thesaurus, you might be able to find other words that are just as logical. Looking up *product*, you would find *merchandise* listed as one of the words. *Merchandise* has a meaning similar to *product*. Therefore, you may prefer using *Merchandise* as the defined term, instead of *Product*.

Once you have settled on a defined term, try to avoid using that same word in the contract in another context. Let's say a provision in the distribution agreement refers to goods other than those supplied by Samar: "During the term of this agreement, Lieber shall not act as a representative or distributor for any product that competes with the Products." Technically, the lower case *product* appearing first in the provision communicates to the reader that the goods in that instance are not those supplied by Samar. Nevertheless, it is confusing to see the same word used in two different contexts in the sentence. You could change the lowercase word; perhaps replace it with *merchandise*: "During the term of this agreement, Lieber shall not act as a representative or distributor for any merchandise that competes with the Products."

If you will be using both the singular and plural form of the defined term in the contract, then you may provide both alternatives when introducing the defined term.

> Distributor shall promote, advertise, and distribute sandals, belts, watchbands, and sunglasses retainers produced by Supplier (the "**Product**" or "**Products**").

Strictly speaking, however, merely providing the singular form of the defined term when giving the definition is sufficient.

4.2 Drafting definitions

A definition should accurately reflect the meaning of the defined term as used in the contract. The following subsections describe guidelines for creating definitions.

4.2.1 Do not create one-shot definitions

Do not provide a defined term if it will be used only once in the contract. Defined terms are often used to shorten what would otherwise be a lengthy sequence of words. If you create a defined term and use it only once, you are unnecessarily creating more words. You are not drafting concisely.

One-shot definition:

Supplier may terminate this Agreement upon one year written notice if Supplier is or Supplier's assets are acquired by a third party. For purposes of this provision, "acquired" means a third party has obtained 50% or more of the capital shares or voting power of Supplier.

More concise:

Supplier may terminate this Agreement upon one year written notice if Supplier is or Supplier's assets are acquired by a third party who has obtained 50% or more of the capital shares or voting power of Supplier.

4.2.2 Do not include substantive provisions in definitions

For clarity you do not want to include a substantive provision[1] as part of a definition. Because definitions serve merely to explain the defined term, they are not expected to include substantive matters. Therefore, if a substantive provision is buried in a definition, a party could easily overlook it. The substantive provision, as a significant point of agreement between the parties, should stand apart. Consider, for example, the following definition:

"**Territory**" means the European Union, where *Distributor shall promote, advertise, and distribute the Product.*

The italicized passage creates an obligation for the distributor. It would be easy for the distributor to overlook this. Delete this passage from the definition and insert it as a separate provision in a logical place.

4.2.3 Do not use "circular" definitions

Circular definitions use the defined term in the definition of that term.

"**Liabilities**" means Distributor's liabilities.

---

1. A **substantive provision** is one that creates obligations, rights, discretionary powers, procedural rules, conditions, declarations, express warranties, performatives, or exceptions. These provisions are discussed in Chapter 7.

Using *liabilities* to define the term *Liabilities* does nothing to enlighten the reader as to what is meant by the defined term beyond merely identifying it as the "Distributor's liabilities."

4.2.4 Do not provide a definition of a defined term within another definition

For clarity, definitions should not include definitions of other defined terms.

> *Definition within a definition:*
> "**Initial Year**" means the period beginning on May 1, 20XX, (the "**Effective Date**") and ending on April 30, 20XX.
>
> *More clear:*
> "**Effective Date**" means May 1, 20XX.
> "**Initial Year**" means the period beginning on the Effective Date and ending on April 30, 20XX.

4.2.5 Use of *including* in the definition

Use the term *including* if you are listing what is covered by the definition.

> "**Territory**" means the United States, including its territories and possessions.

If there is a risk that *including* would be interpreted as limited to the listed items and the parties do not intend this restrictive meaning, then consider prefacing the list with the phrase *including without limitation*. Be mindful, however, that using *including without limitation* in some instances in a contract and using *including* in other instances may create ambiguity. This could lead to *including* being given an unintended restrictive meaning. The examples listed in the inclusionary clause should adequately reflect the categories intended. But do not make the list of examples longer than necessary. The more detailed the list of examples, the more likely the list will be interpreted more restrictively.

4.2.6 Use of *excluding* in the definition

If the parties intend to omit something that might otherwise be included in the definition, provide the definition and then state the exclusions. Signal the beginning of the list of exclusions with *excluding*.

> "**Territory**" means the United States, excluding its territories and possessions.

4.2.7 Precisely identify external documents, statutes, or treaties in definitions

If a definition references an external document, statute, or treaty, identify the outside reference and state whether the definition includes any amendments made after the contract is signed. If the definition is silent about future amendments, then an ambiguity might arise as to whether these amendments affect the meaning of the defined term.

> "**FDA**" means the Canadian Food and Drugs Act (R.S.C. 1985 c. F-27) in effect at any given time.
>
> ———————
>
> "**Lease**" means the equipment lease agreement, dated January 21, 20XX, between Best Equipment Corporation and DX Industries, Inc. in effect at any given time.

4.3 Where to place a definition

> *Legalese is vocabulary used in the legal profession that sounds lawyerly but provides no legally enforceable power. Legalese can confuse or make meanings unclear. Therefore, legalese should be omitted from a contract and replaced with simple vocabulary that communicates meaning more clearly and precisely.*

A definition can be (1) embedded in a sentence or substantive section of the contract, or (2) listed with other definitions in a separate section of the contract.

4.3.1 Embedded definitions

A definition can be embedded

(1) as part of a sentence where the defined term is first applied (**contextual definition**), or

(2) as a separate sentence in the section of the contract where the term is first applied (**sentence definition**).

a. Contextual definition

When a definition is embedded in the sentence where the defined term is first used, the definition always appears immediately before the defined term. The defined term appears in parentheses and quotation marks. If the article *the* will be used whenever mentioning the defined term, the article is placed in parentheses with the defined term, but it is not included within the quotation marks. Sometimes you will see the word *hereinafter* used (e.g., "hereinafter referred to as . . ."). This term is *legalese* and thus should be omitted.

> Distributor shall promote, advertise, and distribute sandals, belts, watchbands, and sunglasses retainers produced by Supplier (the "**Product**" or "**Products**").

b. Definition sentence

If the definition is quite lengthy, it might be clearer to present the definition in a separate, standalone sentence. You can insert this sentence at the beginning of the section where the defined term will be first used. The definition sentence should appear before the defined term is used.

A definition sentence has three components presented in the following order:

1. The defined term as the subject of the sentence.
2. The verb, usually *means* (though sometimes *means* can be replaced by *includes* or *excludes* as explained in the next paragraph).
3. The definition of the defined term.

The defined term is presented in quotation marks. In a definition sentence, the article *the* does not precede the defined term even if the article will be used with the defined term elsewhere in the contract.

> "**Confidential Information**" means information regarding the manufacture, design, pricing, or marketing of the Products and all other information regarding Supplier's business, excluding information that is, or becomes, public or general industry knowledge through no fault of Distributor. Distributor shall not use any of the Confidential Information for any purposes other than in connection with the sale of Products under this agreement. Within 15 days of the termination of this agreement, Distributor shall, at its expense, return all the Confidential Information to Supplier.

Sometimes the operative verb *means* in a definition sentence is replaced by *includes* or *excludes*. These instances are uncommon, though, because using *includes* or *excludes* as the operative verb results in an imprecise definition. *Includes* is used if the defined term is intended to be broadly inclusive, extending to examples that would not ordinarily be included in the definition. Only the examples that go beyond the common meaning of the defined term are explicitly mentioned. The inclusion of more common meanings of the term is implied.

> "**Travel Expenses**" includes lodging and food.

Excludes is used when the defined term excludes something that is otherwise assumed included in the definition. In this instance, only the items explicitly excluded are mentioned. What is included in the defined term is implied.

> "**Employee**" excludes anyone who is not a citizen or resident of the United States and whose duties are primarily performed outside the United States.

4.3.2 A definition section

If your draft includes numerous defined terms, consider presenting all the definitions in a separate section of the contract. A definition section assists the reader in readily locating the definitions of all defined terms used in a contract. This section may be inserted

(1) at the beginning of the middle part of the contract before the core provisions,

(2) at the end of the middle part of the contract after the general provisions,

(3) after the table of contents and before the introductory statement in a lengthy contract, or

(4) in a separate schedule attached to the contract.

Although a definition section is not technically considered a substantive contract section, a definition section appearing in the middle part of the contract—options 1 or 2 above—will follow the same format and enumeration pattern used for the substantive sections.

The defined terms are listed alphabetically. For readability, do not number each defined term. The format of the definition sentence is the same as for an embedded definition sentence. When the definition is embedded elsewhere in the contract (excluding the introduction statement or recitals), cross-reference to the provision where the definition is embedded. See the definition of *Order Form* in the example below.

In the following example, the definition section appears at the beginning of the middle part of the contract (as evidenced by "Article 1"). Note the language prefacing the list of definitions, which acknowledges embedded definitions appearing in the introductory statement and recitals.

Article 1 Definitions

As used in this agreement, terms defined in the introductory statement and recitals have the meanings assigned to them, and each of the following terms has the meaning assigned to it.

"**Agreement**" means this International Distribution Agreement and all schedules and exhibits attached to it, as in effect at any given time.

"**Distributor's Agent**" means an import broker or forwarding agent selected and engaged by Distributor to accept deliveries and oversee Product shipments to the Territory.

"**ICC**" means International Chamber of Commerce.

"**Laws**" means all federal, state, local, foreign, or international laws; treaties; statutes; rules; and regulations in effect at any given time.

"**Marks**" means Supplier's trademarks, service marks, and trade names relating to its Product.

"**Order**" means Distributor's request to purchase Product as designated on an Order Form.

"**Order Form**" has the meaning assigned to it in Section 4.1.

"**Product**" or "**Products**" means sandals, belts, watchbands, and sunglasses retainers produced by Supplier.

"**Territory**" means the European Union.

4.4 Consistently use the defined term

For clarity and precision, consistently use the defined term throughout the contract. For instance, in the distribution contract example, if *Product* has been defined as "sandals, belts, watchbands, and sunglasses retainers produced by Samar," always use the defined term *Product* when referencing these items in the contract. To avoid creating ambiguity, always capitalize the first letter of every word in the defined term. If you forget to do this, a dispute could arise over whether that word or phrase in all lower case letters was intended to have the special meaning assigned to it in the contract or was intended to have the common meaning as used in everyday speech.

Word processing programs typically include a FIND or SEARCH function, which you can use to locate a defined term wherever it appears in the contract. This is an easy, simple, and fast way to ensure the defined term has been properly capitalized wherever used.

Doesn't pick up mis-spellings

Exercises

▶ **Exercise 4-1   Defining *Person***

How would you define the term *Person*? Draft a preliminary definition focusing on a regular, non-legal definition starting with, "A 'Person' is . . ." or "A 'Person' means . . ." Compare your definitions with those of a partner.

Then, find the definitions of *Person* in DA#7 and DA#12 in the "Distribution Agreements" file on the companion website (www.aspenlawschool. com/books/Adams). How is *Person* defined in a contract setting? How does your definition vary from that provided in the contracts?

▶ **Exercise 4-2   Fill in the defined term**

The defined terms in the following definitions have been omitted. Try to reconstruct them based on the key words you see in the passage.

Once you are done, double check the rest of the passage to make sure it follows the rules laid out in this chapter.

> *Example:*
> "_____" means the terms set out in this distribution **agreement** together with the **exhibits** attached hereto and **any documents included by reference** and any subsequent **amendments** approved in writing by both parties. [DA#10]

Answer: Agreement

1. "_____" shall mean any entity or person other than Supplier or Distributor. [DA#15]
2. (i) . . . "_____" means (a) the marks set forth in Schedule D, (b) all designs related to those marks, and (c) all other marks that Manufacturer adds from time to time and authorizes Distributor to use by written notice. The _____ are protected by _____ registration and applications both in the USPTO and other foreign countries. [DA#6]
3. "_____" shall mean the controlling regulatory authorities within the member countries of the European Union, and each of the countries that are member signatories to the European Union agreements. [DA#7]
4. For the purposes of this Agreement, "_____" shall mean all companies; natural persons, partnerships and other business entities controlled by, under common control with or controlling either party to this Agreement. [DA#8]
5. "_____" The duration of this Agreement as provided in Article 2. [DA#11]

6. "_____" shall mean an Abbreviated New Drug Application within the meaning of Section 505(j) of the U.S. Food, Drug and Cosmetic Act. [DA#15]

7. "_____" shall mean that degree of effort, expertise and resources which a person of ordinary skill, ability and experience in the matters addressed in this Agreement would utilize and otherwise apply with respect to fulfilling the obligations assumed under this Agreement. [DA#15]

8. "_____" means the gross receipts representing sales of the Products worldwide, except for sales in the Territory, in finished product form (i.e., packaged and labeled for sale to the ultimate consumer) less deductions for: (i) transportation charges, including insurance, for transporting Product, (ii) trade, quantity and cash discounts on Product, (iii) allowances or credits to customers on account of rejection or return of Product. [DA#19]

9. "_____" means Chronic Fatigue Syndrome. [DA#24]

10. "_____" shall mean any entity engaged in the promotion and sale of the Products whose primary means of promotion, sale or distribution of the Products is via an E-commerce Web Site. [DA#29]

11. "_____" shall mean Licensed Know How and Licensed Patents. [DA# 31]

12. "_____" means a person, company, or other legal entity that purchases a Product for its own internal purposes and not for distribution to, or use on behalf of, others. [DA#36]

▶ **Exercise 4-3   Define a category I**

Assume that you have four distinct items in your product line, Magidraw, Magispell, Magipaint, and Magiflash. When referring to these items, you do not always want to mention all four but instead want to refer to them as a group. Compose a definition for the definitions section of a contract that solves the problem.

▶ **Exercise 4-4   Define a category II**

Assume that you want to make sure that the distributor sells the four product lines (as discussed in the previous exercise) in four countries, Albania, Romania, Bulgaria, and Moldavia. Compose a contract definition that allows you throughout the contract to refer to the four countries collectively after the initial definition.

▶ **Exercise 4-5   Compose definitions**

Compose definition sentences for the terms *Agreement* and *Affiliate*.

The "Definitions Agreement" and "Definitions Affiliate" files in the materials section of Chapter 4 on the companion website (www.aspenlawschool.com/books/Adams) contain a collection of examples you can compare with your definitions. Before you open these files, however, brainstorm what words you can expect in the definitions and compose a first draft. Then, rewrite your draft based on a comparison with examples from the two files.

▶ **Exercise 4-6   Redrafting definitions**

Look at the following definitions and describe what potential problem could arise from the wording. Then, rewrite them.

Example:

For the purposes of this Agreement, "Material Adverse Effect" means any adverse effect on the business, operations, properties, prospects or financial condition of the Company or its Subsidiaries and which is material to such entity or other entities controlling or controlled by such entity or which is likely to materially hinder the performance by the Company of its obligations hereunder. [DA#19]

This is a circular definition that defines *material* by using the word *material*.

Problem 1.   Look at the following definition and explain why it may be problematic.
Then, rewrite it.

"Affiliate" means any company, corporation, firm, individual, trust or other entity which controls, is controlled by or is under common control with a party to this Agreement, and for the purpose of this definition the term "control" means the possession, directly or indirectly, of the power to direct or cause the direction of the management and policies of such firm, person, trust or company, whether through the ownership of voting securities, by contract or otherwise, or the ownership either directly or indirectly, including the ownership by trusts with substantially the same beneficial interests, of 50% or more of the voting securities (or, in relation to any country where ownership of more than 50% of the voting securities is prohibited by law, the maximum percentage permitted, provided such percentage is no less than 30%) of such company, corporation, firm, individual, trust of other entity. . . . [DA#14]

Problem 2.   The following passage can be found in the Definitions section of a contract. What kind of problem do you see in the wording? How can you solve the problem?

1.5 "Products" shall mean each of Company's products listed on the Company price sheet which include, but are not limited to,

Continued

> consumer electronics, MP3/audio products, headphones, cell phone accessories, apparel, helmets, and related products as they may exist from time to time (Company reserves the right to unilaterally delete products no longer supplied by Company, to modify the specification, style, design or color of any products, and to add new products, in each case such change to be effective without prior notice to Distributor). [DA#7]

▶ Exercise 4-7   Consistency check

You have been asked to check the final draft of a contract for consistent use of the word *Person* throughout the document. Go to contract DA#21 in the "Distribution Agreements" file on the companion website and, using the FIND function of your word processor, find the definition of the word *Person*. Then check for consistent use of the word throughout the contract.

▶ Exercise 4-8   Add to your vocabulary list

Add to your vocabulary list at least ten new words from the "Contract Database" file on the companion website (www.aspenlawschool.com/books/Adams). Use the model from section 1.4 in Chapter 1 for guidance. Modify your old lists if you have new information regarding a word.

▶ Exercise 4-9   Pegasus/Azteca deal—drafting defined terms

If you completed the Pegasus/Azteca deal exercises in Chapters 1 and 2, review your emails to Cynthia Adler regarding a proposed contract between Pegasus Snowboards Inc. and Deportes Azteca, Ltda. (Alternatively, your professor will give you a term sheet for this deal.) Review your notes or the preliminary term sheet, as the case may be, and identify the words or phrases that should be defined. For each word or phrase that you have identified, draft a defined term and create a definition.

The Beginning of a Contract

As mentioned in Chapter 3, contracts have three basic parts: the beginning, the middle, and the end. Each part serves a particular purpose and includes distinct components. The purpose of the beginning part of a contract is to introduce the reader to the nature of the agreement and to the contracting parties. In a formal contract, the beginning part of the contract includes the (1) title of the document, (2) an introductory statement, (3) recitals, and (4) a transitional clause. You were introduced to these four components in Chapter 3. In this chapter, you will learn more about each component and suggestions for drafting them.

5.1 The title

Begin the contract with its title. Center the title at the top of the first page of the contract. For emphasis, present the title in bold typeface and use a slightly larger font than that used for the text of the contract. See Figure 5-1.

Contract titles do not include *the, a,* or *an.* Also, do not state the names of the parties in the title. Do, however, create a name for the document that identifies, as clearly and concisely as possible, the nature of the deal. The document is a contract, so logically you would assume that the word *contract* would be at least one of the words used in the title. Although it would be more precise to use the word *contract* in the title to describe this formal understanding between the parties, the word *agreement*, rather than *contract*, is commonly favored for use in the title. Thus, "Distribution Contract" would instead be drafted as "Distribution Agreement." The rationale for this preference is unknown. One contract drafting scholar has

> *In everyday speech,* contract *and* agreement *are often used interchangeably to refer to the document that states the obligations of the parties and other important points of the deal. It is more precise, however, to refer to this document as a* contract. Agreement *has a broader meaning than* contract. *While an agreement can include a contract, it can also refer to less formal situations where two or more persons agree to something, such as a mutual assent to play tennis tomorrow.*

suggested that perhaps *agreement* has been preferred over the years because it sounds more "genteel" than *contract*.[1] Whatever the reason, *agreement* is almost universally used.

International Distribution Agreement

This agreement is dated May 20, 20XX, between Samar Corp., a United States corporation incorporated under Florida law ("**Supplier**"), and Lieber Gmbh & Co., a German corporation ("**Distributor**").

Background

Supplier engages in the business of developing, designing, producing, packaging, and marketing sandals, belts, watchbands, and sunglasses retainers (the "**Products**").

Distributor promotes, sells, and distributes merchandise in the European Union, including merchandise similar to those of the Products.

The parties desire to enter into this agreement for the purpose of granting Distributor the exclusive distributorship of the Products in order to promote, sell, and distribute the Product in the European Union, excluding Cyprus (the "**Territory**").

Therefore, the parties agree as follows: . . .

Figure 5-1 Example of the beginning of a contract

Do not simply entitle the document "Agreement" or "Contract." This description is too general and, if the parties have entered into more than one contract, would be confusing if all or some of the contracts share the same title. Consider including words in the title that adequately communicate the business nature of the contract. For instance, a contract for the cross-border distribution of goods might be entitled *International Distribution Agreement*. A contract for the purchase of assets could be entitled *Asset Purchase Agreement*. If the contract covers the purchase of stock, then state *Stock Purchase Agreement*. All of these examples included *agreement* in the title, but some contracts will not include the word *agreement* in the title—for example, documents might be titled *Guaranty* or *Assignment of Lease*.

For contracts that amend a previous contract or amend and restate the contract, the title should explicitly state this: *Amendment to Equipment Lease; Amended and Restated Loan Agreement*. If amendments have preceded the current draft, state the number of this amendment in the series: *Third Amendment to Equipment Lease; Second Amended and Restated Loan Agreement.*

---

1. Kenneth A. Adams, *A Manual of Style for Contract Drafting* 2 (2d ed., ABA 2008).

5.2 The introductory statement

The text of the contract starts with a one-sentence introductory statement. The sentence begins with a general reference to the contract itself ("This agreement . . .") or a restatement of the title (e.g., "This International Distribution Agreement . . ."). This is followed by naming the contracting parties. The date of the contract can also be included in the introductory statement, though this is unnecessary if the date is explicitly stated elsewhere in the document.

5.2.1 Referencing the contract

The introductory statement begins with a reference to the contract itself. In Figure 5-1 the sample introductory statement begins with "This agreement. . . ." When referencing the contract in the remainder of the document, continue to use the word *agreement* but preface it with the pointing word *this*: "this agreement. . . ." Using the pointing word *this* clarifies that *agreement* refers to the document itself and not another contract.

Alternatively, the contract can begin more formally by restating the contract's full title and giving it the defined term *Agreement*. The defined term will be used throughout the rest of the contract.[2] Although in this instance the contract has been given as a defined term, you will continue to preface *Agreement* with the pointing word *this* whenever referencing the contract elsewhere in the document—for example, "This Agreement is governed by New York law."

5.2.2 The date of the contract

For easy reference, the date of the contract is often stated in the introductory statement. Alternatively, the date can be stated at the end of the contract.[3] Use the same format for presenting the date as is used for dates elsewhere in the contract.[4]

In the United States, the date of contract is assumed to be the date when the parties sign the contract. It is also assumed to be the contract's **effective date**, which is when the contract provisions go into operation. Sometimes the contract's effective date is different from the date when the parties sign

---

2. Format and placement of defined terms were discussed in Chapter 3.

3. See Chapter 14 for a discussion of drafting considerations for the end part of the contract.

4. For example, the twentieth day of May in 20XX is typically expressed in a U.S. contract as "May 20, 20XX." A non-U.S. contract might express the date as "20 May 20XX" or "20XX May 20." The format will depend on the parties' preference.

the contract. If the effective date is different from the date of the contract, (1) state the date of the contract either in the introductory statement or at the end of the contract, and (2) expressly state the contract's effective date in a substantive provision in the middle of the contract as part of the core provisions.[5]

The verb used in the introductory statement will depend on whether the date of the contract appears there. If the date of the contract is included, use the phrase *is dated*. If the date is omitted, use *is made*. Sometimes you will see the phrase *is made and entered into* in a precedent's introductory statement. The words *entered into* add nothing to the meaning and thus are extraneous; therefore, delete *entered into* from contracts you draft. Also, you might find the phrase *dated as of* used in a precedent's introductory statement. Some drafters use *as of* to indicate that the parties signed the contract after the contract's effective date. Unfortunately, *dated as of* has been abused over the years; it has been used too often in situations where the date of the contract and the effective date are the same. Therefore, do not rely on *dated as of* to communicate that the parties signed the contract after the effective date. If the effective date is different from the date the parties signed, expressly state the effective date in the core provisions (as recommended earlier) to ensure clarity.

Date of the contract is included in the introductory statement:
This agreement is dated May 20, 20XX, between Samar Corp., a United States corporation incorporated under Florida law ("**Supplier**"), and Lieber Gmbh & Co., a German corporation ("**Distributor**").

Date is omitted from the introductory statement:
This agreement is made between Samar Corp., a United States corporation incorporated under Florida law ("**Supplier**"), and Lieber Gmbh & Co., a German corporation ("**Distributor**").

5.2.3 Introducing the contracting parties

Use the preposition *between* in the introductory statement when referring to the relationship of two contracting parties. Oftentimes, *by* is coupled with *between*. Because *by* does not have any legal effect, though, you should omit this word.

---

5. See Chapter 10 for a discussion of drafting considerations for the core provisions, including drafting a provision for contract's effective date.

> *Wrong:*
> This agreement is dated May 20, 20XX, by and between Samar Corp., a United States corporation incorporated under Florida law ("**Supplier**"), and Lieber Gmbh & Co., a German corporation ("**Distributor**").
>
> *Correct:*
> This agreement is dated May 20, 20XX, between Samar Corp., a United States corporation incorporated under Florida law ("**Supplier**"), and Lieber Gmbh & Co., a German corporation ("**Distributor**").
>
> ――――――――
>
> *Wrong:*
> This agreement is made by and between Samar Corp., a United States corporation incorporated under Florida law ("**Supplier**"), and Lieber Gmbh & Co., a German corporation ("**Distributor**").
>
> *Correct:*
> This agreement is made between Samar Corp., a United States corporation incorporated under Florida law ("**Supplier**"), and Lieber Gmbh & Co., a German corporation ("**Distributor**").

When there are more than two parties signing the contract, you may still use the preposition *between* or you can use the preposition *among.* However, do not write *by and among*. Similar to *by and between*, the word *by* in *by and among* does not have any legal effect. Therefore, you should omit it.

> *Wrong:*
> This agreement is dated August 9, 20XX, by and among Reye LLC, a New York limited liability corporation ("**Reye**"), Solar Enterprises, Inc., a Delaware corporation ("**Solar**"), and Karl J. Bauer, a Canadian citizen and resident of Vancouver, British Columbia, Canada ("**Bauer**").
>
> *Correct:*
> This agreement is dated August 9, 20XX, among Reye LLC, a New York limited liability corporation ("**Reye**"), Solar Enterprises, Inc., a Delaware corporation ("**Solar**"), and Karl J. Bauer, a Canadian citizen and resident of Vancouver, British Columbia, Canada ("**Bauer**").
>
> ――――――――
>
> *Continued*

> *Wrong:*
> This agreement is made by and among Reye LLC, a New York limited liability corporation ("**Reye**"), Solar Enterprises, Inc., a Delaware corporation ("**Solar**"), and Karl J. Bauer, a Canadian citizen and resident of Vancouver, British Columbia, Canada ("**Bauer**").
>
> *Correct:*
> This agreement is made among Reye LLC, a New York limited liability corporation ("**Reye**"), Solar Enterprises, Inc., a Delaware corporation ("**Solar**"), and Karl J. Bauer, a Canadian citizen and resident of Vancouver, British Columbia, Canada ("**Bauer**").

Identify the contracting parties by their legally recognized names and ensure that the named parties are the appropriate persons to bear duties of performance and liability under the contract. Identifying the appropriate contracting party becomes especially tricky when dealing with an entity operating under an assumed business name or when it is a parent, a subsidiary, or an affiliate. Do not rely on your client or even the representatives of the other contracting party to provide the correct information. Independently verify all party information, including checking with the appropriate government agency that keeps records of this nature.

A contracting party who is a natural person is identified in the introductory statement by that party's full legal name and his or her citizenship or residence, or both.

> Karl J. Bauer, a Canadian citizen and resident of Vancouver, British Columbia, Canada ("**Bauer**")

An entity is identified in the introductory statement by its complete name, the type of entity (e.g., corporation, partnership), and where it is registered.

> Samar Corp., a Florida corporation ("**Supplier**")

If the contract is a cross-border agreement, you may want to be a little more descriptive about the entity.

> Samar Corp., a United States corporation incorporated under Florida law ("**Supplier**")

Sometimes the parties' addresses are included as part of the identifiers. Including the parties' addresses makes for a lengthy, sometimes convoluted introductory statement. Addresses are not essential in the introductory paragraph if they are stated elsewhere in the contract, such as in the recitals or the notice provision.[6]

For conciseness, the parties' names often are shortened for ease of reference. Introduce each party's shortened name as a defined term in the introductory statement. After the party has been fully identified, state the shortened name in quotation marks and parentheses. Examples of this format are shown above and in Figure 5-1.

Choosing the shortened name is a matter of preference. Using Solar Enterprises, Inc. as an example, a party's shortened name can be one or two words from the party's proper name (*Solar*), the party's initials (*SEI*), or a generic name that expresses the party's role in the contract (*Buyer*). Be careful, however, in choosing defined terms for the contracting parties that are spelled similarly. For instance, only one letter differs between *Employer* and *Employee* (the terminal -*e* or -*r*). If these names were used to identify the parties to an employment contract, it would be easy to overlook a typographical error that results in the misuse of *Employer* for *Employee*, or vice versa.

The advantage in choosing a generic name over a shortened proper name of a party is that it saves editing time if the contract is used as a model in future deals because the name does not need to be changed throughout the contract to coincide with a new party's proper name. As is the case with any defined term, consistently use the defined term throughout the contract and ensure that the first letter of each word in the defined term is always capitalized.

5.3 The recitals

Recitals provide background for the contract. Although you are not required to include recitals, they can be helpful in explaining to the reader the nature of the deal. Some state the parties' intentions for entering into the contract. Others might address important events leading up to the contract. And still others might reference transactions or documents related to the contract's business deal. A judge may review a contract's recitals to help interpret the parties' intent, if a dispute arises over an ambiguous substantive provision. Therefore, if recitals are included in a contract, make sure they precisely reflect what is being reported and do not conflict with the substantive provisions.

---

6. Notice provisions are included in miscellaneous provisions in the middle part of the contract. Notice provisions and other miscellaneous provisions are discussed in Chapter 13.

Recitals do not include the substantive provisions of the business deal. The substantive provisions are stated in the middle part of the contract.

Recitals are placed after the introductory statement. Historically, the recitals section opened with the word *Witnesseth* followed by a list of fact clauses, each beginning with *Whereas*. . . . Because *witnesseth* and *whereas* have no legal effect, though, these unnecessary words are omitted from the recitals in modern contracts.[7]

The recitals can begin with a heading, typically titled *Recitals* or *Background*. It is not necessary to number each paragraph of a recital, though some drafters choose to do this. See Figure 5-1 for an example of a recitals section in a modern contract.

5.4 The transitional clause

If recitals are used in the contract, a transitional clause is included to signal the end of the recitals section and the beginning of the middle part of the contract. The transitional clause is a simple statement. The following are some sample transitional clauses.

The parties agree as follows: . . .
Agreed: . . .
Therefore, the parties agree as follows: . . .

See Figure 5-1 for an example of a transitional clause.

5.5 Note: Beginning a lengthy, complex contract

In a lengthy, complex contract, the introductory statement might be preceded by a separate cover page, a table of contents, and a list of defined terms with definitions. A cover page formally introduces the contract by stating the title of the contract. The title is usually typed in large, bold letters and is centered in the middle of the page. Often, the title page also includes the name of the contracting parties and, if appropriate, the date of the contract.

International Distribution Agreement
between Samar Corp. and Lieber Gmbh & Co.
Dated: XXXX

Figure 5-2 Title page example for a lengthy, complex contract

---

7. *Witnesseth* and *whereas* are forms of legalese and thus should not be used in the contract. Avoiding the use of legalese in a contract is discussed in Chapter 8.

A table of contents assists the reader in quickly locating specific sections and subsections in a long contract. Headings and subheadings used in the contract provisions are listed in the table of contents along with the page numbers where they appear. Any schedules and exhibits attached to the contract are also listed in the table of contents. A list of defined terms and accompanying definitions might appear after the table of contents. The format for the definitions is the same as for a definitions section, discussed in section 4.3.2 of Chapter 4.

Exercises

▶ **Exercise 5-1   Phrasing of Introductory Statement**
Compare at least ten introductory statements within one contract category (DA, APA, CA) from the "Contract Database" on the companion website (www.aspenlawschool.com/books/Adams) and enter the information in chart 1 on the next page.
Follow-up tasks:

1. How many introductory statements in the "Distribution Agreements" file DA#1-40 on the companion website use the expression *by and between*?
2. Search for the expression *dated as of* in all introductory statements. Is there a difference between *effective date* and the date the contract was signed by the parties?
3. Edit five of the introductory statements, so they reflect the principles for composing an introductory statement described in this chapter.
4. Do any of the introductory statements in the contract database look dramatically different from the pattern described in this chapter? If so, explain.

▶ **Exercise 5-2   Phrasing of recitals**
Pick one contract category (DA, APA, or CA) from the "Contract Database" file on the companion website and count how many times the recitals start with *witnesseth/whereas*. Then, find the recital section of contracts that do not contain *witnesseth/whereas*.
How do they differ from each other in style, wording, and format?

▶ **Exercise 5-3   Content of recitals**
Analyze at least ten recital sections within one contract category (DA, APA, or CA) from the "Contract Database" file on the companion website.

1. How detailed are the descriptions of the business/background of the parties?
2. What verbs are commonly used when describing the parties? What tenses are commonly used?

Chart 1

	This Agreement/ Agreement as defined term?¹*	Is made/ dated/ dated as of	Date/ effective date?	Between/ between and by/	Party A/ address? Further information? Party as defined term?	Party B/address? Further information? Party as defined term?	If effective date is different: stated in core provision/end of contract?
DA#2	THIS INTERNATIONAL DISTRIBUTION AGREEMENT (this "Agreement")	is made and entered into as of	this second day of June 2009	by and between:	**COMPANY S.A.**, a corporation organized and existing under the laws of Belgium, with its registered office at XXX, Belgium ("Supplier")	and **COMPANY LTD.**, (E.C.) a corporation organized and existing under the laws of the State of Bahrain, with its registered office at XXX, Bahrain ("Distributor")	

* Names of the parties and addresses have been deleted or abbreviated in the contract database.

3. Do any of the recitals contain wording that should not appear in recitals, for example wording found in substantive provisions?

▶ **Exercise 5-4   Use of business names in recitals**

Go to the New York State Corporate Entity Search site (http://www.dos.-ny.gov/corps/bus_entity_search.html) and find at least ten corporations by entering a letter or several letters into the Search Type: **Begins With** section. Find corporations with lengthy names. Then, come up with a shortened name for the businesses that you could use in a contract.

Follow-up task: In the entry, identify the type of entity the business is and its address. Is the business name an assumed name? Is there a parent company? If it is a foreign entity, is its agent in New York? (*Hint:* To find a foreign corporation, you can just enter a country name under Search Type.)

▶ **Exercise 5-5   Add to your vocabulary list**

Add to your vocabulary list at least ten new words from the "Contract Database" file on the companion website (www.aspenlawschool.com/books/Adams). Use the model from section 1.4 of Chapter 1 for guidance. Modify your old lists if you have new information regarding a word.

▶ **Exercise 5-6   Pegasus/Azteca deal—drafting the beginning of the contract**

Draft the beginning of the contract between Pegasus Snowboards Inc. and Deportes Azteca, Ltda. Use the information based on your work for the Pegasus/Azteca deal exercises in Chapters 1 through 4. (Alternatively, your professor will give you a term sheet for this deal.)

The Importance of Clear and Concise Writing

Contract drafting is a skill. As is the case in mastering any skill, you must learn and practice the basics before moving on to more complex tasks. Therefore, before drafting provisions such as Indemnification clauses, Warranties, confidentiality clauses, non-competition clauses, or alternative dispute resolution clauses, you need to understand and work on applying the key principles of contract drafting. This chapter and the following three chapters discuss these key principles and give you exercises on applying them. You may be surprised to discover that a few of these principles are not new to you. Most likely, you will remember some of them from English and writing courses. Contract drafting, however, demands that you give attention to these principles on an extraordinary level, which you might not have encountered previously. A misplaced comma, for example, could cost your client millions.[1]

---

1. In a contract between two Canadian parties, the provision specifying the term of the contract read: "This agreement shall be effective from the date it is made and shall continue in force for a period of five (5) years from the date it is made, and thereafter for successive five (5) year terms, unless and until terminated by one year prior notice in writing by either party." A dispute arose over whether a party could exercise this one-year termination notice at any time or only during the second five-year period. The government regulator deciding the dispute ruled that the second comma treated "and thereafter for success five (5) year terms" as an interrupter and thus the one-year termination notice applied to both the initial five-year period and the second five-year period. If the second comma had not been there, the one-year termination only would have applied to the second five-year period. *See* Ian Austen, "The Comma That Costs 1 Million Dollars (Canadian)," *N.Y. Times* (Oct. 26, 2006), http://www.nytimes.com/2006/10/25/business/worldbusiness/25comma.html.

6.1 The key principles for good drafting

The contract drafter's motto, the one that you will want to practice each time you draft is:

Attention to detail.

The following are the key principles for good drafting. If you apply these principles, you are well on your way to drafting a clear, concise, and precise document:

- **Avoid ambiguity.**
- **Be consistent in format, style, and word usage.**
- **Follow English grammar and punctuation rules.**
- **Prefer simple words and phrases common in English usage.**
- **Prefer short, simple sentence structures.**

The remainder of this chapter introduces you to two different concepts in drafting, ambiguity and vagueness, which will be further explored in the following chapters. **Ambiguity** arises when an expression is capable of two or more reasonable but conflicting meanings. **Vagueness**, however, creates only a certain measure of uncertainty. Ambiguity raises an uncertainty that creates an "'either-or' challenge, while the uncertainty of vagueness lies in marginal questions of degree."[2] Drafters strive to avoid ambiguity. But, a limited degree of vagueness is sometimes unavoidable and perhaps desirable in some instances.

6.2 Avoiding ambiguity

Because ambiguity causes misinterpretation and disagreement, you must do your best to avoid it. Ridding a contract of all ambiguities, however, is a challenge. The best way to accomplish this goal is to follow the other key principles of contract drafting listed above. A noted U.S. authority on legal writing, Bryan A. Garner, recommends "developing a concise, lean, and straightforward writing style, along with sensitivity to words and their meanings.

---

2. Reed Dickerson, *The Fundamentals of Legal Drafting* 39-40 (2d ed., Little, Brown & Co. 1986).

Once a writer has acquired such a style, ambiguities tend to become more noticeable, and therefore easier to correct."[3]

There are three types of ambiguities: semantic, syntactic, and contextual. Each one presents its own set of problems in contract drafting.

6.2.1 Semantic ambiguity

A **semantic ambiguity** arises when a symbol or word has conflicting meanings. Sometimes you can resolve the ambiguity by looking at the symbol or word in relation to the rest of the sentence, or in relation to other words or provisions in the document. For example, the currency symbol $ can mean U.S. dollars, Canadian dollars, Argentine pesos, Chilean pesos, or Mexican pesos. If the contract is between U.S. parties and the contract will be performed entirely in the United States, then it is likely that "$" means U.S. dollars. However, the ambiguity is not resolved if the contract involves either or both of the following: at least one non-U.S. party is from a country that uses the $ for its currency, or some or all performance under the contract will occur outside the United States in countries that use the $ symbol for its currency.

A simple way to resolve a semantic ambiguity is either to define the symbol, word, or phrase (as discussed in Chapter 4), or to use a more precise symbol, word, or phrase to communicate the intended meaning. Thus, if the meaning of $ is ambiguous, you may either define $ or replace $ with the appropriate ISO currency code.[4]

6.2.2 Syntactic ambiguity

Syntactic ambiguity occurs when the relationship between words or phrases in a sentence gives rise to conflicting interpretations. Unlike semantic ambiguity where the conflict arises from the meaning of the symbol or word regardless of where it appears in a sentence, syntactic ambiguity arises because of where the words or phrases appear in the sentence. An example of a syntactic ambiguity is a word or phrase that might modify the word preceding it or the word following it: "Supplier will request Distributor immediately to assign its rights in the property." Does *immediately* modify *request* or *assign*? In this instance, the ambiguity is resolved by

> *A word or phrase that could modify a word coming before or after it is called a **squinting modifier**. The modifier appears to be looking in two directions at once to determine which word it modifies.*

---

3. Bryan A. Garner, *A Dictionary of Modern Legal Usage* 48 (2d ed., Oxford Univ. Press 1995).

4. For U.S. currency, the ISO code is "USD." See Chapter 8, section 8.1.4, for using ISO currency codes.

repositioning the modifier next to the word it modifies: "Supplier will immediately request Distributor to assign its rights in the property." Or, "Supplier will request Distributor to assign immediately its rights in the property."

Another example of a syntactic ambiguity is a word or phrase that appears before or after a series: "tax-free bonds or mutual funds." Does *tax-free* modify only *bonds* or both *bonds* and *mutual funds*? Resolving this ambiguity will require more extensive restructuring of the sentence (as compared to the previous example) to clarify the meaning: "tax-free bonds or tax-free mutual funds" or "mutual funds or tax-free bonds." Additional examples of syntactic ambiguities and approaches for resolving them are discussed in Chapter 9.

6.2.3 Contextual ambiguity

A **contextual ambiguity** arises when two or more provisions in a document conflict with each other:

---

6. Company shall pay all taxes incurred by Employee for residing and doing business in Singapore.

===============

9. Employee shall pay for utilities, residential taxes, and furnishings for his residence in Singapore.

In paragraph 6 of the example, the company is obligated to pay all of the employee's taxes, but paragraph 9 makes the employee responsible for paying residential taxes. If paragraph 6 is the parties' intent, then omit "residential taxes" from paragraph 9. If the company will not be paying the employee's residential taxes, then paragraph 6 should be revised to add the following sentence: "Despite the previous sentence, Company will not pay Employee's taxes on his residence in Singapore."

Contextual ambiguities are often difficult to spot because they require the reader to consider how a provision affects other provisions in the contract. As you draft or review a contract, you will need to be alert to the interaction between provisions to avoid contextual ambiguities. This is yet another reason why you are in a stronger position if you create the first draft. As the original drafter, you are likely to be closely connected to the provisions and have a much greater understanding of their interaction.

6.3 Vagueness

Vague words and phrases hold some measure of uncertainty, but the uncertainty is not to the degree that it creates an "either-or" question. Red, for example, is a vague word.[5] Red includes shades from orange-red to crimson to maroon, and varying hues in between.[6] Though you will strive to state all provisions as clearly as possible, it might not be sufficiently important, doable, or practical to state every provision as precisely as possible.

Vagueness in a provision might depend on whether the contracting parties think details are sufficiently important to mention. For example, if your client wants to purchase a fleet of red trucks for its business, the purchase agreement might merely state "red" for the truck color. Because most trucks are painted a bright red, the client may not find it important to specify the particular shade of red for the trucks. However, if maroon is the signature color of the business, the client might insist on specifying that the trucks be painted that shade.

Sometimes standards of performance are expressed in vague terms, though this can raise issues. To illustrate, let's start with the provision "Distributor shall sell the Product." Here, the distributor has undertaken a duty to sell the product, but the provision does not elaborate on the level of effort the distributor must give to sell the product. Consider, then, the addition of the following phrases and how they might impact the distributor's duty to perform.

> Distributor shall use reasonable efforts to sell the Product.
> Distributor shall use its best efforts to sell the Product.

Reasonable is a standard frequently referenced in common law legal systems, though the standard also is recognized in some civil law systems. The *reasonable* standard also is frequently used in international contracts. *Reasonable* implies an objective standard, but there is no uniform definition for *reasonable*. The phrase *best efforts* also appears in international contracts, but as in the case of *reasonable*, there isn't a uniform definition for what it means. Indeed, many U.S. courts make no distinction between *reasonable efforts* and *best efforts*.

The best way to clarify the meaning of vague words or phrases is to expressly define them in the contract. Therefore, using the previous examples, you should define *reasonable efforts* and *best efforts*. If both are used in the contract, you should consider defining both standards so that the distinction between the two is made clear.

In instances where vague terms are not defined and a dispute arises over the meaning of the terms, the judge will look to governing law for clarification. If governing law does not provide a resolution, then answers become

---

5. Dickerson, *supra* n. 2, at 40.
6. *Id.* at 39, n. 3.

more difficult. The supplier's opinion of *best efforts* in selling its products might be quite different from the distributor's opinion.[7]

Ideally, you should precisely state a party's standard of performance. Sometimes, though, it is not possible to do so, either because the standard is impossible to predict at the time of contracting or because it would be impractical to express every detail of the performance. Aside from impossibility or impracticality, there are other reasons why you may keep the standard of performance vague. Parties who have spent many hours negotiating significant issues may be content to leave details of less important points to those administering or enforcing the provisions.

Although vague words and phrases appear in contracts due to necessity or the parties' preferences, you should strive to limit the use of vague words and phrases. Ensure the provisions identified, either by your client or you, as needing a high level of certainty are as precisely stated as possible.

Exercise

▶ **Exercise 6-1   Add to your vocabulary list**

Add to your vocabulary list at least ten new words from the "Contract Database" file on the companion website (www.aspenlawschool.com/books/Adams). Use the model from section 1.4 of Chapter 1 for guidance. Modify your old lists if you have new information regarding a word.

---

7. *See generally* Rob Park, Note, "Putting the 'Best' in Best Efforts," 73 U. Chi. L. Rev. 705 (2005).

Basic Categories of Contract Provisions

When you receive the results of the parties' negotiations—usually from your client or your supervising attorney—the terms of agreement (also referred to as *agreed terms*) will likely not be presented in a form that you can simply cut and paste into a draft. As the drafter, one of your primary responsibilities will be to create provisions that clearly and concisely state the parties' agreement. Also, because negotiations often focus only on issues of primary importance to the parties, you will often find during the drafting process that other questions must be resolved. Therefore, you

> *Term has different meanings in different contexts. In contract drafting, **term** can mean (1) a word or phrase (e.g., defined term), (2) an important requirement or condition of the parties' agreement, or (3) the duration of the contract or a situation. In the text accompanying this note, the second definition of* term *is being used.*

will need to go back to your client, and perhaps the other contracting party, to work out the remaining details. For each of the parties' agreed terms, you will draft a contract provision that clearly and concisely, and as precisely as possible, reflects the parties' intent.

As the drafter, you will decide how each agreed term will be expressed as a contract provision. This chapter introduces you to eight basic categories of contract provisions: obligations, discretionary powers, procedural statements, conditions, declarations (including representations), express warranties, performatives, and exceptions. Each category, including its purpose and suggested drafting guidelines, is discussed below. You can also refer to the chart at the end of this chapter for a summary of each category.

When deciding how an agreed term should be drafted in the contract, you can review these eight categories to determine which type of provision would best express the parties' intent. While making this decision, you will also consider how to draft the provision to adequately protect your client's interests. Wherever reasonably possible, you will try to shift risk from your client to the other party. This is not an easy task. First, you cannot significantly change the parties' agreed terms. Second, the other contract party will want to shift as much risk as possible from itself to your client. We will discuss more about allocating risk in Chapters 8, 10, 11, and 13. In this chapter, though, you will be introduced to the types of provisions that allocate risk: obligations, representations, warranties, conditions, and exceptions.

> *For purposes of this discussion,* **risk** *means the possibility of something happening that will result in the party taking the risk being responsible for or incurring loss or damages.*

Good drafting is clear, concise, and, as much as possible, precise. Therefore, in this chapter we will suggest a word or phrase to use when drafting a particular type of provision (**operative word** or **operative phrase**). For example, as discussed in section 7.1, we will suggest using the operative word *shall* whenever creating an obligation.[1] Consistently and exclusively using the suggested operative word or operative phrase—such as *shall* in obligation provisions—will help ensure that the provision is interpreted as intended. Nevertheless, the mere use of a particular word or phrase will not magically guarantee that a provision will be interpreted in a certain way. Beyond the word or phrase, the reader will take into consideration its context within the sentence, as it relates to other provisions or, in certain instances, in light of external circumstances (such as the parties' conduct). One final note: If you are a subordinate attorney in your office, your supervising attorney might insist that you draft provisions in a manner different from the recommendations made in this chapter. If your supervising attorney's preferences comply with governing law, then you should defer to your supervisor's preferences in the interest of keeping your supervisor content.

You will find that many of the operative words recommended in this chapter are modal verbs. Before you read further, work the modal verb exercise in Exercise 7-1 at the end of this chapter. This exercise gives a general review of modal verb usage.

7.1 Obligations and corresponding rights

7.1.1 Purpose of obligations

A contract is primarily about the contracting parties undertaking obligations. An **obligation** (also referred to as a *covenant*) is a promise that gives rise to a duty to take action or to refrain from taking action in a specifically stated way (to *perform*, when used as a verb; *performance*, when used as a noun). The party making the obligation is called the **promisor**. With the creation of an obligation comes a corresponding *right* in the party who is entitled to the

---

1. Please note that the rules you might have learned in English language classes on the use of *shall* and *will* do not necessarily apply in contract drafting.

promisor's performance of the obligation (the **promisee**). If the promisor fails to perform (**breaches** its obligation), then the promisee is entitled to a **remedy**, to recover damages or, in some instances, to require performance of the obligation. **Damages** is money that the promisee is entitled to receive for the loss of obligor's performance. In limited circumstances where unique property is involved (such as an antique, an artwork, or land), a court may order **specific performance**, which means the promisor is required to fulfill its promise.[2] Therefore, you will want to draft an agreed term as an obligation if

> *Promise as used in everyday conversation is a pledge without the law imposing a duty to perform. In this book, **promise** is used in the legal sense, meaning it creates a duty in the party making the promise to perform.*

1. a contracting party will be taking action or refraining from taking action, and
2. the party entitled to that performance wants damages or, if available, specific performance in the event the other party fails to perform.

> *If the contract does not expressly provide for permissible remedies in case of a breach, then remedies available under the governing law of the contract will fill in the gap.*

Let's say, for example, that a salesperson wants to sell equipment for a company. She will also agree to refrain from working for any other business while she is working for the company. The company, in return, is willing to pay the salesperson for her services and provide her other benefits, such as health insurance. Each party wants to be able to recover damages if the other party fails to perform as agreed. Therefore, you will express these agreed terms as obligations in the contract. For an example of the salesperson's obligations, see Figure 7-1.

7.1.2 Drafting obligations

The issue then becomes which word or phrase best expresses an obligation. Words or phrases commonly used for obligations include the modal verbs *will*, *must*, or *shall*, or the phrases *agrees to* or *is obligated to*. Any of these words or phrases could arguably communicate the intent to create an obligation. But, to help ensure that a provision will be interpreted as an obligation, you should select the most precise word or phrase.

As an inexperienced drafter, you might look to precedent for guidance. Unfortunately, some precedent can be filled with imprecision and inconsistencies. A poorly drafted precedent might use one word or phrase to express an obligation in one sentence then use a different word or phrase to express an obligation in another sentence. Equally troublesome, words or phrases used to express

---

2. In the United States specific performance is an extraordinary remedy that is only permitted when damages would be inadequate. See section 11.4.3(f) in Chapter 11 for additional discussion of this issue.

obligations might also be used for other purposes in the contract—to express future time, conditions, or procedural statements, for example. The resulting confusion can lead to serious interpretation issues. In a contract dispute over a sloppily drafted contract, the court might interpret a provision arguably intended as something other than an obligation, thus denying any remedy to the party allegedly injured. At the very least, resolving disputes over unclear contract language can wind up costing the parties time and money.

Will. The modal verb *will* expresses a duty to perform, but in contracts it is also used to express future situations, including those that only have the possibility of occurring.

> *Poor drafting:*
>
> *Expressing an obligation:*
> **1.** Employee will work for Company as a sales account executive.
>
> *Expressing a possible future event:*
> **15.** If Employee breaches this Agreement, Company will not pay any travel expenses or other expenses incurred after the date of termination.

To avoid this double duty, and thus avoid problems with ambiguity, the word *will* should be reserved for making procedural statements about possible future situations. (See section 7.3.) Do not use *will* to create an obligation.

> *Better:*
>
> *Expressing an obligation:*
> **1.** Employee shall work for Company as a sales account executive.
>
> *Expressing a possible future event:*
> **15.** If Employee breaches this Agreement, Company will not pay any travel expenses or other expenses incurred after the date of termination.

The harsh sound of must, *however, makes it a good operative word to express obligations in consumer contracts or adhesion contracts to stress duties imposed on the party that has weaker bargaining power.*

Must. The modal verb *must* is a strong word for expressing an obligation, conveying a sense of necessity or of being compelled to perform. Even so, many drafters, especially U.S. drafters, do not use *must* for obligations in business contracts because the word, when used repeatedly, sounds harsh. Obligation provisions appear frequently in a contract, so repeatedly using *must* can be overbearing. Consider using *must* only to signal conditions, as discussed in section 7.4. Condition provisions that use *must* typically do not occur as frequently as obligations in contracts. Also, reserving *must* only for conditions will draw a distinction between conditions and obligations.

Expressing an obligation:
1. Employee shall work for Company as a sales account executive.

Expressing a condition giving rise to a right:
11. To participate in Company's health insurance plan, Employee must notify the Company's Human Resources Department in writing prior to July 1, 20XX.

Agrees to. At first look, the phrase *agrees to* seems like a logical choice for expressing an obligation, but upon closer review, it is too imprecise to convey a legal obligation. Parties *agree to* many different types of provisions in a contract, not just those expressing obligations.

Is obligated to. The alternative phrase, *is obligated to*, appears to be a good option. Unfortunately, it is not as concise as one operative word, which could serve in its place.

Shall. For reasons explained below, the modal verb *shall* is arguably the best operative word to express an obligation.

---

1. Employee shall work for Company as a sales account executive.

---

11. During her employment with Company and for three years after termination of this agreement, Employee shall not directly or indirectly own, manage, or participate in any business similar to the type of business conducted by Company.

Figure 7-1 Examples using shall to express obligations

Admittedly, though, the modal verb *shall*, while communicating a duty to perform, has had a troublesome history of use and abuse, especially in contract drafting. You only need to look at a few poorly drafted precedents to see that *shall* has been overused and misused in many provisions that are not obligations.[3] Nevertheless, many U.S. contract drafting scholars favor *shall* as the operative word to express an obligation. Unlike *will* or *agrees to*, the

---

3. *See, e.g.,* Bryan A. Garner, *A Dictionary of Modern Legal Usage* 940 (2d ed., Aspen Publishers 1995).

modal verb *shall* is easily reserved for use only in expressing obligations. Also, *shall* does not carry an overbearing tone like *must* and is more concise than the phrase *is obligated to*.

Therefore, to state an obligation, use *shall* followed by the base form of the verb describing the promised action. Only use *shall* when expressing an obligation.[4] By doing so, you will avoid confusing obligations with other types of provisions.

Draft the obligation in active voice.[5] The promisor will be the subject of the sentence, a place of emphasis. Also, active voice is more concise than passive voice. Compare the following:

> *Active voice:*
> Distributor shall promote and advertise the Products.
>
> *Passive voice:*
> The Products shall be promoted and advertised by Distributor.

Obligations can also be undertaken by more than one of the contracting parties.

> Supplier and Distributor shall contribute to a cooperative advertising fund, which will be used by Distributor for advertising and promoting the Products in the Territory.

7.1.3 Obligations limited to the contracting parties

Only the contracting parties, those parties signing the contract, can undertake obligations. Thus, obligations cannot be created in third parties (those persons or entities not signing the contract parties to the contract), *Example 1*, or in things that are not capable of acting or forbearing from acting, *Example 2*.

---

4. In contract drafting, use *shall* only to create an obligation and not for any other purpose, even though this might be contrary to more traditional grammar rules (e.g., a traditional British grammar rule provides using *shall*, rather than *will*, in the first person, when referencing simple future time).

5. For a discussion of active voice and passive voice, see Chapter 9. In passive voice, the subject of the sentence is what is being acted upon, not the one performing the action, and the verb is a form of *to be*. One way to identify passive voice is to look for *by* in the sentence, which is often, though not always, used to introduce the actor, for example: "The Product shall be promoted and advertised by Distributor."

> *Example 1:*
> The retailers of the Product shall provide good customer service.
>
> *Explanation:*
> The distribution agreement is between the supplier of the sunglass accessories and the distributor of these products. Because the retailers are not parties to this contract, the contract cannot impose an obligation on the retailers.
>
> ————————
>
> *Example 2:*
> New York law and federal law, as applicable, shall govern the terms of this agreement.
>
> *Explanation:*
> "New York law and federal law" are not contracting parties. Further, they are things, incapable of acting or forbearing from acting. Instead, draft the provision as a procedural statement: "New York law and federal law, as applicable, govern this agreement."

Contracting parties, however, can undertake an obligation to direct third parties to act or refrain from acting.

> *Example 1:*
> Distributor shall cause its agents and employees to protect the confidentiality of the Products and the Confidential Information.
>
> *Example 2:*
> Distributor shall direct retailers of the Product to provide good customer service.

7.1.4 Corresponding rights

Every obligation creates a corresponding right for the promisee. It would be redundant, however, to state both the obligation and the right in a contract. Therefore, you should state the obligation or the corresponding right, ***but do not include both***. To express a right, use the operative phrase *is entitled to* and reserve this phrase only for a right. State the sentence in active voice, so the subject of the sentence is the party receiving the right.

In most instances, you should state the agreed term as an obligation, rather than as a right. For example, let's say that the supplier of a product wants the distributor to provide it with a report of the distributor's monthly sales of the product. It is possible to express this agreed term either (1) as an obligation imposed on the *distributor* or (2) as a stated right of the *supplier*.

Stated as an obligation:
Distributor shall provide Supplier with a complete and accurate report of Distributor's sales of the Products during the preceding calendar month.

Stated as a right:
Supplier is entitled to receive from Distributor a complete and accurate report of the Distributor's sales of the Products during the preceding calendar month.

The obligation implies that the supplier receives a right that the distributor will provide a sales report. Similarly, the right implies that the distributor is obligated to provide a sales report. Either way, it accomplishes the same result. But, to emphasize the promise to perform and the party undertaking that promise, it is preferable to express the agreed term as an obligation.

Of course, the promisee will want to ensure that the contract provides an adequate remedy if the promisor breaches its promise to perform. Therefore, consider including provisions for a remedy in the *exit provisions* section of the contract. These provisions might give the promisee the power to terminate the contract along with the right to receive monetary damages or, if permissible under the contract's governing law, the right to specific performance.[6]

Sometimes a provision will prohibit a right where one might be otherwise implied, as shown in the following example. In this instance, note the use of the phrase *is not entitled to.*

Supplier is not entitled to any damages if Distributor fails to purchase the minimum purchase quantities stated under Section 8.

---

6. If the contract does not expressly provide for permissible remedies under law in case of a breach of performance, then remedies available under the governing law of the contract will fill in the gap. See Chapter 11 for a discussion of drafting remedial provisions.

7.2 Discretionary powers

Contracts often include provisions that give one or both of the contracting parties the *freedom of choice* to act or to refrain from acting. For purposes of this book we will refer to this type of contract provision as a **discretionary power** provision. Draft the sentence expressing a discretionary power in active voice. The subject of the sentence will be the party with the discretionary power.

> **Discretion** *is a noun, meaning the freedom of choice to make a decision about something. Although not relevant to how the word is used here, discretion can also mean (1) that someone is using good judgment to avoid causing others embarrassment, anger, or distress; or (2) that someone has the ability to keep secret information that could cause embarrassment, anger, or distress.*

7.2.1 Use the operative word *may*

When expressing a discretionary power, you could state, "Supplier has the discretion to inspect Distributor's place of business and make an inventory of the Products." But, a more concise way to state a discretionary power is by replacing *has the discretion to* with *may* plus the base form of the verb describing the action. An example of *may* plus the base from of the verb describing the action is the provision in the box below, which uses "may inspect . . . ." For clarity, consistently use the word *may* for expressing a discretionary power. Do not use *may* for any other purpose in the contract. Also, do not use *may not*. It is illogical to draft a negative discretionary power. Rather, if the party does not have a choice, use *shall not* for an obligation that prohibits action or *will not* if it is merely a fact statement.

Correct use of may:
Supplier may inspect Distributor's place of business and make an inventory of the Products.

Incorrect use of may:
Distributor may not modify any Product unless it obtains the prior written consent of Supplier.

Redraft to replace may not *with* shall not *or* will not. *Whether it will be stated as an obligation* (shall not) *or a fact statement* (will not) *depends on the parties' intent:*

Distributor shall not modify any Product unless it obtains the prior written consent of Supplier.
   or

Distributor will not modify any Product unless it obtains the prior written consent of Supplier.

7.2.2 Attempting to expand or restrict a discretionary power

Sometimes drafters add phrases to a discretionary power provision in an attempt to expand or restrict the power. For example, some drafters attempt to expand a party's discretionary power by including the phrase *within [its] discretion,* or *within [its] sole discretion,* or *within [its] absolute discretion.* Alternatively, the drafter may attempt to restrict the party's discretionary power by including the phrase *consent will not be unreasonably withheld.*

> *Example of an attempt to expand the discretionary power:*
> Supplier may, in its sole discretion, withhold consent.
>
> *Example of an attempt to restrict the discretionary power:*
> Distributor shall not assign its rights and delegate its duties under this agreement without Supplier's written consent, which consent will not be unreasonably withheld.

These qualifiers should be used carefully, if at all. If only one provision or only some discretionary power provisions in the contract include phrases attempting to expand or limit the discretionary power, the question arises whether, in the same contract, other discretionary power provisions without qualifiers are subject to a different standard of conduct. Another problem with using one of the qualifiers mentioned above is that it raises the question whether the party with the discretionary power will conduct itself in good faith. Contract law in the vast majority of states implies that all parties will conduct themselves in good faith when performing under a contract. This does not change simply because a contract includes language suggesting a party could act in bad faith.[7]

> *Good faith* in contracts means that the parties will conduct themselves honestly and deal fairly with each other in keeping with the conduct standards of their trade.

> In the United States, some states do not impose a "good faith" standard on parties attempting to form a contract, though they will impose a good faith standard on the parties when performing under the contract.

7.2.3 Using *is not required to*

If a contract provision implies that a party may have an obligation to perform, use the phrase *is not required to* plus the verb to express that the party has the discretionary power to decide whether to perform.

---

7. *See generally* Paul J. Powers, "Defining the Undefinable: Good Faith and the United Nations Convention on the Contracts for the International Sale of Goods," 18 J.L. & Comm. 333 (1999).

> Distributor is not required to reimburse Supplier for any shipments made directly to a customer at Distributor's request.

7.3 Procedural statements

Procedural statements manage or facilitate the contract's administration. Procedural statements are used to create defined terms in a contract. (Drafting defined terms were discussed in Chapter 4.) In addition to creating defined terms, procedural statements can be used to create rules for administrating and enforcing the contract. Unlike obligations, procedural statements do not give rise to a legal remedy if the rules are not followed, though there can be other consequences. Draft procedural statements in active voice, using a verb that expresses the intent of the sentence.

> New York law governs all matters arising under and related to this Agreement.

When expressing a possible future situation, consider using the verb *will* plus the base of the verb that expresses the intent of the sentence.

> Any disputes arising under this Agreement will be submitted to binding arbitration.

Procedural statements are often used to provide details related to an obligation or discretionary power, but they do not replace the need to state the obligation or discretionary power.

> *Example 1:*
> Company shall pay employee a commission of 10 percent of the collected gross revenues. The collected gross revenues will be calculated on the current rate of exchange for currency of the countries where revenues were generated.
>
> *Example 2:*
> Supplier may change the pricing of Products at any given time. These price changes will become effective immediately upon Distributor's receipt of notice. Price changes will not affect purchase orders accepted by Supplier prior to the date the price change becomes effective.

7.4 Conditions

A condition is a possible future occurrence that, ***if it occurs***, will result in a consequence that either

(a) ***creates*** an obligation, a right, a discretionary power, or a situation (sometimes referred to as a *condition precedent*) or

(b) ***terminates*** an obligation, a right, a discretionary power, or an existing situation (sometimes referred to as a *condition subsequent*).

Conditions can be expressed in the following formats:

1. A sentence in which the condition is stated in a dependent clause[8] or a phrase,[9] and the consequence stated in an independent clause.[10]
2. A sentence in which the consequence is stated in a phrase and the condition is stated in an independent clause.
3. A sentence expressly stating the provision is a condition.

7.4.1 The condition stated in a dependent clause or a phrase and the consequence stated in the independent clause

A condition and consequence can be expressed in one sentence with the condition expressed as a dependent clause or a phrase, and the consequence stated in the independent clause. You may place the condition clause or phrase either at the beginning or at the end of a sentence. Placement of the condition clause or phrase in the sentence depends on the length of the clause or phrase. Longer clauses or phrases should be placed at the end of a sentence to promote readability.

---

8. A dependent clause needs an independent clause for grammatical and logical completion. It has a subject and a verb and cannot stand alone or be disconnected from the independent clause. For example: "If John buys the product, he will pay immediately." The subject *John* in combination with the verb *buys* creates a dependent clause. It cannot stand alone.

An independent clause has a subject and a verb, and usually can stand alone. The subject *he* and the verb *will pay* form an independent clause that can stand alone.

You can state, "He will pay immediately," but you cannot state, "If John buys the product."

9. A phrase is a construction that lacks the subject/verb combination of a clause. "In the office" is a phrase. Often, a phrase is a reduced clause, as in "Upon Distributor's receipt of notice . . . ," which is derived from the dependent clause, "After Distributor receives notice . . . ."

10. *See supra* n. 8.

> *Example of a "condition" clause placed at the beginning of a sentence:*
> If Products have not been delivered, Distributor may cancel all outstanding purchase orders at the time Supplier terminates this agreement.
>
> *Example of a "condition" clause placed at the end of a sentence:*
> Price changes will become effective immediately upon Distributor's receipt of notice.

The condition clause is written in the present tense. Never use *shall* in the dependent condition clause because the clause is stating a condition, not an obligation. The consequence caused by the occurrence of the condition is found in the main clause of the sentence. Use *shall* in the main clause when the condition creates or terminates an obligation. Use *may* in the main clause when the condition creates or terminates a discretionary power. If the condition creates a situation or terminates an existing situation, state this consequence in the active voice and use a present tense verb that expresses the intent of the main clause.

> *Example of a condition creating an obligation:*
> If Distributor rejects any of the Product because it is defective, then Supplier shall repair or replace the rejected Product.
>
> *Example of a condition creating a discretionary power:*
> If Distributor rejects any of the Product because it is defective, Supplier may repair or replace the rejected Product.
>
> *Example of a condition terminating an existing situation:*
> If Distributor is judged by a court to be bankrupt, then this Agreement terminates.

A condition that is uncertain to occur begins with *if* or *subject to*, but a condition that probably will occur can begin with the adverbs *when, after,* or *upon.*

> When this agreement ends, Distributor may dispose of any unsold Products.

Sometimes an obligation, right, discretionary power, or situation will be in effect so long as a condition exists and remains the same. In this instance, begin the condition with *so long as* or *as long as.*

> A party's delay in performing or failure to perform its obligations under this agreement will be excused so long as the force majeure event continues.

7.4.2 The consequence stated in a phrase and the condition stated in a independent clause

If a party's right is conditioned on that party's performance of an obligation, then state the condition in the independent clause. The party's right is stated in a dependent phrase at the beginning of the sentence. To signal the party's right, begin with *to* or *in order to* in the phrase. In the independent clause, use the modal verb *must* plus the base form of the verb describing the action. The use of *must* signals to the reader that the independent clause is a condition that must be performed before the party receives the stated right.

> To reject any Product that is defective, Distributor must notify Supplier in writing of its rejection of the Product and the reason for its rejection no later than 10 calendar days after receiving the Product.

7.4.3 Sentence expressly stating the condition

A sentence might also explicitly state that a provision is a condition.

> As a condition to termination of this Agreement due to Supplier's breach, Distributor must
>
> > (1) give written notice to Supplier of its intent to terminate that includes a description of the breach, and
> > (2) gives Supplier the option to remedy the breach no later than 30 calendar days after receipt of Distributor's notice of intent to terminate.

7.5 Declarations

A **declaration** is a formal statement expressly stating that the facts referred to in the statement are true. In contracts, declarations are used to express representations or acknowledgements.

7.5.1 Representations

Representations are statements made by a party regarding *present or past facts, or both,* made with the intent to induce the other party to enter into the contract. A representation cannot be made about anything in the future. A statement regarding a future situation over which the party has control should be drafted as an obligation.

To determine whether a party truthfully represented a fact, a court will look at whether the fact was true at the time the statement was made. In the case of a representation in a written contract, the court will look at the date the parties signed the contract unless another date for determining accuracy is explicitly stated. Therefore, when drafting representations, you must be mindful of the effective date for representations and ensure that your client is correctly stating the facts as of that date. See also section 10.5.4 in Chapter 10 for a discussion of issues with timing and making representations.

a. Types of representations

In a business contract, three types of representations are commonly made:

    (a) representations relating to the contract,
    (b) representations relating to the contract's subject matter, and
    (c) representations relating to the status and authority of the party making the statement.[11]

Representations relating to the contract focus on the legal capacity of the parties entering into the contract. Using the distribution agreement as an example, the supplier may make a representation that it has taken the corporate action necessary to sign the agreement and to carry out its obligations. An example of a representation relating to the contract's subject matter might be the supplier's representation that it has obtained all the necessary business and other governmental licenses, permits, and authorizations to perform its obligations. Lastly, in a representation relating to the party making the statement, the supplier might state that it is a corporation in good standing and validly existing in the state of its incorporation.

> There are three types of misrepresentation: innocent, negligent, and fraudulent. **Negligent misrepresentation** occurs when the representing party fails in its duty to use reasonable care to ascertain and communicate the truth of its statement. For **innocent representation** the representing party makes a false statement but has no duty to ascertain the truth of the statement. In **fraudulent misrepresentation** a party knowingly or recklessly makes an untrue statement. Negligent and innocent misrepresentations (and, in many jurisdictions, fraudulent misrepresentation) require a showing that the statement was important to the transaction. All three claims require that the party knew or should have known the statement was important and, by making the statement, intended to induce the other party to act or refrain from acting.

---

11. Charles M. Fox, *Working with Contracts: What Law School Doesn't Teach You* 11-12 (P.L.I. 2002).

b. Drafting representations

When expressing a representation, the sentence structure is typically as follows:

① The subject of the sentence is the party making the representation.
② The present tense of the verb is used.
③ The fact or series of facts follow the operative word or phrase.

No magic operative words will guarantee a court finding that a statement is actually a representation. Nevertheless, certain words are commonly used when drafting representations: *represents and warrants* or merely *represents*. These words show the party's intent to make a representation. There is disagreement, however, among drafting scholars as to whether *and warrants* is a necessary addition.

Some argue that using the operative phrase *represents and warrants* is helpful in the instance of an innocent misrepresentation or a negligent misrepresentation.[12] Merely stating *represents* without *and warrants* arguably limits an injured party's remedies under U.S. common law to **rescission** (avoiding the contract) and **restitution** (returning property that was received under the contract or, if this is not possible, the monetary value of the property).[13] By adding *and warrants*, the party making the representation is now also making a promise that the representation is true. A failed promise gives rise to damages. Thus, the injured party will have the option of bringing a claim for breach of warranty and, if successful, can recover damages.[14] Additionally, bringing a claim for a breach of warranty sidesteps the need to show an injured party's justifiable reliance on the representing party's statement, an essential element in a successful claim for innocent or negligent misrepresentation.

Other drafting scholars argue that using the word *represents* or merely *states*[15] is sufficient to communicate the parties' intent to make a statement of fact.[16] Adding *and warrants* is redundant, providing nothing of legal significance that isn't already communicated by using *represents* or *states*.[17] The

---

12. For a thorough discussion of this position, *see* Tina L. Stark, *Drafting Contracts: How and Why Lawyers Do What They Do* 11-16 (Aspen Publishers 2007).

13. *Id.*

14. *Id.* Damages, however, can be recovered for fraudulent misrepresentation in addition to rescission.

15. *See* Kenneth A. Adams, *The Koncise Drafter Blog*, "Using 'States' Instead of 'Represents and Warrants,'" http://www.koncision.com/using-states-instead-of-represents-and-warrants (May 21, 2012).

16. *See* Kenneth A. Adams, *A Manual of Style for Contract Drafting* 284-291 (2d ed., ABA 2008). *See also* Kenneth A. Adams, *The Koncise Drafter Blog*, "Revisiting Represents and Warrants: Bryan Garner's View," http://www.koncision.com/revisiting-represents-and-warrants-bryan-garners-view (Dec. 14, 2011).

17. *See supra* n. 15.

authors of this book agree. Relying on mere words—*represents,* or *represents and warrants,* or any other word (e.g., *states*)—to summon the preferred remedy for misrepresentations is a flawed solution. **The exit provisions of the contract should state the specific remedy (including monetary damages) available to an injured party in the event a misrepresentation, no matter if the statement is innocent, negligent, or fraudulent.** Furthermore, this is the best way to avoid concern that magic words might trigger the application of common law default rules for misrepresentations.

Nevertheless, you might find that others insist on using *represents and warrants* when making a representation. This is one point on which you could yield to their stylistic preference (perhaps in return for their yielding to a request from you on something you find of real substantive importance).

The following is an example of a representation that might be made by a distributor.

Using "represents" as the operative word:
Distributor represents that it has all necessary business and governmental licenses, permits, and authorizations to market, sell, and distribute the Products in the Territory.

Using "represents and warrants" as the operative phrase:
Distributor represents and warrants that it has all necessary business and governmental licenses, permits, and authorizations to market, sell, and distribute the Products in the Territory.

For a long series of representation statements, consider enumerating and tabulating the sentence. (See Chapter 9 for guidelines on enumerating and tabulating contract provisions.)

Supplier represents that it

(1) is a corporation in good standing and validly existing under the laws of the Delaware;

(2) has taken all corporate action necessary to sign this agreement and to perform its obligations under this agreement; and

(3) has obtained all the necessary business and governmental licenses, permits, and authorizations to perform its obligations under this agreement.

7.5.2 Acknowledgements

An **acknowledgement** is a formal statement by a party recognizing that facts, usually provided by the other contracting party, are correct. Unlike a representation, an acknowledgement does not create a remedy for either party if the facts are incorrect. The purpose of including an acknowledgement in a contract is to justify an expectation of future conduct. The party or parties making the acknowledgement are the subject in a sentence, which is drafted in active voice. The recommended operative word is *acknowledge*. Reserve this verb only for expressing an acknowledgement.

> *Example 1:*
> Distributor acknowledges that Supplier has an established reputation for excellence with the public as a manufacturer and marketer of the highest quality sunglass gear. During the term of this agreement, Distributor shall act in a manner that will uphold Supplier's reputation.
>
> *Example 2:*
> Consultant acknowledges that damages for any breach by Consultant of this confidentiality clause will be an inadequate remedy. Therefore, in the event Consultant breaches this confidentiality clause, Company will be entitled to injunctive relief.

7.6 Express warranties

In contract law, an **express warranty**[18] is a promise made by a party that the subject of the warranty (goods or services) is as stated and will continue to remain so. Unfortunately, there is no operative word or operative phrase that guarantees that a judge will interpret a provision as a warranty. In some instances, governing law might not even require that a party show a specific intent to create a warranty.[19] Whether a court will interpret a provision as a warranty often depends not only on the language of the provision but also on the facts and circumstances of the agreement, all examined in light of the contract's governing law.

---

18. Warranties can be expressly stated in the contract or implied by law. Implied warranties are generally discussed in Chapter 10.

19. *See, e.g., James River Equip. Co. v. Beadle Co. Equip., Inc.,* 646 N.W.2d 265 (S.D. 2002) (court held a written statement of hours of usage next to an equipment listing, which was attached as an exhibit to an asset purchase agreement, was an express warranty). Warranties can also arise from oral assurances, written representations, brochures, advertisements, samples, models, pictures, plans, and blueprints, as well as through course of dealing, course of performance, and trade usage. *See generally* Robert A. Feldman & Raymond T. Nimmer, *Drafting Effective Contracts: A Practitioner's Guide* § 5.05[A][4] (2d ed., Aspen Publishers 2011).

Express warranties can be found in service contracts and in contracts for the sale of goods. In service contracts, express warranties might include fact assertions about the workmanlike conduct of the services that are being provided. In a contract for the sale of goods, express warranties might make fact assertions that the delivered goods are, or that goods delivered in the future will be, free from defects in material and workmanship.

Because an express warranty is a promise, the failure of that promise is a breach. Governing law might impose damages for a breach of warranty or the contract might state the remedies for a breach of warranty.

When drafting an express warranty, the party making the warranty should be the subject of the sentence. The verb most commonly used is *warrants*, though this is no guarantee that the provision will be interpreted as a warranty or that other provisions using other words will not be interpreted as warranties.

> Supplier warrants that the Products are free from defect in materials and workmanship and conforms to the Supplier's standard product specifications.

Again, as is the case when drafting any other types of provisions, it is important that you know the governing law of the contract and draft express warranties accordingly. See Chapter 10 for further discussion on warranties and drafting warranty disclaimers.

7.7 Performatives

Performatives recognize actions taking place simultaneously with the signing of the contract. A performative is drafted using active voice, and the verb is drafted in the present tense. Thus, in the case of the distribution agreement example, the performative documents the supplier's grant to the distributor of the exclusive right to sell the snowboards and related products.

> By signing this Agreement, Supplier grants to Distributor during the period of this Agreement and subject to the provisions of this Agreement the exclusive right to sell and distribute the Product in the Territory.

Using the phrase *by signing this agreement* conveys the immediacy of the action, that the act is being accomplished by the execution of the contract.

Alternatively, a performative can be expressed by using the adverb *hereby* before the active verb.

> Supplier hereby grants to Distributor during the period of this Agreement and subject to the provisions of this Agreement the exclusive right to sell and distribute the Product in the Territory.

7.8 Exceptions

Exceptions are situations excluded from a provision in a contract. Examples of words or phrases that create exceptions include *except, except as otherwise provided, unless,*[20] *however, despite,* or *notwithstanding anything to the contrary*. To promote readability and understanding, state the rule before stating the exception(s).

There are three basic ways to express an exception. You can state the exception

1. as a dependent clause, and the rule is stated in an independent clause,
2. in a separate sentence from the sentence stating the general rule and where one sentence or, ideally, both sentences reference the other sentence, or
3. in a separate sentence that serves as a general exception to the entire contract.

7.8.1 The rule and the exception stated in one sentence

Ideally, the rule and exception are stated in one sentence: The rule is stated as an independent clause and the exception is stated as a dependent clause or a phrase. The exception clause is almost always placed at the end of the sentence, after stating the general rule.

> *Dependent clause:*
> The parties shall equally bear the costs of arbitration, except that the parties shall, at their own expense, pay for their own travel fees and their own attorney's fees and expenses.
>
> *Phrase:*
> The parties shall equally bear the costs of arbitration, except for payment of their own expense, payment of their own travel fees and their own attorney's fees and expenses.

---

20. *Unless* can also be used as a condition. Whether the word means an exception or condition will depend on the context in which the word is used.

7.8.2 The rule and the exception stated in separate sentences

If stating the rule and exception in one sentence make the sentence too long, break it into two sentences (the rule sentence followed by the exception sentence). Ideally, the sentence stating the exception immediately follows the sentence stating the rule.

> Supplier may change its net distributor prices, and each price change will be effective when Supplier notifies Distributor of the change. Despite the preceding sentence, no price change will apply to orders already accepted by Supplier.

If the exception and rule must appear in difference sections of the contract, then ensure that the exception is cross-referenced to the rule and vice versa.

> 3.1 Supplier may change its net distributor prices, and each price change will be effective when Manufacturer notifies Distributor of the change.
>
> ══════
>
> 3.4 Except as provided in Section 3.1, no price change will apply to orders already accepted by Supplier.

7.8.3 General exceptions to the entire contract

Sometimes an exception will apply to an entire contract, overriding all other provisions in the contract. The sentence might begin one of the following phrases: *despite any other provision in this agreement;* or *notwithstanding anything to the contrary in this agreement.* Use these sparingly, though, as the danger of creating an ambiguity is great. In the following example, the supplier is not liable for the damages specified.

> Notwithstanding anything to the contrary in this agreement, Supplier is not liable for special, incidental, or consequential damages.

The example exception applies to all provisions. The distributor will want to ensure that this general exception does not shield the supplier from liability in instances where the distributor would want it imposed.

Exercises

▶ **Exercise 7-1   Understanding the use of modals**

Look at the chart on pages 101 and 102 categorizing the use of modal verbs in English. To get a feeling for their use, read the examples, analyze their function, and paraphrase them in the *Paraphrase* column.

▶ **Exercise 7-2   Evaluating modals in the context of contracts**

Decide the function of the modal verbs in the following contract provisions.

Example:

> Exceptions. The Receiving Party's obligations under Section 8.2 with respect to any Confidential Information of the Disclosing Party will terminate if and when the Receiving Party <u>can</u> document that such information: (a) was already known to the Receiving Party at the time of disclosure by the Disclosing Party; . . . [DA#36]

Function: Ability

> *Ex. 1:*
> AMENDMENT. This Agreement <u>cannot</u> be changed, modified or amended unless such change, modification, or amendment is in writing and executed by the party against which the enforcement of such change, modification or amendment is sought. [DA#40]

Function: _____

> *Ex. 2:*
> Obligations and Covenants of Distributor. Subject to all other terms, provisions and conditions of this Agreement, Distributor <u>shall</u>:
> (a) Use Distributor's best efforts to advertise, sell and distribute the Products;
> (b) Order the Products solely from the Company; . . .
> [DA#13]

Function: _____

Modal Verb	Example	Function	Paraphrase
Can	She can play the piano.	Ability	She is able to play the piano
	You can come in!	Permission	
	Can I come in?	Request for permission	
	They can always change their plans if they want to.	Option/Choice	
Cannot	You cannot come in!	Prohibition	
	I cannot do it.	Lack of Ability	
Could	I think she could do it.	Ability/possibility	
	Could I come in?	Polite request	
	She could have done it, but she was afraid.	Expressing contrary-to-fact statement in the past	
May	You may be right.	Possibility in the Present or Future/Uncertainty	
	She may get accepted into the program.		
	You may come in.	Permission/Option	
	May I come in?	Request	
May not	You may not come in!	Prohibition (stronger than "cannot")	
		Command	

Continued

Modal Verb	Example	Function	Paraphrase
Shall	We shall see.	Future (not frequent in American English)	
	They shall return soon.		
Shall (not)	Distributor shall deliver bi-weekly	Legal Obligation	
Shall not	You shall not come in!	Prohibition (stronger than "cannot")	
Should	You should study more!	Moral Obligation, Advice	
Should not	They shouldn't do this.	Advice	
Will	They will come at 8pm.	Future	
	I will do it.	Willingness	
Will (not)	Distributor shall deliver bi-weekly	Legal Obligation (often British English)	
Will not	He will not win.	Future Time	
Must	You must promise me.	Obligation	
	It must arrive before 5, or it will be invalid.	Necessity/Precondition	
	This watch must be expensive.	Logical conclusion/ Assumption	
Must not	You must not enter!	Prohibition	

Ex. 3:

> ***Proprietary Right.***
> . . . All products authorized by Company which are sold by the Distributor directly or through its sales distribution channel <u>must</u> bear an authorized Company name, trademark or logo, and no other except those authorized by Company in writing. [DA#38]

Function: _____

Ex. 4:

> Distributor <u>can</u> suggest changes or adjustments to be made by Manufacturer to the product, whenever commercial surveys or legislation would require such changes or adjustments. [DA#32]

Function: _____

Ex. 5:

> ***Distribution Rights:***
> . . . If Distributor has not enrolled at least 20 patients in a controlled, mutually designed . . . clinical trial by June 1, 2004, Distributor <u>will</u> lose its exclusive right to market, distribute and sell the Products in the Territory. [DA#19]

Function: _____

Ex. 6:

> ***Reporting Responsibilities.***
> . . . Supplier <u>may</u> also request at its sole discretion any other information that is reasonable in the normal course of business. [DA#9]

Function: _____

Ex. 7:

> Corporation <u>shall not</u> charge Distributor for Products a price that is higher than the lowest price charged by Corporation for such Products to other international distributors. [DA#1]

Function: _____

Ex. 8:

> Amendment. This Agreement <u>may not</u> be amended, modified, released or discharged except by an instrument executed in writing by the Parties hereto. [DA#13]

Function: _____

Ex. 9:

> LICENSES AND PERMITS. The Distributor agrees that it shall obtain any and all licenses and permits which <u>may be required</u> under all applicable law in order to perform the duties and obligations hereunder. [DA#1]

Function: _____

Ex. 10:

> Supplier has no independent obligation to determine what marking or labeling <u>may</u> be required by applicable laws and regulations of the Territory. [DA#12]

Function: _____

Ex. 11:

> Appointments <u>will not</u> be issued without a valid purchase order. [DA#15]

Function: _____

Ex. 12:

> Except as provided elsewhere herein, this Agreement <u>can be</u> modified only by a specific written agreement duly signed by persons authorized to sign agreements on behalf of Distributor and the Company. [DA#27]

Function: _____

▶ **Exercise 7-3 Evaluating modals in a contract**

In the following contract passage, modal verbs have been deleted. Reinsert the correct modal verbs and discuss your choice with a partner. When you are done, look up the original draft on the companion website (www .aspenlawschool.com/books/Adams), and explain if you agree or disagree with the original drafter's choice.

Excerpt from Contract DA#9

3. Distributor responsibilities

3.2 Reporting Responsibilities.

Distributor [. . .] provide a daily report to Supplier, including the following informational headings: Daily POS, Daily Inventory, Daily Distributor Backlog, Daily DPA Claims and Weekly Forecast. Distributor [. . .] also provide at least a weekly report to Supplier concerning customer backlog on Distributor of Supplier Products, including the following informational headings: Supplier valid part number, quantity, resale price, requested delivery date, end customer, ship-to location and ship-to company. Supplier [. . .] also request at its sole discretion any other information that is reasonable in the normal course of business. Supplier [. . .] provide details, format, timing and other requirements. The reporting format is to be via electronic data interchange (EDI) transaction or another acceptable reporting method, if agreed to by Supplier.

3.3 Covenants.

(a) Both parties [. . .] conduct business in a manner that reflects favorably at all times on the Products and the good name, goodwill and reputation of the other party.

Continued

(b) Neither party [...] engage in deceptive, misleading, or unethical practices that are or might be detrimental to the other party, the Products, or the public, including, but not limited to, disparagement of the other party or the Products and use of misleading advertising.

(c) Neither party [...] make false or misleading representations with regard to the other party and [...] make no representations to customers or to the trade with respect to the specifications, features or capabilities of the Products that are inconsistent with the literature distributed by Supplier.

(d) Both parties [...] maintain the confidentiality of the other party's proprietary information, pursuant to the terms of the Mutual Non-Disclosure Agreement attached hereto as Attachment I and executed concurrently with this Agreement.

(e) Distributor [...] not make shipments to customers located out of Territory unless authorized to do so by Supplier.

(f) In cases where below list pricing is granted to a particular OEM or CM, Distributor [...] claim debits solely against Products shipped to an OEM Customer or such OEM Customer's designated contract manufacturers in order to meet the volume requirements of said OEM . . . .

▶ **Exercise 7-4 Turning *right* provisions into *obligation* provisions**

As discussed in section 7.1.4, in most instances, stating the provision as an obligation, rather than as a right is often the preferred mode of expression. Look at examples in section 7.1.4, and then express the rights in the following two passages as obligations.

Examples:

Ex. 1:

Distributor (or its representatives) shall be entitled at any time, but in any event no more than once in any twelve month period during the Term, upon 30 days advance notice in writing, to access the Approved Facilities in the company of a representative of Supplier to review and audit the Approved Facilities or the Manufacture of the Finished Product. [DA#14]

Re-write: _____

_____

> *Ex 2:*
> Prior to filling orders for such products Supplier shall be entitled to request and receive documentary evidence of all such outstanding Purchase Orders and an accounting of Distributor's then current inventory of Supplier Products. [DA#30]

Re-write: _____

▶ **Exercise 7-5   Evaluating the effects of discretionary powers I**
   You represent the distributor of a line of audio products, headphones, and cell phone accessories. Counsel for the manufacturer, the Company, has sent you a draft of the contract containing the following provision.

> Company reserves the right to unilaterally delete products no longer supplied by Company, to modify the specification, style, design or color of any products, and to add new products, in each case such change to be effective without prior notice to Distributor. [DA#7]

What is the meaning of the expression *reserves the right*? Can you think of alternative expressions that have the same meaning? What kind of concerns do you have with the wording of the provision? Which party in this deal appears to have more power? What changes would you suggest for the provision?

▶ **Exercise 7-6   Evaluating the effects of discretionary powers II**
   The following two versions of a provision (displayed in a chart) reflect the power balance between a manufacturer and a distributor. Use a comparison chart to outline the power balance between the manufacturer and the distributor in the *Product Changes* provision that follows below.

Version A:

> Manufacturer may create printed promotional materials sent to Distributor at the beginning of each new sales season. Distributor can reject modifications in promotional materials within 30 days after receiving Manufacturer's print design.

Manufacturer	Distributor
May create printed promotional materials.	Can reject modifications

In Version A, manufacturer can create printed materials, but the distributor has a right to reject those materials.

Version B:

> Manufacturer may create printed promotional materials sent to Distributor for each new sales season.

Manufacturer	Distributor
May create printed promotional materials.	Input by distributor is not required.

In Version B, the distributor has no influence with regards to printing materials created by the manufacturer.

Exercise:

> PRODUCT CHANGES. End of life. Manufacturer may, at its sole discretion, declare any Product to be obsolete, or discontinue the manufacture and/or sale of any Product ("Product Deletion"). In the event of any such Product Deletion, Manufacturer shall give Distributor at least (180) days advance written notice thereof. Distributor may, in its sole discretion, within ninety (90) days after receipt of such notice, notify Manufacturer in writing of Distributor's intention to return any or all Products in its inventory affected by such Product Deletion per the terms in section 8. Manufacturer shall, within thirty (30) days after receiving Product so returned, issue to Distributor full credit for all such Product. Any such credit shall be in the amount of the actual net invoice price paid by Distributor for the affected Products less any prior credits. Products so returned shall be shipped freight collect.[21] [DA# 40]

▶ **Exercise 7-7   Completing provisions that contain conditions**

The following provisions are not complete. Guess what might follow in the second part. Complete the missing part, but remember, there might be more than one way to complete the section. Find similar provisions in the

---

21. Freight will be paid by person receiving the freight.

"Contract Database" file on the companion website (www.aspenlawschool. com/books/Adams), and see how other lawyers have drafted provisions containing conditions. Look for key words in the first part of each provision below, which can help you locate similar provisions in the "Contract Database" file.

Example:

> In the event of any breach or default by the other party in any of the terms or conditions of this Agreement, and if such breach is not remedied within 30 days from the date of notification to their satisfaction thereof, the non-defaulting party . . . [second part is missing].

Key words: breach, default, remedied, notification

Guess: The rest of the provision probably deals with the consequences of a breach, such as termination of the agreement

Your version: . . . can terminate the Agreement without further notice.

Original version: . . . may immediately terminate this Agreement by giving written notice to the other party (termination for cause). [DA#10]

Other versions: . . . may terminate Agreement at any time immediately upon written notice to the other party. [modified from DA#1]

. . . can terminate Agreement after written notice specifying the alleged breach in reasonable detail. [modified from DA#4]

1. "If the parties are unable to agree upon a single arbitrator within five business day period, the parties . . ."
   Key words: _____
   Guess: _____
   Your version: _____
2. "If Distributor agrees that the Product does not conform to the Specifications, Supplier . . ."
   Key words: _____
   Guess: _____
   Your version: _____
3. "If there is a foreign language translation of this Agreement, . . ."
   Key words: _____
   Guess: _____
   Your version: _____
4. "Discontinued Product. If during the term of this Agreement, Supplier discontinues a Product(s), Supplier . . ."
   Key words: _____
   Guess: _____
   Your version: _____

5. "In the event of a conflict or inconsistency between the terms of this Agreement and those of any order, quotation, solicitation or other communication from one party to the other . . ."
Key words: _____
Guess: _____
Your version: _____

▶ **Exercise 7-8   Drafting rules and exceptions**

In a first draft, you initially wrote down a list of rules and exceptions for provisions in a shortened form. Under which heading would each provision be inserted? Compose the full provision. Can you find similar provisions in the "Contract Database" file on the companion website? Keywords from your own draft can help you find the correct provision.

Example:

> **Rule:** The term of this agreement shall begin on the date the last party signs the agreement (the "**Effective Date**") and ends on the fifth anniversary of the Effective Date.
> **Exception:** Terminated earlier than the fifth anniversary of the Effective Date as provided under this agreement.

Key words: term, begin, end, anniversary, terminate, effective date
   Heading: Term and Termination
   Full provision—three variations:

> The term of this agreement begins on the date the last party signs (the "**Effective Date**") and ends on the fifth anniversary of the Effective Date, unless terminated earlier as provided under this Agreement.
>
> ═══════════
>
> Except for early termination under this Agreement, the term of this agreement begins on the date the last party signs (the "**Effective Date**") and ends on the fifth anniversary of the Effective Date
>
> ═══════════
>
> The term of this agreement begins on the date the last party signs (the "**Effective Date**") and ends on the fifth anniversary of the Effective Date, if not terminated earlier as provided under this Agreement

Expand the following sentences to full provisions. Find headings and look for key words.

1. **Rule:** If there are expenses or charges involved in the fulfillment of the agreement, the Distributor will have to pay for these.
   Exception: Expressly provided in the agreement
2. **Rule:** No party may assign its rights under or related to this agreement without the other party's prior written consent.
   Exception: Either party can make an assignment without the other party's consent to any of the following: (i) the assignor's successor in a consolidation or merger; (ii) the assignor's successor in an acquisition of all or substantially all of the assets, equity, or beneficial interests of the assignor; or (iii) an entity under common control with, controlled by or in control of the assignor.
3. **Rule:** The parties agree that the terms in the section below should have the meanings they are given below for all purposes of the agreement. Also, the definitions of the terms should be applied equally in the singular and the plural forms.
   Exception: Otherwise specified
4. **Rule:** The parties should not be regarded as each other's employee, agent, partner, co-venturer, or legal representative.
   Exception: Otherwise provided in the agreement
5. **Rule:** Distributor is prohibited from selling, leasing or renting any equipment outside the territory. This applies to direct or indirect actions.
   Exception: Provided in Section 2.2
6. **Rule:** Any expenses or charges connected with the fulfillment of Distributor's obligations under this agreement shall be exclusively borne by Distributor.
   Exception: If another provision in the agreement provides otherwise
7. **Rule:** Distributor will not have additional rights or interests in the trademarks or trade names.
   Exception: Limited right granted in the previous section

▶ Exercise 7-9   Adding provisions to a contract

You represent Tortech Corp., a company that produces automotive tools, in a deal with Villanova S.A., a Spanish distributor. You have drafted the International Distribution Agreement. While on a business trip, Jim Brown, a partner in your firm, is calling you about adding some provisions. The audio recording and transcript can be found in the materials section of Chapter 7 on the companion website (www.aspenlawschool.com/books/Adams).

Take notes and turn his suggestions into contract provisions. Draft the provisions first. Then, look up key words from your draft and, on the companion website, find passages in the sample contracts that deal with the same topic.

▶ **Exercise 7-10   Add to your vocabulary list**

Add to your vocabulary list at least ten new words from the "Contract Database" file on the companion website. Use the model from section 1.4 of Chapter 1 for guidance. Modify your old lists if you have new information regarding a word.

▶ **Exercise 7-11   Pegasus/Azteca deal—identifying basic provisions**

Identify the agreed terms that will be drafted into the middle part of the contract, if you have not already done so in the Pegasus/Azteca deal exercise at the end of Chapter 3. Use the information based on your work for the Pegasus/Azteca deal exercises in Chapters 1 through 4. (Alternatively, your professor will give you a term sheet for this deal.) For each agreed term, identify how it can be best expressed in the contract (e.g., an obligation, a discretionary power, a procedural statement, a condition).

Categories of Contract Provisions

Category	Explanation	Suggested operative word or phrase	Example(s)
Obligation	An obligation is a promise imposing a duty on the party making the promise to act or to refrain from acting. An obligation creates a right in another party to the promisor's performance of its obligation.	Affirmative: *shall* + base form of the verb Negative: *shall not* + base form of the verb	Affirmative: "Licensee shall pay a royalty of 10% to License Owner." Negative: "Licensee shall not sell Products outside of the Territory."
Right	A right entitles the party receiving the obligation to performance of that obligation.	Affirmative: *is entitled to* Negative: *is not entitled to*	Affirmative: "License Owner is entitled to a royalty of 10%." Negative: "Manufacturer is not entitled to any damages if Distributor fails to purchase the minimum purchase quantities stated under Section 8."
Performative	A performative recognizes an action taking place simultaneously with the signing of the contract.	*"By signing this agreement,* [name of party] + present tense of verb]." **or** *hereby* + present tense of verb	"By signing this agreement, License Owner grants to Licensee the right to use its name on Licensee's Products." "License Owner hereby grants a license to Licensee the right to use its name."
Discretionary power	A discretionary power gives a party a choice to act or to refrain from acting.	Use *may* + base form of the verb. **or**	Affirmative: "Licensee may renew this agreement for another five-year period."

Continued

Category	Explanation	Suggested operative word or phrase	Example(s)
		To signal a discretionary power in what might otherwise imply an obligation: *is not required to* + base form of the verb.	Negative: "Licensee is not required to reimburse License Owner for travel expenses in connection with the marketing of the Product."
Procedural statement	Procedural statements create defined terms and rules for administering or enforcing the contract.		
	Rules for administering or enforcing the contract.	Use the verb's present tense, or when expressing a possible future situation, use *will* + base form of the verb.	"United States law governs all matters arising under or related to this agreement." "Royalties will be based on the Net Sales Price of the Products." "Arbitration proceedings will be conducted in English."
	Defined terms.	*means* **or** *has the meaning; includes;* **or** *excludes.*	"**Net Sales Price'** means the invoiced billing price for Products less any returned damaged goods." "**Closing'** has the meaning given in Section 3.1." "**Travel Expenses'** includes lodging and food." "**Employee'** excludes anyone who is not a citizen or resident of the United

		The operative word or phrase depends on the circumstance and how the condition is expressed.	
Condition	A condition is a possible future occurrence that, *if it occurs*, will result in a consequence that either i) *creates* an obligation, a discretionary power, or a situation, or ii) *terminates* an obligation, a discretionary power, or an existing situation.		States and whose duties are primarily performed outside the United States." *Ways to express:* 1) A one-sentence statement establishing the condition(s) and the result(s). 2) A one-sentence statement creating a right by the party performing the stated condition(s). 3) A sentence expressly stating the condition(s).
1) A sentence establishing the condition(s) and the result(s).		*if; in the event; subject to*—potential to happen *when; after; upon*—anticipated that it will happen *as long as; so long as*—exists and remains the same	*Example of a condition giving rise to an obligation:* "If License Owner rejects any Product samples, Licensee shall redesign that Product." *Example of a condition giving rise to a discretionary power:* "When this agreement ends, Distributor may dispose of any unsold Products." *Example of a condition giving rise to a state of affairs:* "If Licensee files for bankruptcy or discontinues its business, then this agreement terminates."
2) A sentence creating a party's right by that party performing the stated condition(s).		The right: *to; in order to* The condition: *must* + base form of verb	"To reject any sample of the Product, License Owner must notify Licensee in writing of its rejection of the Product."

Continued

Category	Explanation	Suggested operative word or phrase	Example(s)
3) A sentence expressly stating the condition(s).		As a condition to [state the object of the condition], [state condition(s) using *must* + base form of the verb]	"As a condition to License Owner's termination of this agreement for cause, License Owner must give notice to Licensee of its intent to terminate stating the reason for its termination."
Declaration	A declaration is a formal statement expressly stating certain facts are true. In contracts, declarations are most often used to express representations or acknowledgements.		
Representation	A party declares the truth of past facts or present facts, or both, of which the party has or should have personal knowledge.	*represents* **or** *represents and warrants*	"License Owner represents that it has the power to grant Licensee an exclusive license under the terms of this agreement." "License Owner represents and warrants that it has the power to grant Licensee an exclusive license under the terms of this agreement."
Acknowledgement	A party recognizes or admits the truth of facts,	*acknowledges*	"Licensee acknowledges that License Owner has an established reputation for excellence with the public as a manufacturer and marketer of the highest quality athletic gear."

			"Licensee acknowledges that monetary damages for his breach of this confidentiality provision will be an inadequate remedy for License Owner."
Express warranty	A party promises goods or services are as stated and will continue remain so.	*warrants*	"Manufacturer warrants that the Product will be free from defects in material and workmanship for a period of one year from the date of delivery."
Exception	An exception states circumstances where a rule is not applicable.	*except; except as otherwise provided; unless; however; despite; notwithstanding anything to the contrary*	*Example of the rule and the exception stated in one sentence:* "The term of this agreement is five years, unless sooner terminated as provided in this agreement." *Example of a rule stated in one sentence and the exception stated in the next sentence:* "Licensed Owner shall not grant to any other person or entity the right to use its name on merchandise sold in the Territory. Despite the previous sentence, Licensed Owner may grant such a license if Licensee gives its prior written approval and the merchandise does not compete with the Products." *Example of an exception to the entire contract:* "Despite any other provision in this agreement, the parties have all rights and remedies available under the law governing this agreement."

Word Choice

In Chapter 7, you learned how words can be used to create various contract provisions—such as rights, obligations, conditions, or exceptions—found in the middle part of the contract. In this chapter, we address word choice for more general usage in the contract. Before reading further, work through Exercise 8-1 at the end of the chapter as a warm-up exercise.

8.1 Choosing simple and concise words

To promote clarity and precision, use simple words and phrases that are in common English usage. Pretentious legal language when a simple word will do (**legalese**), unnecessarily complicated phrases (**verbosity**), and needless repetition (**redundancy**) have no place in a contract. Legalese, verbosity, and redundancy hinder the reader's understanding. Even worse, it may result in misunderstanding and expensive litigation.

Pretentious language sounds scholarly, professional, and self-important. Those who use pretentious language in drafting erroneously believe it implies a special meaning or a point of great significance.

In 1996, the UK tax office, HM Revenue & Customs, began rewriting tax legislation in plain English. A 2009 progress report noted that the office saved approximately £70 million annually in administrative costs. For other success stories of governments and businesses using plain English, see http://plainenglishfoundation.com/index.php/plain-english/successstories.

8.1.1 Legalese

The following list provides examples of legalese.[1] It's not unusual to find these words in contracts, perhaps because the drafters mistakenly thought the words suggested professionalism or a lawyer-like tone. In truth, these words confuse understanding and complicate readability. A good drafter eliminates legalese from a contract. Indeed, studies have shown that rewriting a document in

---

1. Based on lists found in Reed Dickerson, *The Fundamentals of Legal Drafting* 207 (2d ed., Little, Brown & Co. 1986), and Tina Stark, *Drafting Contracts* 202 (Aspen Publishers 2008).

plain English—that is, removing legalese—increases reader comprehension and can save significant money because fewer issues arise.

List of common legalese

above   (as an adjective; e.g., "the above payment schedule")
above-mentioned
aforementioned
aforesaid
before-mentioned
foregoing
henceforth
hereby
herein
hereinabove
hereinafter
hereinbefore
hereto
heretofore
hereunder
hereunto
hereupon
herewith
said   (replacing *the, that,* or *those*; e.g., "said party"; "said agreement")
same   (replacing a pronoun; e.g., "Distributor shall prepare the report and deliver same to Supplier.")
such   (replacing *the, that,* or *those*; e.g., "such party"; "such agreement.")
thereby
therefrom
therein
thereof
thereon
thereto
thereunder
thereunto
therewith
to wit
under-mentioned
unto
whatsoever
whensoever
whereas
whereby
wherein
wheresoever
whereupon
whosoever
within-named
witnesseth

8.1.2 Coupled synonyms[2]

In contracts written in English, the use of *coupled synonyms* dates back over 500 years when both English and French were commonly spoken in England. At various periods in England's history, these languages were used alternatively as the principal language of the law.[3] In those days, coupled synonyms—usually a mix of Latin, French, and English words—clarified meaning to a multilingual society.[4] When English became the primary language in England, contract drafters continued to use coupled synonyms as an ornamental literary style.[5] In today's world, English language contracts may still include coupled synonyms. Coupled synonyms, such as those found in the following list,[6] have long since lost their original function. Because coupled synonyms are redundant, choose one of the words in the coupled synonym and omit the others.

alter or change	kind and nature
assumes and agrees	made and entered into
any and all	null and of no effect
bind and obligate	null and void
by and between	or and on behalf of
by and with	over and above
convey, transfer, and set over	pay, satisfy, and discharge
covenant and agree	power and authority
deemed and considered	release and discharge
due and owing	represents, warrants,
due and payable	and covenants
each and every	rest, residue, and remainder
fair and reasonable	sole and exclusive
faith and credit	stipulate and agree
final and conclusive	suffer or permit
free and clear	then and in that event
full and complete	true and correct
full force and effect	type and kind
furnish and supply	under and subject to
indemnify and hold harmless	understood and agreed
just and reasonable	unless and until
kind and character	void and of no effect

2. *See* David Mellinkoff, *Mellinkoff's Dictionary of American Legal Usage* 129 (West 1992).

3. David Mellinkoff, *The Language of the Law* 120-121 (Little, Brown & Co. 1983).

4. John Gibbons, *Forensic Linguistics: An Introduction to Language in the Justice System* 43 (Blackwell Pub. Co. 2003).

5. Mellinkoff, *supra* n. 3, at 121.

6. Based on lists found in Dickerson, *supra* n. 1, at 208, and Stark, *supra* n. 1, at 205.

8.1.3 Replacing unnecessarily formal expressions

If you naturally tend to use unnecessarily formal expressions in drafting contracts, make a conscious effort to replace those formal expressions with plain English equivalents. The list that follows contains suggestions for replacing unnecessarily formal expressions with plain English expressions.[7] The right column lists suggested replacements for formal expressions in the left column, opposite.

Formal expression	Plain English expression
above	[Reference the specific location where it appears (e.g., section, previous sentence).]
attains the age of	becomes . . . years old
at the time	when
by means of	by
cease	stop
commence	begin, start
contiguous to	next to
corporation organized and existing under the laws of	corporation
does not operate to	does not
during such time as	while
during the course of	during
effectuate	carry out
endeavor (used as a verb)	try
for the duration of	during
for the purpose of holding	holding
for the reason that	because
forthwith	immediately
in case	if
in cases in which	when, where (state "whenever" or "wherever" only when necessary to emphasize the exhaustive or recurring applicability of the rule)
in lieu of	instead of, in place of
inquire	ask
institute	begin, start
in the event that	if
is able to	can
is binding upon	binds
is empowered	may

Continued

---

    7. Based on lists found in Dickerson, *supra* n. 1, at 209-213, and Stark, *supra* n. 1, at 205-206.

Formal expression	Plain English expression
is unable to	cannot
loan (as a verb)	lend
necessitate.	require
party of the [first] part	[the party's name]
provision of law	law
State of [Illinois]	[the name of the state, e.g., Illinois]
sufficient number	enough
until such time as	until
utilize, employ (in the sense of "use")	use

8.1.4 Coupled words and numerals

a. Generally

You also might find in your review of contracts that numbers are presented sometimes in a coupled word and numeral format. Examples of this usage include the following:

> on the fifteenth (15th) day of the month
> three (3) copies of the report
> one-half (1/2) of the original sales price
> fifteen percent (15%) of the royalties

The reason for expressing numbers in this coupled format is that, in the event the numeral is incorrect because of a typographical error, the reader may rely on the word to interpret the parties' intent. The logical remedy, however, is to ensure that the numbers are typed correctly, which is one of your primary responsibilities as the drafter. Therefore, to avoid repetition, choose to express numbers either in words (Contract A below) or in numerals (Contract B below) and use the chosen form consistently throughout the contract. There are two exceptions to this consistency rule:

1. A number appearing at the beginning of a sentence is always expressed as a written word, even when numerals are otherwise used throughout the contract.

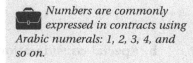

Numbers are commonly expressed in contracts using Arabic numerals: 1, 2, 3, 4, and so on.

2. "Nominal numbers" (numbers that identify something) should always be expressed in numerals. Examples of nominal numbers include the street number in a mailing address (e.g., 134 Main Street) or a telephone number (001-999-832-1000).

If the number appears in the middle or at the end of a sentence:

<u>Contract A</u>	<u>Contract B</u>
. . . on the fifteenth day of the month.	. . . on the 15th day of the month.
. . . three copies of the report.	. . . 3 copies of the report.
. . . one-half of the Original Sales Price.	. . . ½ of the Original Sales Price.
. . . fifteen percent of the Royalties.	. . . 15 percent of the Royalties.

If the number appears at the beginning of a sentence:

<u>Contract A</u>	<u>Contract B</u>
Three copies of the report . . .	Three copies of the report . . .
One-half of the Original Sales Price . . .	One-half of the Original Sales Price . . .
Fifteen percent of the Royalties . . .	Fifteen percent of the Royalties . . .

You will also find that drafters often observe additional exceptions to the consistency rule. Here are examples of exceptions commonly followed:

> *Cardinal numbers* (e.g., 1, 2, 3, 4, and so on) refer to quantities, such as "one report" or "two stock certificates."
>
> *Ordinal numbers* refer to a position in a sequence (e.g., "First Vice President" or "99th annual event").

- Express *cardinal numbers* less than 10 as words (e.g., one, two, three, four . . .)
- Express *ordinal numbers* as words (e.g., first, tenth, hundredth), except for hyphenated ordinal numbers, which are expressed as numerals (e.g., 42nd, 75th, 201st).

No matter the format you choose to observe, be consistent in adhering to that format throughout the contract.

b. Special considerations for expressing monetary amounts

Some contracts include the coupled word and numeral format when presenting a monetary amount. Perhaps the drafter feared accidentally mistyping a numeral, or omitting or misplacing a decimal separator.

Five Thousand One Hundred Fifty-Seven and 25/100 Dollars ($5,157.25)

Mistyping or omitting a word that expresses the number, however, is just as easy to do. Attention to detail is critical in any case. In the case of monetary figures, numerals are easier to read than words. Therefore, use only numerals to express monetary figures. Ensure the numbers are correct, and if used, ensure the decimal separator is correctly placed.[8] If only zeroes appear after the decimal separator, consider omitting the zeroes. Thus, in the case of U.S. dollars, "25,525.00 USD" becomes "25,525 USD." Also, for expressions of huge monetary amounts, drafters customarily replace multiple zeroes with words for easier readability. For example, in the case of U.S. dollars, "1,000,000 USD" becomes "1 million USD"; "1,300,000 USD" becomes "1.3 million USD"; "1,000,000,000 USD" becomes "1 billion USD"; and "1,500,000,000 USD" becomes "1.5 billion USD."

In cross-border agreements, express monetary amounts using the appropriate symbol for the currency, preferably the ISO currency code. Be careful about using currency symbols, other than the ISO currency code. Currency symbols might be shared by more than one currency. For instance, the symbol $ is the currency sign for U.S. dollars, Canadian dollars, Chilean pesos, Mexican pesos, and Argentine pesos. Using the ISO currency code will clarify the monetary amount expressed: 2,000 USD; 2,000 MXN; 2,000 CAD.

ISO currency codes are three-letter abbreviations for currencies used around the world. The International Organization for Standardization, based in Switzerland, created these codes. These codes are used in currency markets, such as currency futures.

8.2 Avoiding ambiguities arising from single words or phrases

We have discussed how legalese, redundancies, and verbosity can result in semantic ambiguities, but these are not the only instances where a word or

---

8. The decimal separator, typically either a period or a comma, varies depending on the currency. The numbers appearing to the left of the decimal separator are often placed in groups, split by a separator for ease of reading. The amount of digits in a grouping (e.g., three or four) and the type of separator used (e.g., a comma, a period, or a space) depends on the currency. For example, British and U.S. currencies use the period for the decimal separator, and digits to the left of the period are separated into groups of three digits, separated by a comma: 2,486.27.

phrase can create ambiguity. The following subsections address a few of the more common semantic ambiguities that occur in English language contracts.

8.2.1 Confusing English words

Some English words sound similar (or even the same) but have different meanings and spellings. When drafting a contract provision, you need to be mindful of similar-sounding words and ensure that you use the appropriate word. The following is a list of similar-sounding words used in contracts that are commonly confused:

Words	Definition
affect	a verb meaning *to influence*
	a noun meaning either *an emotion* or *a sensation*
effect	a noun meaning either *in force* or *a result*
	a verb meaning either *to cause something to happen*
accept	a verb meaning *to agree*
except	a preposition meaning *other than*
advise	a verb meaning either *to recommend; to give advice;* or to *consult*
advice	a noun meaning either *an opinion; a recommendation;* or *formal information* (usually from a distance)
capital	a noun meaning either *cash for investment; net worth;* or *a seat of government*
	an adjective meaning either *financial capital* or *principal*
capitol	a noun meaning *a building for a law-making body*
insure	a verb meaning *to be covered by insurance*
ensure	a transitive verb either *to safe-guard* or *to make certain*
assure	a transitive verb meaning either *to convince someone* or *to make something certain*
its	an adjective indicating possession
it's	a contraction of *it is*

Continued

Words	Definition
guarantee	a verb meaning either *to promise something* or *to accept responsibility for another's obligations*
	a noun meaning *the party to whom the guarantee is made*
guaranty	a noun meaning *a pledge to pay another's debt or otherwise to perform another's obligation if that debtor or obligor fails to perform*
	═══
precedence	a noun meaning *priority* or *a preceding occurrence of priority*
precedents	the plural form of the noun "precedent," meaning either *an established practice* or *a decision subsequently used to justify a similar act*
	═══
principal	an adjective meaning either *primary* or *initially invested*
	a noun meaning either *the most significant participant*; *the represented person*; or *the initial amount invested*
principle	a noun meaning either *an important law*; *a standard of conduct*; or *the primary source*
	═══
than	a conjunction used to state a preference when making a comparison
then	an adverb used to convey time an adjective expressing existing at the time specified
	═══
warrantee	a noun meaning *a party to whom a warranty is made*
warranty	a noun meaning *a promise that everything is as represented*

8.2.2 Words and phrases conveying time standards and duration

Do not undervalue the importance of clearly expressing time in contracts. Stating the time of day is challenging when the parties reside in different time zones or the business takes place in different time zones. And do not assume that a year is a 12-month period, or that a month always means a calendar month, or that a week is seven days, or that a day means a 24-hour period. Even expressing duration can create problems if you don't use concise words. The following subsection offers suggestions for concisely expressing time and duration. The discussion of days, months, and years is based on the Gregorian calendar, which is used in business throughout the world.

a. Time standards

Expressing the time of day. Ambiguities can arise when referencing the time of day in a contract. The United States and Great Britain commonly use the 12-hour time system to express hours in the day. (See Figure 8-1.) In the 12-hour time system, the first 12 hours after midnight (12:00[9] A.M.) are written with an A.M. suffix, and the 12 hours following noon (12:00 P.M.) are written with a P.M. suffix. It can be confusing, though, because 1:00 A.M. follows 12:00 A.M., and 1:00 P.M. follows 12:00 P.M. Therefore, when using the 12-hour time system, it is clearer to refer to 12:00 P.M. as *noon*. Referring to 12:00 A.M. as *midnight*, however, can prove confusing because a day can be interpreted to have two midnights: one that starts the day and one that ends the day.

> A.M. *is the abbreviation for the Latin term* ante meridiem, *which means "before midday."*
>
> P.M. *is the abbreviation for the Latin term* post meridiem, *which means "after midday."*

It is more precise, however, to use the 24-hour time system when specifying the hour of a day in a contract. (See Figure 8-1.) Using the 24-hour time system also eliminates the need for the suffixes A.M. and P.M.

	AM												PM											
12-hour Clock	1	2	3	4	5	6	7	8	9	10	11	12	1	2	3	4	5	6	7	8	9	10	11	12
24-hour Clock	1	2	3	4	5	6	7	8	9	10	11	12	13	14	15	16	17	18	19	20	21	22	23	24

Figure 8-1 12-Hour and 24-Hour Time Systems

The time zone can be added to the hour, minutes, and (in the case of the 12-hour time system) the suffix A.M. and P.M. It might be clearer to state the time zone in reference to a city where countries have different time zones. For example, while China uses only one time zone, the United States has nine different time zones.[10] Referencing a city instead of a time zone may be especially useful to avoid confusion in those countries that observe daylight savings time during part of the year. Thus, "13:00 CET"[11] could be written as "13:00 Paris time."

Expressing the month, day, and year. There also are different formats for expressing months, days, and years. For example, the 15th day of October 20XX could be expressed in a typical U.S. contract as "October 15, 20XX."

---

9. The colon is the U.S. format. The British replace the colon with a period when using the 12-hour time system.

10. For a map of the U.S. time zones, go to http://www.time.gov.

11. *CET* is the abbreviation for the *Central European Time* zone.

A non-U.S. contract might express the date as "15 October 20XX" or "20XX October 15." The format will depend on the parties' preference.

Expressing days. If time is being expressed in days, the question arises whether *days* means (1) calendar days, which includes all seven days of the week and holidays; or (2) business days, which are only the days the parties are open for business. Unless the term *days* is specifically defined in the contract, U.S. courts usually interpret it to mean calendar days.

Expressing weeks. When a time period is measured by weeks, the question becomes when does a week begin and end? Do the parties intend a week to mean a business week? In the United States a business week typically begins on a Monday and runs through the following Friday. Or, do the parties intend a week to begin on another day? These ambiguities can be easily resolved by specifically defining the term *week* in the contract, unless it is otherwise made explicit by the context.

Expressing months. The term *month* also creates ambiguity in a contract. A month usually means a calendar month. Does it start on the first day of the calendar month, though, or does it start on another day relevant to the contract, such as the 15th day in a calendar month? If *month* is being used to express duration, how long does a *month* last? Is it a 30-day period or is it tied to the calendar, in which case a *month* could be greater or less than 30 days? Because of these ambiguities, specifically define the term *month*, unless the context makes the meaning evident.

Expressing years. Time periods measured in years can also present problems. When does the *year* begin and end? Does it begin on January 1? Or does it begin at another time relevant to an important starting point in the contract? Perhaps the parties intend for the year to mean a "fiscal year." A fiscal year is a 12-month period used for reporting a business's financial condition, which may begin at any point in the calendar year. For example, a fiscal year of a business might begin on July 1 and end on June 30 of the following year. As is the case with other time measurements, you should define the meaning of *year* as used in the contract, unless evident from the context.

Warning about holidays. Finally, be mindful of holidays, both religious and secular, that may affect timing in a contract. Anticipate when holidays will interfere with performance and specifically address these issues in the contract.

b. Miscellaneous expressions of duration

Words and phrases that express time periods also can be ambiguous. Interpretation problems can arise even when specific dates are used, such as in the following examples.

by . . .

Ambiguous:	**Supplier shall ship the Product *by* January 20, 20XX.**
Problem:	The term *by* has the same problem as *through*: It is unclear whether the parties intended the time period to include January 20, 20XX. This ambiguity could be eliminated by inserting "before."
Better:	**Supplier shall ship the Product *before* January 21, 20XX.**

through . . . or until . . .

Ambiguous:	**Supplier shall ship the Product *through* June 20, 20XX.**
	Supplier shall ship the Product *until* June 20, 20XX.
Problem in both examples:	Whether June 20, 20XX, is included in either of these statements is unclear. The beginning date also is not evident. Assuming that the beginning date was specified by a previous provision, the ambiguity of *through* or *until* can be resolved by adding the phrase *and including*.
Better:	**Supplier shall ship the Product *through and including* June 20, 20XX.**
	Supplier shall ship the Product *until and including* June 20, 20XX.

from . . . to . . .

Ambiguous:	**Supplier shall ship the Product *from* January 20, 20XX, *to* June 20, 20XX.**
Problem:	Some courts may find that *from* does not include January 20, 20XX and *to* does not include June 20, 20XX. If the parties' intent is to include these dates, the provisions could be stated more clearly.
Better:	**Supplier shall ship the Product during the time period *beginning on* January 20, 20XX, *and ending on* June 20, 20XX.**

---

within . . .

Ambiguous: **Supplier shall ship the Product *within* 21 days.**

Problem: One problem with this statement is that the starting or ending date of this time period has not been identified. And, even if the starting or ending date were identified, it is unclear whether the 21-day period would include that beginning or ending day. For these reasons, *within* should not be used when specifying a time period.

Better: **Supplier shall ship the Product *before* the twenty-first day after the day on which the Supplier receives Distributor's written request for shipment.**

---

between . . . and . . .

Ambiguous: **Supplier shall ship the Product *between* January 20, 20XX, *and* June 20, 20XX.**

Problem: Most U.S. courts would probably interpret this statement to mean that the dates were not included in the time period. To eliminate doubt, the provision could be rewritten using "beginning on" and "ending on."

Better: **Supplier shall ship the Product *beginning on* January 20, 20XX, *and ending on* June 20, 20XX.**

Also, note that the following words are consistently interpreted, at least by U.S. courts, to *not include* the referenced date:

Supplier shall ship the Product 21 days *following* receipt of Distributor's request.
Supplier shall ship the Product *after* January 20, 20XX.
Supplier shall ship the Product *before* June 20, 20XX.
Supplier shall ship the Product *prior to* June 20, 20XX.

8.3 *Deem*

The verb *deem* is commonly used to establish, for purposes of the contract, a circumstance that otherwise might not be true. The circumstance is sometimes referred to as a *legal fiction*. The following example from a distribution agreement creates a legal fiction:

> Any orders accepted by the Supplier that cannot be fulfilled because of a decree, statute, or regulation will be deemed to have been rejected when submitted to Supplier for acceptance or rejection.

Thus, the parties will treat the order as rejected, although the supplier had originally accepted it, if a decree, statute, or regulation prevents the supplier from filling the order.

Limit your use of *deem* to instances where the parties intend to create a legal fiction. Otherwise, avoid using *deem*, which generally is considered an archaic word for *consider, regard,* or *think.*

> ***Archaic:***   Supplier may allocate production among Distributor, other distributors, other dealers, and others that Supplier deems appropriate.
>
> ***Better:***   Supplier may allocate production among Distributor, other distributors, other dealers, and others that Supplier considers appropriate.

8.4 Phrases to avoid

Below are phrases that you will come across when reviewing contracts and model forms. These phrases have been overused and abused in contracts for many years. Because these phrases create ambiguity, you will want to avoid using them in contracts.

The Kentucky Supreme Court has called the use of and/or *a "much condemned conjunctive-disjunctive crutch of sloppy thinkers."* Raine v. Drasin, *621 S.W.2d 895, 905 (Ky. 1981).*

8.4.1 Avoid *and/or*

The phrase *and/or* in a contract provision is intended as a shortened method of expressing both the conjunctive and disjunctive. Using this phrase in a contract can make a contract provision unclear:

> Supplier may inspect Distributor's sales records and/or its place of business.

In the example, does the supplier have the power to inspect either the distributor's records *or* its places of business, or can the supplier do both? For clarity, a respected book on English grammar, *The Elements of Style,*[12] recommends replacing the phrase *and/or* with *and . . . or both.* Applying *and . . . or both,* the previous example would read as follows:

> Supplier may inspect Distributor's sales records or its place of business or both.

The meaning is now clear that the supplier may take either action or both.

8.4.2 Avoid *provided that* or *provided, however, that*

The phrases *provided that* or *provided, however, that* signal the beginning of a *proviso.* A **proviso** is an imprecise phrase used in contracts to create an exception, a condition, or a limitation that overrides a preceding clause in the sentence. Also, it is used to add a substantive provision. Sometimes *provided that* or *provided, however, that* are underlined or italicized in the contract for emphasis.

> *"Provide" when used as a verb does not create a proviso and can be used in drafting a provision: "Distributor shall provide Supplier both Spanish and English copies of all publicity and advertising."*

Provisos create ambiguity because they do not signal whether the proviso is intended as an exception, a condition, a limitation, or an addition. The meaning of the proviso must be determined by its context, which can sometimes be a challenge because the proviso often occurs in long, convoluted sentences. Even worse, more than one proviso might be tacked on to the sentence, thus creating even greater ambiguity. For these reasons, you should avoid using provisos. The following examples illustrate how provisos can be revised to more clearly express the parties' intent.

> #### An "exception" provision:
>
> ***Ambiguous:***   Supplier may change prices for the Product; *provided, however,* that no price change will affect purchase orders submitted by Distributor and accepted by Supplier prior to a price change.
>
> *Continued*

---

12. *And/or* is "[a] device, or shortcut, that damages a sentence and often leads to confusion or ambiguity." William Strunk, Jr. & E.B. White, *The Elements of Style* 46 (4th ed., Allyn & Bacon 2003).

Better:	Supplier may change prices for the Product, except that no price change will affect purchase orders submitted by Distributor and accepted by Supplier prior to a price change

A *"condition" provision*

Ambiguous:	Distributor may reject any Product that fails to meet acceptance specifications, *provided* that the rejected Product is returned freight prepaid before the 10th day after the day on which Supplier receives Distributor's written notice of rejection.
Better:	Distributor may reject any Product that fails to meet acceptance specifications on the condition that the rejected Product is returned freight prepaid before the 10th day after the day on which Supplier receives Distributor's written notice of rejection.

A *"limitation" provision with an added substantive provision*

Ambiguous:	Supplier may repair or replace the rejected Product promptly after receiving it, *provided, however, that* Supplier elects to do so no later than 30 days after receiving the rejected Product; and *provided* further that Supplier will pay all transportation costs to deliver the repaired or replaced Product to Distributor.
Better:	Supplier may repair or replace the rejected Product as promptly as possible but in no event later than 30 days after receiving the rejected Product. Supplier will pay all transportation costs to deliver the repaired or replaced Product to Distributor.

8.5 Avoid contractions

In informal English, it is common to shorten certain words or numbers by using contractions. An apostrophe is used in a contraction to mark any omitted words or numbers. Examples of contractions include *it's* for *it is; don't* for *do not; they'd* for *they had;* or *'16* for *2016.* Because contracts are formal documents, though, do not use contractions.

8.6 Choosing words that allocate risk

While negotiating a business deal, the parties will identify possible risks that they will take on by entering into a contract. Each party's goal is to ensure that its own risk is as slight as possible. Reducing one party's risk usually means the risk burden shifts to the other party. In other words, reducing one party's risk increases the other party's risk. Understandably, these conflicting interests create tension as each party attempts to negotiate terms, shifting the risk to the other party. Despite the parties' attempt to shift risk, governing law might limit the extent to which, or the manner in which, risks are allocated.

Who bears the burden of risk and the degree of that risk can be expressed in the contract through the use of carefully worded provisions. One of the most hotly negotiated and perhaps dangerous phrases that can shift the risk between parties is a "knowledge" qualifier used in a party's representation of fact. Consider the following representation appearing in a distribution agreement:

> Distributor represents that to the best of its knowledge there are no legal actions that could jeopardize its licenses or permits to distribute the Product in the Territory. For purposes of the previous sentence, "knowledge" means the facts and circumstances actually known by the Distributor.

In the example, the *knowledge* language shifts the risk from the distributor to the supplier. The distributor's knowledge does not include what it *should* know. If it is later discovered that legal actions existed, the supplier must show that the distributor *actually* knew about this litigation at the time it made the representation in order to recover damages. For this reason, the supplier will resist including the knowledge qualification in the distributor's representation. Conversely, the distributor, who does not want to bear risk for something *of which it is unaware,* will advocate for including this qualification in its representation. Therefore, standards relating to the level of knowledge of the representing party can be a point of intense negotiations. See section 10.5.1 in Chapter 10 for additional discussion on knowledge qualifiers in representations.

Another means for shifting risk in a representation is through *materiality qualifiers*. Consider the following representation that uses the qualifying phrase *material adverse effect*:

> Company represents that there are no outstanding judgments, writs, orders, injunctions, or decrees of any court, government agency, or arbitration panel against Company that are likely to have a Material Adverse Effect.
>
> For purposes of this agreement, "**Material Adverse Effect**" means any unfavorable change affecting the affairs of the Company's business, operations, property, prospects, or Company's financial condition and which is likely to hinder the Company's performance of its obligations under this agreement.

The inclusion of the phrase *Material Adverse Effect* results in the representing party bearing less risk than in a case where the phrase is excluded from the representation. The representing party will breach its representation only if the subject matter satisfies the definition given for *Material Adverse Effect*. Section 10.5.2 in Chapter 10 provides further explanation of materiality qualifiers in representations.

In addition to representations, an obligation is another example of a provision that allocates risk. The party undertaking the obligation accepts the risk of carrying out the performance. If the party fails to perform as promised, then the party entitled to that performance may receive damages. However, proper phrasing of the obligation related to the level of performance can increase or decrease the promisor's obligation. Qualifying language often used to define the level of a party's performance include *reasonable efforts, best efforts, due diligence*, and various phrases referencing particular industry or professional standards. For instance, "Distributor shall use its best efforts to market, sell, and distribute the Products in the Territory," or "Supplier shall use reasonable efforts to fill orders on or before 30 calendar days after receipt of a written order." Qualifiers for obligations are also discussed in Chapters 10 and 13.

The following are some other examples of words and phrases frequently used to qualify standards of performance.

adequate	reasonable care
convenient	satisfactory
due care	substantial
immediate	sufficient
material	temporary
ordinary course of business	to the extent permitted by law
practicable	undue
prompt	

Exercises

▶ **Exercise 8-1   Replacing legalese I**

On your first day of working on a contract in English, you are revising a few contract provisions. When you are asking your supervising attorney about the meaning of the words *herein, hereto, hereof, thereto,* and *thereof,* she says, "They are outdated ways of saying *in, to, of, to,* and *of.*" She suggests that you revise the provisions looking at the following example based on provisions from two different contracts:

> All notices, consents, requests, instructions, approvals, and other communications provided for **herein** shall only be validly given, made, or served if in writing . . . [DA#21]
>
> ════
>
>   All notices and other communications required or provided for **in this Agreement** shall be validly given, made, or served if in writing . . . [DA#23]

Revise the provisions below following the supervising attorney's advice, and keep in mind that words such as *herein, hereto, hereof, thereto,* and *thereof* do not always refer to the agreement.

Ex. 1:

> The terms and conditions *herein* contained, constitute the entire and only contract between the Parties *hereto* with respect to the subject matter *hereof* and shall supersede all previous communications, representations and agreements, either written or oral, between the Parties in respect of such subject matter. [DA#1]

Ex. 2:

> This Agreement shall be effective as of the Effective Date and shall remain in force for five years (the "Term"), unless terminated prior *thereto* as provided *herein*. [DA# 29]

Ex. 3:

> If any provision of this Agreement shall be held to be invalid, illegal or unenforceable, the validity, legality and enforceability of the remaining provisions shall in no way be affected or impaired *thereby*. [DA#17]

▶ **Exercise 8-2   Drafting a provision more precisely—legalese and other drafting conventions**

Compare the following three assignment provisions. Based on your comparison, compose a fourth version that does not contain legalese. Also, consider anything else you have learned so far about drafting a provision.[13]

Assignment. Neither Party may assign this Agreement or any rights hereunder except upon prior written consent of the other Party, which consent may be withheld in such other Party's sole discretion. Notwithstanding the foregoing, either Party may assign its rights and obligations to an Affiliate of such Party, although no such assignment shall relieve the Party of its primary responsibility for performance hereunder. This Agreement shall be binding upon, and inure to the benefit of, the permitted assigns and successors of the Parties hereto. [DA#24]

Assignment. This Agreement shall be binding upon and inure to the benefit of the parties hereto and their respective successors and assigns. Notwithstanding the foregoing, Distributor may not assign or otherwise transfer its rights hereunder or any interest therein without the prior written consent of Supplier. [DA#22]

ASSIGNMENT. Either party may assign this Agreement to an entity that acquires, directly or indirectly, substantially all of its assets or merges with it. Except as set forth in this section, neither this Agreement nor any rights under this Agreement, in whole or in part, will be assignable or otherwise transferable by either party without the express written consent of the other party. Any attempt by either party to assign any of its rights or delegate any of its duties under this Agreement without the prior written consent of the other party will be null and void. Subject to the above, this Agreement will be binding upon and take effect for the benefit of the successors and assigns of the parties to this Agreement. [DA#11]

▶ **Exercise 8-3   Replacing legalese II**

You just received a marked-up draft of a contract you are working on. Follow the advice of your reviewer, shown on the note below.

> John. Please re-write this passage. It's poorly written. Too long and too much legalese. Break up the passage into shorter sentences and get rid of the legalese, and you'll be ok.
>   P.S.: No one says "covenants and agrees" anymore!!!

---

13. In Chapter 13, we discuss in greater detail the legal basis for an assignment provision.

> 2. **Patent Indemnity.** Company covenants and agrees, at its own expense, to indemnify, defend and hold harmless each Distributor and its customers from and against every expense, damage, cost and loss (including attorneys' fees incurred) and to satisfy all judgments and decrees resulting from a claim, suit or proceeding insofar as it is based upon an allegation that the commodities or any part thereof furnished by Company or any process which is practiced in the customary use of the commodities is or has been infringing upon any patent, copyright or proprietary right, if Company is notified promptly of such claim in writing and given authority, and full and proper information and assistance (at Company's expense) for the defense of same. [DA#17]

▶ **Exercise 8-4   Replacing coupled synonyms**

Rephrase the provisions with coupled synonyms. Can you find any other redundancies?

Ex. 1:

> Dispute Resolution. Any and all disputes, controversies or claims concerning or relating to this Agreement (a "Dispute") will be addressed in accordance with the procedures specified in this Section 15.7, which will be the sole and exclusive procedures for the resolution of such Disputes. [DA#38]

Ex. 2:

> It is a company duly organized under the laws of the country identified in its address on the signature page of this Agreement and has all requisite corporate power and authority to enter into, deliver and perform its obligations under this Agreement. When duly executed and delivered by it, this Agreement will constitute an obligation which is valid, binding on and enforceable against it. [DA#12]

▶ **Exercise 8-5   Numbers as numerals or words**

Rewrite the following provisions, so that numbers appear either in numerals or in words.

Example:

> Obtain directly from Supplier and authorized Supplier distributors one hundred percent (100%) of its requirements of Supplier products. [DA#9]

Note: One hundred percent should be written either as a word or a numeral.

Ex. 1:

> In consideration for being granted the exclusive right as the Distributor for the Territory, Distributor shall pay to Corporation a Distributor Fee in the amount of $10,000.00 payable $5,000 upon execution of the Agreement and $5,000 at the start of the sixth month following the Effective Date. One-half of the entire amount of the above Distribution Fee shall be set off and deducted at the rate of $100 per unit from the amounts payable to the Corporation by the Distributor for the purchase of Products pursuant to the terms of this Agreement. [DA#1]

Ex. 2:

> *Payments.* For the first one million dollars ($1,000,000) of Company B Fees payable to Company B by Company A pursuant to this Agreement, the Company B Fees shall be payable in shares of the common stock of Company A ("Shares"), based on a price per share of $4.50 (the "Share Price"). [DA#35]

Ex. 3:

> Distributor would achieve a Ceiling Price of two hundred and ten US Dollars (US$210.00) per Unit with a Transfer Price of sixty US Dollars (US$60.00). [DA#24]

▶ **Exercise 8-6   Composing provisions—time references**

You represent a beverage manufacturer in a distribution and service deal. Today, you are looking up notes from a meeting you had with the manufacturer three weeks ago to start drafting provisions they requested.

Example:

> **Notes from meeting:**
>
> **Obligation:** *supplier promises secondary technical support assistance: by telephone, telefax and Internet*
>
> **Purpose:** *to identify and resolve technical problems*
>
> **Duration:** *6 A.M. to 5 P.M., Monday-Friday*
>
> **Exception:** *supplier holidays*

Your draft:

Support by Supplier

From 06:00 to 17:00 Pacific Standard Time, Mondays through and including Fridays, excluding Supplier holidays, Supplier shall provide secondary technical support assistance to Distributor by telephone, telefax, and Internet for problem identification and resolution.

Start drafting provisions based on the following notes:

Clement & Hampton
415 N. Oakton Blvd. Suite 340b
Chicago, Ill. 60642

Meeting with Barton's Lemonade, Corp.
Re: Distribution and Service Agreement
Mon., May 8, 2012 Jim Barton, CEO, Jeff Rathers, Production Manager, Elizabeth Hull, Sales
Barton wants exclusive dealership with BevDist, Inc.

1. Obligation: supplier promises secondary technical support assistance: by telephone, telefax and Internet
Purpose: to identify and resolve technical problems
Duration: 6 A.M. to 5 P.M., Monday-Friday
Exception: supplier holidays

2. Condition: if not otherwise agreed
Consequence/covenant: distributor pays company
Time frame: 4 P.M. (at the latest), every Friday
Purpose: for beverages that the distributor bought in the week that preceded this business week.
Exception: business week ends on a Thursday
Consequence/covenant: distributor pays company
Time frame: 4 P.M. (at the latest), on Thursday

3. Duration of term of agreement: from effective date: for one year (initial term)
Renewal: automatic renewal for an additional year: on one year anniversary of effective date
Exception: no renewal if terminated 60 days (the latest time possible) before the following anniversary of the effective date

▶ **Exercise 8-7 Turning notes into provisions**

Jackie Howard, a partner in your law firm, calls you with instructions as to what she wants to be included in some contract provisions. You represent the manufacturer in the deal. Take notes, and compose the provisions accordingly.

Example:

Jackie Howard: So in a provision on a license fee, I'd like you to include a provision that states that in exchange for exclusivity in the territories and within the markets, we will pay them a non-refundable, up-front fee of $15,000 through December 31, 2004.

Your version: License Fee. As consideration for exclusivity within the Territories and within the Markets, Distributor shall pay to Manufacturer a non-refundable upfront fee of $15,000 through and including December 31, 2004. [based on DA#36]

Note: State "through and including December 31, 2004" if you want to include the 31st of December. Don't forget the heading and capitalize defined terms. Also, are you expressing a discretionary right or an obligation? Also, keep in mind who Jackie refers to when she says "us" or "they."

Listen to the telephone conversation with Jackie Howard and take notes for this activity. The audio recording and transcript can be found in the materials section of Chapter 8 on the companion website (www.aspenlawschool.com/books/Adams).

▶ **Exercise 8-8 And/or**

Rewrite the passage below to express *and/or* in a less ambiguous way.

> Warranty Service. Distributor shall, according to the recommendations of Supplier, arrange for Supplier's performance of warranty service where appropriate, both within the Territory and/or at Supplier's facility in Belgium. [DA#2]

▶ **Exercise 8-9 Deem**

In order to get an idea of how to use the word *deemed*, look up instances in the sample contracts from the "Contract Database" file on the companion website by using the FIND function of your word processing program. Compare the following three Severability clauses.[14]

---

14. You will have a chance to compose a severability clause in Chapter 13.

> Severability. If any provision of this Agreement is **deemed to be unlawful** or unenforceable, such provision **is deemed severable**, and the other provisions shall remain in full force and effect. [DA#4]
>
> ———
>
> Severability. If and to the extent that any provision of this Agreement is **held to be illegal**, void or unenforceable, such provision shall be given no effect and **shall be deemed** not to be included in this Agreement but without invalidating any of the remaining provisions of this Agreement. In such event the parties shall negotiate with a view to finding the nearest permissible provision to that **found to be illegal**, void or unenforceable. [DA#14]
>
> ———
>
> Severability. In case any provision of the Agreement **will be** invalid, **illegal** or unenforceable, the validity, legality and enforceability of the remaining provisions will not in any way be affected or impaired thereby. [DA#12]

1. Which of the following expressions is used incorrectly? Explain.
   a) deemed to be unlawful
   b) held to be illegal
   c) found to be illegal
   d) will be illegal
2. In the context of a Severability clause, would either one of the following expressions make sense?
   a) is deemed severable
   b) shall be deemed not to be included

▶ **Exercise 8-10   Provided that**

Rewrite the *provided that* clauses so that they clearly express the parties' intent; also make other revisions based on what you have learned so far.

Ex. 1:

> Termination Without Cause. Distributor shall have the right to terminate this Agreement with or without cause at any time on or after January 15, 2002, provided that Distributor shall have given Supplier written notice of termination at least 12 months in advance of the termination date. [DA#3]

Ex. 2:

> Insolvency. Either party may terminate this Agreement immediately on delivery of written notice to the other party (i) upon the institution by or against such other party of insolvency, receivership, or bankruptcy proceedings or any other proceedings for the settlement of such party's debts; provided that, with respect to involuntary proceedings, such proceedings are not dismissed within 120 days, (ii) upon such other party's making an assignment for the benefit of creditors, or (iii) upon such other party's dissolution or ceasing to do business. [DA#3]

Ex. 3:

> Distributor will provide complete and accurate copies of all such agreements to Manufacturer within thirty (30) calendar days after the execution thereof; provided that business and economic terms may be deleted from such agreements. [DA# 36]

Ex. 4:

> Licensee and Licensee's Authorized Distributors shall not have any right to modify or to create derivative works from Licensor Technology, provided that Licensee may develop and market Licensee Applications that incorporate the Licensor Technology in unaltered and unmodified form. [DA#35]

Ex. 5:

> Distributor shall have the right to sell and distribute the Software through its agents, provided that each of its agents is located in the Territory and agrees in writing to comply with the provisions of this Agreement. [DA#28]

Ex. 6:

> Packing Manufacturer shall, at its expense, pack all Products in accordance with Manufacturer's standard packing procedure, which shall be suitable to permit shipment of the Products to the Territory; provided, however, that if Distributor requests a modification of those procedures, Manufacturer shall make the requested modification at Distributor's expense. [DA#10]

▶ **Exercise 8-11   Notwithstanding**

Part A: Before you start part B of this exercise, look up instances of the use of *notwithstanding* in the sample contracts DA#1-DA#40 by using the FIND function of your word processing program. With what other words or in what combinations does *notwithstanding* frequently appear? Try to replace *notwithstanding* in at least five sentences.

Part B. Look at the following provision and rephrase subsection (e) to clarify the reference "Notwithstanding the above." What does the word *above* refer to?

The Company reserves the right, in its sole discretion and without incurring any liability to Distributor, to:

(a) Alter the specifications for any Product;

(b) Discontinue the manufacture of any Product;

(c) Discontinue the development of any new product, whether or not such product has been announced publicly;

(d) Commence the manufacture and sale of new products having features which make any Product wholly or partially obsolete, whether or not Distributor is granted any distribution rights in respect of such new products; obsolete. In this case, Company shall provide Distributor with a right of first refusal to distribute such new products under the terms and conditions of this Agreement; and

(e) Withdraw any Product from marketing at any time. Notwithstanding the above, the Company shall use reasonable efforts to provide Distributor with prompt written notice of any such decisions and shall fill all accepted Purchase Orders from Distributor for any such altered or discontinued Products of which manufacturing and commercial deliveries have commenced. [DA#27]

▶ **Exercise 8-12   Allocation of risk I**

Using the FIND function of your word processing program, look up the words *material, timely,* and *substantial* in at least ten contracts in the "Contract Database" file on the companion website (www.aspenlawschool.com/books/Adams). Discuss with a partner, and determine if there is a party that benefits more from the use of one of these words.

▶ **Exercise 8-13   Defining *adversely* in greater detail**

Look at the following examples of *adversely affect* or *adversely reflect.* Is there a description or definition of the word *adverse?* What does *adverse* mean in the context of these provisions?

Make a list of possible situations in which the events described below could "adversely" affect ownership and operation of a business. Who decides what *adversely* means? Could the drafter use a more precise adverb instead of *adversely*, a definition, or examples?

Ex. 1:

> Termination by Distributor. Upon the occurrence of any of the following, Distributor may terminate the Term by giving Manufacturer written notice and if such occurrence is not cured within thirty (30) calendar days thereafter: . . .
>
> (c) the conviction of Manufacturer or any principal or manager of Manufacturer for any crime tending to adversely affect the ownership or operation of business . . . [DA#36]

Ex. 2:

> Events of Default. Supplier, at its sole option, may terminate this Agreement immediately without prejudice to any other remedy to which it may be entitled at law, in equity, or otherwise under this Agreement, upon the occurrence of any of the following events of default by providing written notice to Distributor: . . .
>
> (c) The conviction of Distributor or any principal officer of Distributor of any crimes that, in the opinion of Supplier, may adversely affect the ownership, operation, management, business or interest of Distributor or Supplier; or . . . [DA#2]

Ex. 3:

> Termination Upon Notice Without the Right to Cure . . .
>
> A. Is convicted of a felony involving fraud, a crime involving moral turpitude, or any other crime or offense which Supplier reasonably believes will adversely reflect upon the Company, the Beverages, the Licensed Marks, or the goodwill of the Company or Supplier's system of distribution. [DA#20]

Ex. 4:

> Distributor's incurable material breach of this Agreement include the following:
>
> (1) If Distributor has falsely made any of the representations and warranties set forth in this Agreement, or knowingly maintains false books or records or submits any false reports to the Company; or

Continued

(2) Distributor (or its principals) are convicted of a felony, a fraud, a crime involving moral turpitude, or found liable in a civil claim for fraud or any unfair or deceptive act or practice; or . . . . [slightly modified DA#27]

▶ **Exercise 8-14   Allocation of risk II**

Analyze the following contract provisions in terms of risks and obligations for each party.

Mark all adjectives and adverbs, and analyze how their use affects the level of risk and obligation. Also mark all verbs and modal verbs, and discuss how their use affects the level of risk and obligation for each party. Are modal verbs used correctly?

2. Dealer's obligations

a. The Dealer agrees to promote the sale of the Products in the Territory aggressively; to contact all potential users and customers and to sell as large a quantity as possible; to avoid transactions which might call upon Company to accept obligations inconsistent with Company's terms and conditions of sale or at unreasonable prices; to refrain from representing, promoting, selling, or arranging to sell products, accessories, or lines competitive with the Products in the Territory within the term hereof; and to avoid any and all activity inconsistent with the foregoing.

b. Dealer will maintain a sales organization, conduct promotional activities, advertise and distribute promotional material as may be mutually agreed upon from time to time.

c. Dealer will supply Company with the resale prices for the Territory and will provide assistance in contract negotiations if and when orders are placed by Dealer for direct contracting by Company with Dealer's customers.

d. Dealer agrees to actively work on and use all reasonable efforts in securing the release of bid bonds, performance bonds, bank letters of guarantee and customer holdbacks in connection with orders placed by Dealer, or directly by customers with Company.

In the event that the Dealer requires Company's assistance in securing the releases of the above, Company will provide Dealer with reasonable support and assistance in securing any such releases. In such event Dealer and Company with mutually agree upon cost sharing for such assistance.

e. In situations where Company is selling directly to a foreign government or government agency, Dealer will not represent Company unless Dealer warrants to Company that neither Dealer nor any employee or sub-agent of Dealer holds an official position with said government or government agency.

Continued

f. In order to further promote and support the sale of the Products, Company may, from time to time, wish to provide technical, marketing, or other support in the Territory to assist the Dealer organization in such activities. It is envisioned that such support by Company shall be provided on a cost sharing basis, to be mutually determined on a case-by-case basis.

g. In certain situations, in addition to the normal responsibilities set forth above, Company may direct Dealer to perform additional services such as assisting in market surveys; providing maintenance or technical services, support and assistance; assisting Company personnel traveling in the Territory; reviewing and editing sales literature for suitability in the Territory; and/or, providing reasonable assistance to customers not within Dealer's Territory as defined herein. Dealer agrees to provide such additional services or assistance, for which Dealer may request reasonable compensation for such services or assistance. [DA#26]

▶ **Exercise 8-15   Add to your vocabulary list**

Add to your vocabulary list at least ten new words from the "Contract Database" file on the companion website (www.aspenlawschool.com/books/Adams). Use the model from section 1.4 in Chapter 1 for guidance. Modify your old lists if you have new information regarding a word.

▶ **Exercise 8-16   Pegasus/Azteca deal—drafting the provisions**

Applying the concepts discussed in this chapter, draft the provisions for the Pegasus/Azteca deal. Use the information based on your work for the Pegasus/Azteca deal in Exercise 7-11 in Chapter 7.

Sentence Structure

9.1 Drafting simple and concise sentences

Choosing words that clearly, concisely, and precisely express the parties' intent is important, but the meaning of a well-chosen word can still be ambiguous in a poorly constructed sentence. Short sentences are easier for the reader to understand. Therefore, you should use short sentences in contract provisions whenever possible. One legal writing scholar recommends striving for sentences approximately 20 words in length, but not exceeding 29 words.[1] Although this is a sensible guideline, every sentence does not need to satisfy this limitation. You may find that a well-written, long sentence is necessary to adequately express the parties' intent. Also, varying sentence length helps maintain the reader's interest. And a short sentence surrounded by longer sentences will add emphasis. What you do want to avoid is needlessly complex sentences.

9.2 Subject, verb, and object placement

Place the subject, verb, and direct object of a sentence close to each other. Any phrase that is inserted between the subject and verb or inserted between the verb and object can disrupt a sentence's logical sequence. Fortunately, this problem can be easily remedied by

(1) shifting the phrase to the beginning or the end of the sentence (see Figures 9-1 and 9-2), or

(2) removing the phrase and stating the information in a separate sentence (see Figure 9-3).

---

1. Bryan A. Garner, *A Dictionary of Modern Legal Usage* 663 (2d ed., Oxford U. Press 1995).

Original draft:
Distributor shall deliver to Supplier, *no later than the fifteenth day of each calendar month*, a complete and accurate financial statement showing Distributor's sales of the Products during the preceding month.

Revised:
No later than the fifteenth day of each calendar month, Distributor shall deliver to Supplier a complete and accurate financial statement showing Distributor's sales of the Products during the preceding month.

Figure 9-1 Shifting the phrase to the beginning of the sentence

Original draft:
Supplier, *upon written notice to Distributor,* may change prices of the Products.

Revised:
Supplier may change prices of the Products *upon written notice to Distributor.*

Figure 9-2 Shifting the phrase to the end of the sentence

Original draft:
Upon receipt of a Purchase Order from Distributor, Supplier shall, unless otherwise instructed in writing by Distributor, ship the Products by marine freight.

Revised:
Supplier shall ship the Products upon receipt of a Purchase Order from Distributor. Supplier shall ship the Products by marine freight, unless otherwise instructed in writing by Distributor.

Figure 9-3 Removing the phrase and conveying the information in a separate sentence

Be careful, however, that you do not change the original meaning of the provision when shifting the phrase (see Figure 9-4).

> *Original draft:*
> Distributor represents and warrants:
>
> 1. No litigation, arbitration, or other proceeding is pending or, to Distributor's actual knowledge, is threatened against Distributor, or any of its properties or assets.
> 2. . . .
>
> *Revised:*
> Distributor represents and warrants:
> 1. To Distributor's actual knowledge, no litigation, arbitration, or other proceeding is pending or threatened against Distributor, or any of its properties or assets.
> 2. . . .

Figure 9-4 When shifting a phrase, do not change the provision's original meaning

In the original draft shown in Figure 9-4, the distributor represents there is no pending proceedings, known or unknown, against it. But as to threatened proceedings, the distributor only makes a representation about what it actually knows, not about threatened proceedings of which it is unaware. In the revised version, *distributor's actual knowledge* now modifies both pending and *threatened* proceedings. Thus, it is not making a representation about pending or threatened proceedings *of which it is unaware*. This revised version is more favorable to the distributor because it reduces the scope of its representation. The other party will not appreciate this revision if the provision as written in the original draft had been a negotiated point of agreement.

9.3 Active voice versus passive voice

Sentences written in active voice are often clearer and more concise than those written in passive voice. Therefore, you should strive to use active voice. Ultimately, however, it always depends on the context as to whether you want to use passive or active voice.

In active voice, the one performing the action of the verb is the subject of the sentence. In passive voice, the one receiving the action is the subject of the sentence.

Active Voice	**Passive Voice**
Distributor shall promote the Products.	The Products will be promoted by Distributor.

If the doer of the action is omitted from a sentence written in passive voice, the omission will leave the audience guessing as to the doer's identity. This can create ambiguity, if the doer of the action is not obvious. For example, in the following sentence, the identity of the party delivering the product is unknown.

> The Products will be delivered every Friday before 5 P.M. to Distributor's warehouse.

The contracting parties probably know, or should know, who will be making deliveries. But those who were not involved in the contracting process, including a judge, would not readily know. When the doer of the action is important, use active voice so that the doer of the action is the subject of the sentence.

> Supplier shall deliver the Products to Distributor's warehouse every Friday before 5 P.M.

Although active voice is preferred in contract drafting, there are two situations where you might consider using passive voice[2]:

1. When the action is more important than the doer of the action.

> All disputes arising out of or relating to this agreement are to be settled by binding arbitration under the Rules of Conciliation and Arbitration of the International Chamber of Commerce.

Note that the doer of the action is identified in a *by* . . . phrase.

2. When the doer of the action is obvious, unimportant, or unknown.

> Notices required under this agreement will be in writing and mailed by registered or certified mail, postage prepaid, to the last known address of the other party.

---

2. A third situation, irrelevant for contract drafting, is a situation where the speaker wants to avoid blame by hiding the doer of the action. "Mistakes have been made," is a prime example often used by representatives of large organizations or political parties to deflect blame.

Therefore, if you do not have a good reason for using passive voice, revise the sentence so that it is stated in active voice.

9.4 Nominalizations

9.4.1 Generally

Nominalizations are commonly found in English language contracts. Verbs, adjectives, and adverbs can be turned into nouns by adding a suffix. Verbs, for example, are turned into nouns by adding suffixes such as *-ure, -ment, -ence, -al, -ance, -ity, -tion*, or *-sion*. Using nominalizations unnecessarily complicates ideas, contributes to wordiness, and hinders the reader's understanding. By turning a verb into a noun, for example, it loses its active character and becomes more of a thing or object. In writing, a style that uses nominalizations looks static and impersonal.

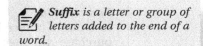 *Suffix is a letter or group of letters added to the end of a word.*

> *First version (nominalization):*
> Shipment of Product shall be done by designated Shipping Company.
>
> *Second version (preferred version):*
> A designated Shipment Company shall ship Product.

9.4.2 Empty verbs in nominalizations

The verbs used in the verb-noun combination of a nominalization are often just filler words or empty verbs that do not add to the overall meaning. The "empty" verbs most frequently used in nominalizations are *make, have, do, provide, give.* For example, *make a statement, have an assessment, provide an explanation, be in agreement,* or *give an evaluation.* In most cases, simply drop the "empty" verb and replace the nominalization with the base form of the verb if the "empty" verb is truly just a filler.

> *First version (nominalization):*
> Distributor shall make a comparison of similar products in the Territory.
>
> *Second version (preferred version):*
> Distributor shall compare similar products in the Territory.

However, in some instances the nominalization cannot just be reduced to the verb, especially if the verb in the verb-noun combination is not just a filler. In the list of replacement suggestions for nominalizations above, it is suggested that the expression *enter into an agreement* be replaced with the verb *agree*. This replacement makes sense in many cases, but the example below illustrates a case where it would not be advisable.

First version:
In order to induce Distributor to enter into this agreement and to purchase the Securities, the Company hereby represents to Distributor . . . .

Second version:
In order to induce Distributor to agree and to purchase the Securities, the Company hereby represents to Distributor . . . .

Although the second version is grammatically correct, the word *agree* does not describe what the company wants the distributor to do. It is not just agreeing, but it is negotiating, re-negotiating, and finally signing a formal document, the contract.

In the phrase *enter into this agreement*, the verb *enter* summarizes all of these actions and, thus, cannot be eliminated, since it is not just an empty filler.

Just as there are filler words in nominalizations that do not add meaning, there are other nominalization expressions in contract provisions that can be stated more concisely.

Examples of nominalizations stated more concisely

Nominalization	*replace with*	**Adjective, adverb**
goods of merchantable quality		merchantable goods
in a professional manner		professionally
in a reasonable fashion		reasonably

Similarly, constructions containing the expressions *it is*, *there is*, or *there are* often also serve as unnecessary fillers. Therefore, you should avoid these expressions, wherever possible.

> ### *Replacement Suggestions for it is and there is/are*
>
> | **Empty subject** | *replace with* | **Full clause** |
> |---|---|---|
> | It is agreed . . . | | The Parties agree . . . |
> | There is a requirement . . . | | The Parties shall . . . |
> | It is necessary that . . . | | The Parties shall . . . |
>
> Exception: If "there is" could be replaced by the verb "exist," it is not a filler expression, e.g., "There are three categories of damages."

9.5 Using *a/an/the*

Preciseness and specificity lie at the heart of contract drafting, and articles such as *the* or *a* are among the most important linguistic tools to create different levels of specificity. After all, you want to make sure that you, your client, the other party's counsel, the other party, and any outsiders, such as a court or shareholders, "are on the same page."[3] In other words, they should share the same knowledge when talking about contract terms.

Since the rules of usage for articles in English are very complex, we will give a brief, general overview of the subject and then focus on the areas that are important for contract drafting. If you want an in-depth overview of article rules, you can refer to the grammar guides listed on the companion website (www.aspenlawschool.com/books/Adams).

9.5.1 General rules for article usage

First, the indefinite article *a/an* and the regular plural form (*-s, -es*) without an article are often used to refer to that noun more generally. The receiving party in an information exchange may not be able to identify exactly what the other party is referring to with regard to that noun.

> The client wants to purchase **a** car.
> The client wants to purchase cars.

---

3. The idiom *to be on the same page* is an American usage, which means that everyone talks about the same thing.

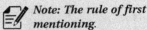

Note: The rule of first mentioning.

When a noun is introduced the first time with an indefinite article, the second time you refer to it, you should use the definite article if you refer to the same noun.

Judging from the written passage only, the receiving party (listener, reader) would not know what kind of car(s) the client intends to purchase. The information is very general.[4]

Second, the definite article *the* increases the level of specificity, and the writer can add follow-up information by describing the noun in greater detail.

Singular:
The client wants to purchase a car. **The car** should be a luxury car.

Plural:
The client wants to purchase cars. **The cars** should be luxury cars.

The information provided in Examples 1 and 2 in the box above is still quite general, but at least the receiving party now knows that the car should be a luxury car. Thus, we can specify a noun with the definite article and still have a more general or abstract reference (a luxury car, luxury cars). The level of shared knowledge of both parties has increased, yet the receiving party still cannot identify exactly what the noun refers to.

Finally, the definite article *the* is used to give a very specific reference, or a reference in which the reader/listener can identify concretely to what the noun is referring. The level of shared knowledge between the two parties is quite high. (See Figure 9-5.)

The client wants to purchase a car. The car should be a luxury car. The client wants to buy **the Mercedes XYZ**, which was offered at the car show.

9.5.2 Count versus non-count nouns

There is a general distinction in English between count and non-count nouns. **Count nouns** are commonly described as nouns that can take on the definite article *the* or the indefinite article *a/an* and that have a plural

---

4. The indefinite article *a/an* can be used with more specific reference if it means *one*: "The car should have **a** 2005 Brand A audio system, a hardwood instrument panel, and a Brand B anti-theft system."

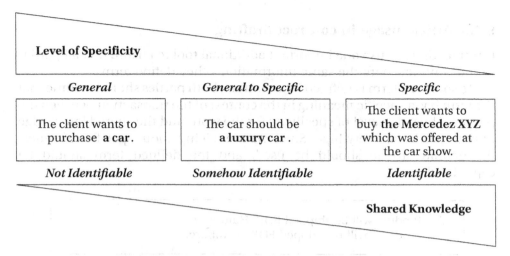

Figure 9-5 Level of specifity and shared knowledge in article usage (Figure by Peter K. Cramer, 2012.)

ending (often *-s* or *-es*). The three rules discussed in section 9.5.1 apply without major exceptions.

Non-count nouns[5] are defined as nouns that cannot normally be counted because they refer to abstract entities, such as *negligence*, or non-countable entities, such as *water*.[6] Non-count nouns do not usually take on the definite or indefinite articles, nor do they have plural endings. To make them quantifiable, or even countable, adjectival modifiers such as *much, no, some, little, all*, or units of measurement, such as *ounces, liters, kilograms, pieces*, or *slices*, are used.

They can take the definite article (but not the plural ending) when they are used for specific reference to describe the noun or the class it represents in greater detail.

> Supplier shall provide *the support* and consultation that is necessary for additional installation at reasonable and customary charges for such services.
>
> Distributor shall collaborate with consumer advocacy groups to gain *the support of the* Target Population.

---

5. For a more detailed discussion, *see* Betty Schrampfer Azar and Stacy A. Hagen, *Understanding and Using English Grammar* (4th ed., Pearson Educ. 2009).

6. The concept of countability and plural use differs from language to language. In English, for example, the word *information* does not take the plural (e.g., *much information*), whereas in other languages, you could say *many informations*.

9.5.3 Article usage in contract drafting

Contract drafters use one important additional tool to ensure that all parties to the contract share the same information—they define terms.

As soon as a term is defined in a contract, both parties should assume that the term has a specific meaning in the context of the transaction between the parties. Thus, the level of specificity for the word and the shared knowledge of both parties are very high. Since we are talking about specific reference, the definite article should be used, and the defined term should be capitalized.

The Product will be shipped FOB, Hamburg.
The Products will be shipped FOB, Hamburg.

Note, though, that some contract drafters eliminate the article because they assume that by defining a word, the meaning of the definite article is included in the defined term.

Product will be shipped FOB, Hamburg.
Products will be shipped FOB, Hamburg.

As a matter of fact, definitions often are phrased in a way that shows that the word *the* should be part of the defined term.

"Product" means **the** interactive CD-ROM **product** of Supplier specified on the applicable Schedule. [DA#22]

In conclusion, with so many different rules and exceptions for the use of or omission of the article, it can become quite confusing for the non-native drafter to decide which choice is correct.

Since there is no mathematical formula for making this determination, the drafter should keep in mind the basic goal: identification and specificity are at the heart of contract drafting. Thus:

1. Using singular nouns with the indefinite article (*a/an*) or plural nouns without an article keeps the level of specificity and shared knowledge low.
2. Using the definite article increases identifiability, specificity, and shared knowledge for all parties.

9.6 Use of pronouns

English pronouns are used as a "placeholder" for nouns and other nominal constructions, such as gerunds, and refer to the original noun, gerund, or other nominal construction they replace. The most commonly used pronouns are personal pronouns, such as *I, you, he, she, it, we, you, they*; possessive pronouns, such as *my, your, his, her, its, our, your, their*; or relative pronouns, such as *which, that, who, when, where, what*, or *how*.

If your language does not separate the pronoun from the verb, be sure to use a separate pronoun and verb when you draft in English. Many Latin-based languages and Asian languages do not separate pronoun and verb.

Spanish: tiene: **he, she, it** has
Japanese: wakarimas: **I understand**

The easiest way to remember the use of personal pronouns in English in general is that English uses the natural gender with only a few words and assigns the pronoun *it* to the remaining words. Thus, unlike in other languages, almost every word other than words like *boy, man, girl*, or *woman*, is referred to by the pronoun *it*.

One major exception, though, can be found in contract drafting, where words such as *distributor* or *supplier* normally do not refer to a concrete person—a man or a woman—but to a legal entity—a construct or thing.

> Manufacturer shall have ownership rights to all of its advertising.

Manufacturer is not Mr. Smith, who owns the company, but Mr. Smith's company.

An easy way of understanding what or who the pronoun refers to is to replace the pronoun with its original noun construction.

> The Effective Date of this Agreement shall be the date **it** is signed as accepted by a duly authorized officer of Supplier. [DA#16]
>
> The Effective Date of this Agreement shall be the date **this Agreement** is signed as accepted by a duly authorized officer of Supplier. [DA#16]
>
> ———
>
> Distributor agrees that **it** will not (and will not permit any other person under **its** control to) change or modify the Products in any manner. [DA#6]
>
> Distributor agrees that **Distributor** will not (and will not permit any other person under **Distributor's** control to) change or modify the Products in any manner. [DA#6]
>
> ———

Continued

> Consultant agrees that if **his** consulting relationship with the Company is terminated for any reason, **he** will return all Company property. [CA#25]
>
> Consultant agrees that if **Consultant's** consulting relationship with the Company is terminated for any reason, **Consultant** will return all Company property. [CA#25]

9.6.1 Non-defining use of the relative pronoun

Relative pronouns, such as *which, who,* or *that,* are used in sentences following the noun or nominal construction to provide either additional but non-essential information, or information that is needed to define the noun or nominal construction in greater detail.

> Participants, who are included in the list, will be notified.
> *Meaning: [Maybe all]* Participants will be notified. *[By the way]* They are included in the list.

In the example above, the relative pronoun is used to give additional information about all participants. It does not help to distinguish one group of participants from another group. When it is used in this sense, it is called *non-defining* or *non-essential*. A comma is inserted directly before the pronoun. The information may be interesting or insightful but is not absolutely necessary for understanding.

9.6.2 Defining use of the relative pronoun

> Participants who are included in the list will be notified.
> *Meaning: [Only]* Those participants *[out of a larger group of participants]* who are included in the list will be notified.

In the example above, the relative pronoun is used to define and narrow down the category of participants to some participants of a larger group. When a pronoun is used in this sense, it is called *defining, restrictive,* or *essential*. Note the omission of the comma before the pronoun.

Drafters are often confused by the actual grammar rule and the different names given to relative clauses based on their function, such as *defining, restrictive,* or *essential*; or *non-defining, non-restrictive,* or *non-essential*. The following pointers can help you make a decision as to which pronoun construction you should use.

> 1. Should the additional information apply to **all** members of a category/the entire category?
> *Yes* → *Answer: non-restrictive use*
> Could the additional information be deleted without changing the basic meaning of the sentence ?
> *Yes* → *Answer: non-restrictive use*

Example: *Distribution contracts, which are difficult to draft* [**all of them**], *should be drafted by Mr. Miller.*
Meaning: We could easily say: *Distribution contracts should be drafted by Mr. Miller.*

> 2. Should the additional information apply to **some but not all** members of a category to help the reader/listener identify those specific members of that category?
> *Yes* → *Answer: restrictive use*

Example: *Distribution contracts that are difficult to draft* [**the ones that are difficult to draft**] *should be drafted by Mr. Miller.*
Meaning: *Out of a selection of distribution contracts, Mr. Miller should draft only the ones that are difficult to draft.*

> 3. Likewise, insertion of the word *only* before the noun that is modified can help you understand if the relative clause is used restrictively. These helping words should not appear in the actual contract provision.

Example: [**Only**] *Distribution contracts that are difficult to draft should be drafted by Mr. Miller.*

> 4. By inserting the expression *by the way, it/they* at the beginning of the relative clause, you can often quickly understand if the information is additional and non-restrictive. These helping words should not appear in the actual contract provision.

Example: *Distribution contracts,* [**by the way, they**] *are difficult to draft should be drafted by Mr. Miller.*

Important note: One easy rule to follow to avoid creating misunderstanding is to use the pronoun *that* instead of *which*[7] when restricting a category. Also, do not put a comma before *that* or *which* when you are using it in a defining, restricting sense.[8]

9.7 Choosing appropriate prepositions

As mentioned in Chapter 1, learning to use the correct preposition in English is one of the most challenging tasks for non-native speakers. The good news for contract drafters is that the incorrect use of a preposition in most cases is probably not going to cause any misunderstandings, or even worse, litigation.[9] Still, your client or your supervising attorney might doubt your proficiency in English, resulting in your being given less demanding tasks. Fortunately, you have several ways of checking whether you are using the correct preposition, as discussed below.

9.7.1 Dictionaries

A dictionary can be consulted at any time and, in most cases, will help you find the answer to your question about the correct use of a preposition. The companion website (www.aspenlawschool.com/books/Adams) includes recommendations of reliable print and online dictionaries. As to the kind of dictionary, always consult a legal dictionary, such as *Black's Law Dictionary*, or an online legal dictionary when first looking up a word for contract drafting.

Even though you may be able to find the preposition commonly used with a verb, legal meanings can differ widely from everyday meanings of words, as the following example shows.

Use of the verb inure *in a regular dictionary*

Inure
     inure somebody to something: *phrasal verb*
to make someone become used to something unpleasant, so that they are no longer upset by it:
Nurses soon become inured to the sight of suffering.

Longmann Dictionary of Contemporary English
http://www.ldoceonline.com/dictionary/inure

---

7. The exception to this rule is when *that* is being used with a preposition.

8. Sometimes you will have to put a comma in front of a defining pronoun, if punctuation rules require you to do so.

9. This is most likely to be the case with phrasal verbs, such as *depend on*. In cases where a verb can take more than one preposition, however, use of the wrong preposition could be costly—for example, "The Work shall be done for the Customer" as opposed to "The Work shall be done by the Customer."

> ### *Use of the verb* **inure** *in a legal dictionary*
>
> ***To inure***
> To take effect; to come into use:
> [For example,] the settlement proceeds must inure to the benefit of
> the widow and children.
>
> *Black's Law Dictionary* 900 (Bryan A. Garner, ed., 9th ed. 2011)

9.7.2 Large collections of legal text

The second source you should consult is the contract database available in this book or other collections of legal texts. By using the FIND function of your word processing program, you can look up instances of certain English words and the prepositions they take in several contracts. For the most part, you will probably look up verbs such as *rely, insist,* or *enter,* or adjectives such as *dependent, entitled,* or *related.* If possible, look up at least five instances from five different contracts to be sure you understand the usage, and always double check with a dictionary. With less commonly used words, such as *inure,* you can first try to find out meaning and possible use of prepositions and then, if the original word is archaic and replaceable, decide to use a more current word once you draft your version of a provision.

9.8 Dangling participles

Legal writers are encouraged to create concise and brief sentences to increase readability and comprehension. However, in an effort to do so, some writers reduce their constructions so much that they create the kind of comprehension problems they wanted to avoid. In some of these reduced constructions, for example, you can find *dangling participles.* The word *dangling* implies that something is not fully connected; a participle is a verbal construction that ends in an *-ing* or an *-ed.*

Normally, a full clause containing a subject and a verb can be reduced to a participial construction when it is part of a complex clause that contains another subject and verb.

> ***Long version:***
> When the Contractor submits a proposal, the Contractor shall send three copies to the local Zoning Board.
>
> ***Shortened version:***
> When submitting a proposal, the Contractor shall send three copies to the local Zoning Board.

In the shortened version, the noun *Contractor* is deleted from the first clause since it is repeated in the following clause. The verb *submits* is replaced by the participle *submitting*. This leaves the phrase *When submitting a proposal.*

As long as the subject of the first clause and the subject of the second clause are identical, the first clause can be reduced by deleting the subject and turning the verb into a participle.[10]

Long version:
After the Zoning Board replies, the Contractor has three weeks to comment on the notes of the Zoning Board.

Incorrect reduction (dangling participle):
After replying, the Contractor has three weeks to comment on the notes of the Zoning Board.

However, in this complex clause #1, the subject of the first clause, *Zoning Board*, is not identical to the subject of the second clause, *Contractor*. As a result, the reduction in clause #2 could lead to the erroneous interpretation that the contractor is the replying entity.

9.9 Enumerating and tabulating complex sentences

9.9.1 Enumeration

Hindu-Arabic numeration is preferred because it is the most cross-culturally recognized numeration system. An alphabetical enumeration system is acceptable so long as the letters are presented in the order of the alphabet of the language used for the contract. Do not use Roman numeration in a contract where the contracting party is from a culture that does not recognize this numeration system.

Enumeration is a format for listing items. Enumeration is used in contract drafting for both large-scale organization and small-scale organization. In Chapter 3, we discussed using enumeration for large-scale organization, numbering sections and subsections as a way to organize contract provisions. Enumeration can also be used for small-scale organization by numbering a series of items within a sentence. Complex sentences that include an extended list or series of lengthy clauses can be expressed in a more organized and readable format by using enumeration.

---

10. The sentence can also be inverted: *The Contractor shall send three copies to the local Zoning Board when submitting a proposal.*

The enumeration pattern can be any of the following:

- Hindu-Arabic: numeration: 1, 2, 3 . . .
- Alphabetical: A, B, C . . . ; or a, b, c . . .
- Roman numeration: I, II, III . . . ; or i, ii, iii . . .

Enumeration also makes it easier to precisely reference an item in a list—e.g., "Section 2.1(3)." For this reason, do not use bullet points or other generic symbols as an enumeration pattern.

Figure 9-6 illustrates how a sentence with a lengthy series of items is made clearer and more readable by using enumeration.

Without Enumeration:
2.1 Distributor shall make a minimum purchase of the Products of 275,000 USD before the first anniversary date of this agreement, 300,000 USD before the second anniversary date of this agreement, 325,000 USD before the third anniversary date of this agreement, and 350,000 USD before the fourth anniversary date of this agreement.

With Enumeration:
2.1 Distributor shall make a minimum purchase of the Products as follows: (1) 275,000 USD before the first anniversary date of this agreement, (2) 300,000 USD before the second anniversary date of this agreement, (3) 325,000 USD before the third anniversary date of this agreement, and (4) 350,000 USD before the fourth anniversary date of this agreement.

Figure 9-6 Using enumeration in lengthy sentences

When enumerating items within a sentence, each item in the series is prefaced by the number or letter in the sequence. The number or letter is placed inside parentheses—e.g.: (1), (2), (3); (a), (b), (c). This format is shown in the enumeration example in Figure 9-8. Alternatively, a period is placed after each number or letter—e.g.: 1., 2., 3.; or a., b., c. (See section 9.9.2(a) for a discussion and examples of sentence form tabulation.) Typically, the latter format (where the period is placed after each number or letter) is used only in list form tabulation. (See section 9.9.2(b) for a discussion and examples of list form tabulation.)

In addition to organizing a list of items, enumeration can also be used to remedy ambiguities. In Figure 9-7, the first provision as written makes it unclear whether the word *polarized* applies only to sunglasses or to both sunglasses and goggles. The following enumerated examples clarify both alternatives.

> *Without Enumeration:*
> Distributor shall market and distribute polarized sunglasses and goggles in the Territory.
>
> *With Enumeration:*
> *"Polarized" applies only to "sunglasses."*
> Distributor shall market and distribute (1) polarized sunglasses and (2) goggles in the Territory.
>
> *"Polarized" applies to all items*
> Distributor shall market and distribute polarized (1) sunglasses and (2) goggles in the Territory.

Figure 9-7 Using enumeration to clarify meaning

9.9.2 Tabulation

For added visual clarity, you may also tabulate the enumerated items. **Tabulation** is a formatting technique that sets off the enumerated items from the surrounding text by placing it in a separate, indented block. Figure 9-8 tabulates the enumerated provision in Figure 9-6.

> Distributor shall make a minimum purchase of the Products as follows:
>
> (1) 275,000 USD before the first anniversary date of this agreement,
> (2) 300,000 USD before the second anniversary date of this agreement,
> (3) 325,000 USD before the third anniversary date of this agreement, and
> (4) 350,000 USD before the fourth anniversary date of this agreement.

Figure 9-8 Using tabulation for visual clarity in lengthy sentences

The following occasions may warrant the use of tabulation:

1. When there is a long list of items. (See Figure 9-6, which shows a sample provision in sentence form.) You also may express the provision in list form.
2. When the items are stated in lengthy phrases or clauses. (See Figure 9-12, which shows a sample provision in list form.) You also may express the provision in sentence form.

3. When two or more sentences are closely related. (See Figure 9-9, which shows a sample provision in sentence form.) You also may express the provision in list format.
4. When it is unclear whether a modifier applies to one or all of the items and the items are lengthy phrases or clauses. (See Figure 9-10, which shows a sample provision in sentence form.) When the modifier applies to all the listed items, you may express the provision in list form if the modifier can be logically inserted in the introductory language.

You may tabulate in either a sentence form or a list form.[11] Determining which form to use depends on your preference and whether one form is more helpful to clearly express the intent of the provision.

a. Sentence form

In the sentence form of tabulation, the words introducing the series (the **introductory language**) and the enumerated items in the series are part of the same sentence.

The rules for a sentence form of tabulation are the following:

1. The introductory language begins the sentence.
2. The first letter of the first word of each item begins with a lowercase letter.
3. Each item must have parallel sentence structure, meaning each item has the same grammatical form. For example, changing the verb voice from one item to the next will break the parallel structure. See the tabulated sentence in Figure 9-9 for an example of parallel sentence structure in which each item begins with the verb *is*. Also, note the parallel structure of the tabulated sentence in Figure 9-10 in which each item begins with the indefinite article *a* or *an*.
4. The next to the last item in the series ends with the conjunction *and* or *or* to indicate whether the list is cumulative or alternative.
5. End each item with either a comma or a semi-colon, except for the last item.
6. The last item on the list ends with a period if that item ends the sentence.

Figure 9-9 exemplifies the sentence form of tabulation.

---

11. *See* Reed Dickerson, *The Fundamentals of Legal Drafting* 115-126 (2d ed., Little, Brown 1986).

Without enumeration and tabulation:
Distributor represents to Supplier that it is a corporation organized and existing under the laws of Delaware. Distributor also represents to Supplier that it is fully licensed in all States where it will sell and distribute the Products.

Enumerated and tabulated:
Distributor represents to Supplier that Distributor

(1) is a corporation organized and existing under the laws of Delaware, and
(2) is fully licensed in all States where it will sell and distribute the Products.

Figure 9-9 Tabulation—sentence form

Tabulation can also clear up ambiguities created by a modifier that appears before or after the series, thus raising the question whether it modifies one or all items in the series. For example, in the unedited provision in Figure 9-10, it is ambiguous whether the phrase "covering the calendar year immediately succeeding its submission" applies only to "method of distribution" or to all of the items in the series. This is clarified in the enumerated and tabulated version of the provision. By tabulating the items and bringing the end phrase "covering the calendar year immediately succeeding its submission" back to the original left margin, it becomes clear that the end phrase modifies all the enumerated and tabulated items. If the phrase "covering the calendar year immediately succeeding its submission" only modified one of the items, then the phrase would have been placed within that item.

Without enumeration and tabulation:
Before December 31 of each year this agreement remains in effect, Distributor shall provide Supplier with a written marketing plan for the sale of each Product that includes a marketing timetable, an advertising strategy, a sales projection, and a method of distribution covering the calendar year immediately succeeding its submission.

Enumerated and tabulated:
Before December 31 of each year this agreement remains in effect, Distributor shall provide Supplier with a written marketing plan for the sale of each Product that includes

(1) a marketing timetable,
(2) an advertising strategy,
(3) a sales projection, and
(4) a method of distribution

covering the calender year immediately succeeding its submission.

Figure 9-10 Using sentence form of tabulation to clarify meaning

b. List form

Similar to the sentence form of tabulation, the list form of tabulation can be used for a series of items that is either cumulative or alternative. But, unlike the sentence form, the list form is especially useful when the items in the list can be cumulative, alternative, or both. For introductory language expressing this option, see Example C in Figure 9-11.

The rules for a list form of tabulation are the following:

1. The introductory language carries the burden of signaling
    (a) whether the provision is an obligation (*shall*), a discretionary power (*may*), a representation (*represents*), or other type of contract provision, and
    (b) whether the list that follows is cumulative, alternative, or a choice, typically by using *all, one,* or *one or more* to modify the noun *following.*
    See the examples in Figure 9-11.
2. The introductory language forms a complete sentence that ends with a colon or a period. See the examples in Figure 9-11.

Example A: Introductory language indicating an obligation and a cumulative list
Supplier shall provide to Distributor all of the following:

Example B: Introductory language indicating a discretionary power and an alternative list
Supplier may provide to Distributor one of the following:

Example C: Introductory language indicating a discretionary power and a choice list
Supplier may provide to Distributor one or more of the following:

Example D: Introductory language indicating a procedural statement and a cumulative list
Seller's obligations to make its Deliveries at Closing are subject to the satisfaction or waiver by Seller of each of the following conditions.

Figure 9-11 Examples of introductory language for list form of tabulation

3. The first letter of the first word in each item on the list is capitalized.
4. Each item ends with a period.
5. The same grammatical structure is used for each item.
6. Because the introductory language specifies whether the list is cumulative, single alternative, or open choice, the conjunction *and* or *or* is omitted from the enumerated list.

Figure 9-12 exemplifies the list form of tabulation.

Unedited:
Supplier shall provide Distributor with samples of the Products, promotional literature, and price lists; make available to Distributor special purchase offers and quantity discounts of the Products; and make available to Distributor consultation services with Supplier's marketing representatives.

Enumerated and tabulated list form:
Supplier shall provide to Distributor all of the following:

1. Samples of the Product, promotional literature, and price lists.
2. Special purchase offers and quantity discounts of the Products.
3. Consultation services with Supplier's marketing representatives.

Figure 9-12 Tabulation—list form

9.9.3 Sub-tabulation

Extremely complex sentences might require more than one level of tabulation. For clarity and ease in referencing, use a different enumeration format for each level of tabulation. The sub-tabulated items are further indented to separate them visually from the items listed at the higher tabulation level. Sub-tabulation can make reading more difficult, so use it sparingly and strive to avoid sub-tabulating beyond the second level of division. Figure 9-13 shows correct sub-tabulation.

To use Supplier's Trademarks, Distributor

(a) must comply with Supplier's quality control standards
   (i) by complying with all relevant laws and regulations, and
   (ii) by not using any Trademarks on or in connection with any goods or services other than Supplier's Products, and
(b) must permit Supplier's representatives to inspect Distributor's facilities without notice and during normal business hours to confirm that Distributor is using Supplier's Trademarks as required in this agreement.

Figure 9-13 Example of sub-tabulation

9.9.4 Avoid overusing enumeration and tabulation

Enumeration and tabulation are helpful organizational tools, but they should not be overused in a document. Excessive enumeration and tabulation can hinder clarity and readability, especially if used more than once in the same section or subsection. You should consider using enumeration and tabulation only if the sentence is complex, or to make clear whether a modifier applies to all items or just one item in a series. For lengthy sentences, do not enumerate or tabulate if the sentence can be split into two or more sentences without giving up clarity and conciseness. And do not use enumeration or tabulation when the sentence is clear and easy to read. For instance, the following sentence is clear and simply stated: "The balls will be painted blue, white, and green." Enumerating or tabulating this sentence will not make it clearer or easier to read.

Exercises

▶ **Exercise 9-1   Sentence length**

You are supervising a new associate, who is still learning how to draft contract terms. Mark up the following passages in the margin of the document, suggest changes, and make revisions based on what you have learned so far. Help the new associate by providing sample answers. For more complex editing tasks, you can use the style sheet from the companion website (www.aspenlawschool.com/books/Adams) to create margin notes.

Examples:

Ex. 1:

> In the event Company, on the one hand, or Distributor, on the other hand, breaches or otherwise fails to perform any part of this Agreement, then the party hereto not in breach may notify in writing the party in breach and demand that such breach or such failure to perform be corrected within a stipulated period, which period, shall not be less than thirty (30) days following notification. [DA#7]

Ex. 2:

> During the term of this Agreement, the Distributor shall have the limited, non-exclusive, royalty-free right to use the Trademarks in connection with the promotion and sale of Products in the Territory, provided however that the Distributor obtain the Corporation's prior written consent to use the Trademarks in catalogues,

Continued

> promotional materials, and advertising materials, a mock up or example of which is first submitted to the Corporation and provided further that failure of the Corporation to reply to any request for its consent within a period of 7 days after receipt of the request and the mock-up or sample shall be deemed as an approval for the relevant use included in such request. [DA#1]

▶ **Exercise 9-2   Subject, verb, and object placement**

Rewrite the following provision by shifting around the inserted phrase "without Supplier's prior written consent."

> Distributor agrees that it will not use, without Supplier's prior written consent, any mark which is likely to be similar to or confused with the Marks. [DA#25]

▶ **Exercise 9-3   Use of active versus passive voice I**

Attached to one of the final drafts of a contract, you find the following Post-it™ Note asking you to go over passages that contain passive constructions.[12] When you are done, send your revisions to a partner (by email or written draft).

> Babara. I see a lot of passive constructions in this contract. Please, see below the passages I pointed out. Can you rewrite them in active voice, if necessary? Some of these passives may be ok, but I'm not 100% sure. Can you send your revised terms to Monica for a final check? Thanks,
> Bill

Passage 1:

> Reasonable efforts to promptly check delivered Products for defects will be used by Distributor. Supplier will be notified of any discovered defect. [DA#32]

---

12. Some of the sample passages have been slightly altered from the original for the sake of the exercise.

Passage 2:

> Purchase orders can be submitted to the Company by facsimile, first class mail, postage prepaid or other electronic means. [adapted from DA#13]

Passage 3:

> This Agreement and the rights and obligations hereunder may not be assigned, delegated or transferred by either party without the prior written consent of the other party. [DA#32]

Passage 4:

> Products distributed by Distributor for further distribution may be distributed only through subdistributors approved by Supplier. Distributor is specifically excluded from selling Products to the accounts listed on Schedule A ("Excluded Accounts"). [DA#34]

Passage 5:

> The Distributor has assured the Company that it possesses the necessary technical and commercial competence and the ability to structure the organization necessary to ensure efficient performance of its contractual obligations hereunder and this agreement is entered into in substantial reliance on the Distributor's representation of that competence. [adapted from DA#1]

Passage 6:

> The failure by a party to take any action in case of default relating to any provision of this Agreement by the other party or the allowing or toleration of a deviation from any provision of this Agreement shall not be considered to be a relinquishment of right. [DA#32]

▶ **Exercise 9-4   Use of active versus passive voice II**

Review the following Notice Requirement provision. As you can see, the provision is full of passive constructions. Would you change these constructions to active constructions, or would you keep them? Explain your reasoning.

When you are done, find at least four similar provisions in the contracts database and compare their wording.

---

16. Notices

Any notice, demand or communication required or permitted to be given by any provision of this Agreement shall be deemed to have been sufficiently given or served for all purposes if (a) delivered personally, (b) deposited with a pre-paid messenger, express or air courier or similar courier, or (c) transmitted by telecopier, facsimile, email or other communication equipment that transmits a facsimile of the notice to like equipment that receives and reproduces such notice. Notices will be addressed to a party at the party's address, facsimile number or email address as set forth below. Notices shall be deemed to have been received (i) in the case of personal delivery, upon receipt, (ii) in the case of messenger, express or air courier or similar courier, two days after being deposited, and (iii) in the case of telecopier, facsimile, email or other communication equipment, the day of receipt as evidenced by a telecopier, facsimile, email or similar communication equipment confirmation statement. [DA#34]

▶ **Exercise 9-5   Nominalizations**

Decide which nominalizations in the following provisions should be rewritten, and correct any grammar or style mistakes:

Examples:

Ex. 1:

WHEREAS, the Parties wish to define their rights and therefore enter into this Agreement that reflects all of the rights of both Parties referred to as the Company and Distributor. [DA#13]

Ex. 2:

Supplier shall make deliveries of Product(s) to Distributor's facility within the period that is no more than [. . .] days before or [. . .] calendar days after Distributor's specified delivery date. [adapted from DA#15]

Ex. 3:

> Supplier shall make the final determination as to the existence and cause of any alleged defect. Expendable items (such as lamps and fuses) are not warranted. [DA#16]

Ex. 4:

> The nullity of a provision of this Agreement shall not have the result that the Agreement as a whole is void. [DA# 32]

Ex. 5:

> Respond to all customer leads supplied by Supplier in a timely fashion, and bid only Supplier Products for all such leads and, if requested, provide an audit of all leads supplied by Supplier. [DA#34]

▶ **Exercise 9-6   Empty subjects**

Rewrite the following provisions if you detect unnecessary wording.

Provision 1:

> It is agreed that if any provision of this Agreement is capable of two constructions, one of which would render the provision void, and the other which would render the provision valid, then the provision shall have the meaning which renders it valid. [DA#20]

Provision 2:

> It is not intended that this provision should restrict Supplier's use of the information for market analysis or other information processing purposes or commission or bonus payments, so long as the confidentiality of the information is assured. [DA#10]

Provision 3:

> It is the desire, intent, and agreement of the Parties that this Agreement be enforced to the fullest extent permissible under the law and public policy applied by any jurisdiction in which enforcement is sought. [DA#21]

Provision 4:

> If there is a foreign language translation of this Agreement, the English version shall be the governing language. [DA#4]

▶ **Exercise 9-7   Using the correct article**

Review the following excerpt. Why did the drafter use the indefinite article before *Return Material Authorization* and then the definite article in the next two instances?

> Distributor must request and receive from Supplier **a** Return Material Authorization **number** for each return prior to shipping Product to Supplier. **The** Return Material Authorization **number** has to be written clearly on **the** Return Material Authorization **form**. [DA#9]

▶ **Exercise 9-8   Using the indefinite or definite article I**

Explain the difference between Version 1 and Version 2.

Version 1:

> The first order will consist of a pallet of 500 boxes of automotive gear. A shipment shall be sent to the U.S. by October 5, 2012.

Version 2:

> The first order will consist of a pallet of 500 boxes of automotive gear. The shipment shall be sent to the U.S. by October 5, 2012.

▶ **Exercise 9-9   Using the indefinite or definite article II**

Is the definite article used correctly in the following sentence?

> Product shall be sent from the Korea to the U.S.A.

▶ **Exercise 9-10   Explaining the use or omission of the indefinite or definite article**

In the following example, explain the use or omission of articles in the context of specific or non-specific reference, as well as the level of knowledge sharing. Which of the nouns are countable?

> IN NO EVENT SHALL THE COMPANY BE LIABLE FOR LOSS OF USE OR PROFITS, LOSS OF BUSINESS, EXPENSES OR COSTS ARISING FROM OR ALLEGED TO ARISE FROM BUSINESS INTER-RUPTION, ATTORNEYS' EXPENSES OR CONSEQUENTIAL, CONTINGENT, INCIDENTAL OR SPECIAL DAMAGES CAUSED OR ALLEGED TO BE CAUSED IN WHOLE OR IN PART BY THE NEGLIGENCE, TORT, STRICT LIABILITY, BREACH OF CONTRACT, BREACH OF WARRANTY OR OTHER BREACH OF DUTY OF OR BY THE COMPANY. [DA#27]

▶ **Exercise 9-11   Restrictive and non-restrictive use of relative clauses I**

Explain whether the relative pronouns in the following provisions are used correctly. How does the insertion of a comma or its omission change the meaning of the construction? Use the pronoun *that* if applicable to avoid confusion.

Examples:

Version A:

> Neither party shall engage in deceptive, misleading, or unethical practices, which are detrimental to the other party.

Explanation:

In this example, the drafter makes a general comment on deceptive, misleading, or unethical practices: They are **all** detrimental to the other party.

The relative pronoun *which* is used in a non-defining way.

Version B:

> Neither party shall engage in deceptive, misleading, or unethical practices which are detrimental to the other party.

Explanation:

In this example, the drafter makes a specific comment on deceptive, misleading, or unethical practices: There are deceptive, misleading, or unethical practices, but **only the ones** that are detrimental to the other party are the ones that the parties are prohibited from engaging in.

The relative pronoun *which* is used in a defining way. It could also be replaced with the pronoun *that*.

Provision 1:

> Any differences or disagreements between the parties arising out of or in connection with the performance by either party of its obligations under this Agreement will be resolved by mutual agreement of the parties. Any such differences, which cannot be resolved through management intervention, shall be deemed a dispute and be adjudicated by a court of competent jurisdiction in the State of California. [DA#26]

Provision 2:

> Each of the Parties shall throughout the duration of this Agreement maintain records and otherwise establish procedures to assure compliance with all regulatory, professional, and other legal requirements which apply to the promotion and marketing of the Product in the Territory. [DA#24]

Provision 3:

> "Trademarks" shall mean those trademarks, service marks, and other proprietary words and symbols, which Manufacturer may designate in writing from time to time and under which Manufacturer markets or promotes the Product. [DA#10]

Provision 4:

> This Agreement sets forth the terms and conditions under that Supplier will grant Distributor certain rights in and to certain Product(s) as designated in the schedules executed simultaneously with the execution of this Agreement and such additional schedules as Supplier and Distributor may subsequently execute from time to time (the "Schedules"). [DA#22]

Provision 5:

> Supplier may, in its sole discretion, extend the Scheduled Closing Date for a period of not more than sixty (60) days (hereinafter referred to as the Extended Closing Date) upon notice to any prospective distributor who has signed the Distribution Agreement, and has paid the Initial Fee as required herein. [DA#20]

Provision 6:

> All such taxes, duties and fees will be for the account of Distributor who shall promptly pay Supplier upon demand therefore. [DA#34]

▶ **Exercise 9-12   Restrictive and non-restrictive use of relative clauses II**

With a partner, go over examples of the use of *which* and *who* in the sample contracts DA#1 through DA#40, and discuss whether they are used restrictively or not.

▶ **Exercise 9-13   Prepositions I**

Before looking up the following words in a dictionary, guess what preposition they take, and if they also appear with other constructions such as with the infinitive *to* or the pronoun *that.*

entitle(d), respond, provide(d), apply(ied), dispose(d), subject (noun), to subject (verb)

For each use you can find, make one example.

When you are done, look up these words in a legal dictionary. Then, find examples in the contract database on the companion website (www.aspenlawschool.com/books/Adams).

▶ **Exercise 9-14   Prepositions II**

In the following contract provisions, prepositions, the infinitive *to,* and the pronoun *that* have been omitted. Re-insert the correct form(s). Keep in mind that there might be several grammatically correct answers.

> The Parties agree . . . the procedure . . . a Product recall and FDA notifications shall depend . . . whether the issue arose . . . activities performed . . . Distributor or . . . activities performed . . . Supplier. [DA#15]

> Upon termination of this Agreement Distributor shall refrain . . . use . . . any signs, equipment, advertising matter, or material which refer . . . or are related . . . Supplier and . . . acts and omissions that indicate or suggest a relationship . . . Supplier. [DA#30]

> If any dispute arises . . . the parties regarding any matter . . . this Agreement, the parties will refer the dispute . . . senior executives . . . each party, who will attempt . . . resolve the dispute . . . ten (10) business days . . . the referral date. [DA#27]

> If there are questionable accounts, Distributor will consult . . . Company for clarification. In addition, Distributor agrees (i) . . . provide to Company . . . Company's request, but not more than . . . a semi-annual basis, a list . . . the names . . . Distributor's then current Customers, and (ii) not to sell, distribute or dispose . . . any of the Products . . . factory outlet stores, warehouse or parking lot sales, swap meets, or similar outlets. Company shall treat Distributor's customer list . . . confidential information. [DA#7]

▶ **Exercise 9-15   Dangling participles**

Rephrase any dangling participles contained in the following clauses.

> Unless terminated by written notice at least 60 days prior to each consecutive anniversary date, the parties can renew the Agreement for an additional one (1) year period on each anniversary of the Effective Date. [based on DA#10]

> Arising out of or in connection with this Agreement, the parties shall settle any and all disputes in accordance with the Rules of Conciliation and Arbitration of the International Chamber of Commerce. [based on DA#2]

> If caused by by fire, embargo, strike, failure to secure materials from the usual source of supply, or any other circumstance beyond Supplier's control that prevents Supplier from making deliveries in the normal course of its business, Supplier shall not be liable for any failure to deliver. [based on DA#2]

> After terminating this Agreement, (i) Distributor's right to act as licensee and distributor of the Products shall cease. . . . [based on DA#13]

▶ ## Exercise 9-16   Tabulation

1. Compare enumeration and tabulation in the following contracts: DA#4, DA#12, and DA#9 vs. DA#16, DA#25, and DA#23
2. Tabulate the following provision in sentence style format:

> Any notice or other document given under this Agreement shall be in writing in the English language and shall be given by hand or sent by prepaid airmail, by fax transmission or e-mail to the address of the receiving Party as set out in Clauses 14.3 below unless a different address or fax number has been notified to the other in writing for this purpose. [adapted from DA#14]

3. Tabulate the following provision in list style format:

> Each Party hereby represents and warrants to the other that it has the corporate power and authority and the legal right to enter into this Agreement and to perform its obligations hereunder and has taken all necessary corporate action on its part to authorize the execution and delivery of this Agreement and the performance of its obligations hereunder; and the execution and delivery of this Agreement and the performance of such party's obligations hereunder do not and will not conflict with or violate any requirement of applicable laws or regulations, and do not and will not conflict with, or constitute a default under, any contractual obligations of it. [adapted from DA#10]

▶ **Exercise 9-17   Add to your vocabulary list**

Add at least ten new words to your vocabulary list from the "Contract Database" file on the companion website (www.aspenlawschool.com/books/Adams). Use the model from section 1.4 in Chapter 1 for guidance. Modify your old lists if you have new information regarding a word.

▶ **Exercise 9-18   Pegasus/Azteca deal—drafting the provisions**

Applying the concepts discussed in this chapter, review and revise your draft of the provisions from the Pegasus/Azteca deal exercise in Exercise 8-16 in Chapter 8.

Core Provisions

The middle part of the contract begins with the **core provisions**, a phrase used in this book to refer to the substantive provisions appearing before the exit provisions. The core provisions

- establish the consideration for the contract by stating the parties' primary performance or their exchange of primary obligations;
- state the term of the contract, including any options for renewal or extension;
- address payment of money;
- if applicable, state closing information and deliveries; and
- provide details of the parties' performance and obligations.

The unique nature of each business deal makes it impossible to address all provisions that might be included in the core provisions. Therefore, this chapter focuses on drafting concerns for core provisions commonly found in contracts: provisions relating to primary performance, the exchange of primary obligations, term of the contract, monetary provisions, and closing provisions. This chapter also introduces you to provisions that are intensely negotiated: representations, warranties, disclaimers, non-competition clauses, confidentiality clauses, and indemnification clauses. The discussion gives you some examples of these provisions, but these examples are intended only to give you a basic awareness of what these provisions might include. An enforceable provision depends on the nature of the business deal and the requirements mandated by governing law. Therefore, you must be familiar with the type of transaction involved and the underlying business of the transaction. Equally important, you must research the governing law of the contract to ensure that you are complying with the law and creating an enforceable provision.

10.1 Primary performance or primary obligation provisions

⚖️ *An obligation assumed without consideration might still be enforced under other legal theories, such as promissory estoppel. A discussion of alternative theories of enforcement is beyond the scope of this book.*

The core provisions often begin by stating the exchange of the parties' primary performance or primary obligations to perform. These provisions establish the contract's *consideration*, a common requirement for an enforceable contract.[1] In the United States, **consideration** is an exchange of promises or performance, and the promises or performance must have economic value. A contract often includes many promises or performance, but these initial provisions establish the mutuality of the parties' bargain. Thereafter, additional provisions detail the obligations, conditions, exceptions, and other aspects of the parties' association flowing from these primary provisions. In the United States, consideration is not established through formalistic means, such as simply stating the word *consideration* (e.g., "in consideration of the mutual promises in this agreement . . .") or signing a contract under seal.[2]

10.1.1 Primary performatives

✏️ *Performative is derived from the word* perform; *thus, "it indicates that the issuing of the utterance is the performing of an action. . . .".J.L. Austin,* How to Do Things with Words *6-7 (J.O. Urmson and Marina Sbisà, eds., 2d ed., Harvard Univ. Press 1975).*

Performatives can appear anywhere in the contract. But if a particular performance is at the heart of the parties' consideration, the performative expressing this performance should be stated at the beginning of the core provisions. A *performative* provision does not assert a fact nor does it state a promise to do something in the future. By the expressed words and signing the contract, a party actually *does* what it is saying. Thus, for example, in a license agreement where the owner of patents or trademarks for products is giving another party the exclusive right to use these patents or trademarks, the agreement may start with the following performative.

By signing this agreement, License Owner grants the Company an exclusive license to manufacture, use, and market the Licensed Product in the Territory subject to the provisions of this agreement.

or

License Owner hereby grants the Company an exclusive license to manufacture, use, and market the Licensed Product in the Territory subject to the provisions of this agreement.

---

1. There are a few exceptions to the consideration requirement. For example, an agreement to modify a contract for the sale of goods does not require consideration. *See* UCC § 2-209(1).
2. See Chapter 14, section 14.3, for a discussion of seals.

Other examples of primary performative provisions are appointing an agent in an agency agreement (Example 1), an assignment of a security interest as collateral for a loan (Example 2), or the creation of a joint venture (Example 3).

Example 1:
XYZ Corporation hereby appoints LM Company, Inc. as its agent subject to the provisions of this agreement.

Example 2:
As security for payment of the Loan, Borrower hereby assigns and grants to Bank a security interest in all of Borrower's accounts described in **Schedule A**.

Example 3:
By signing this agreement, the parties create a joint venture to develop, manufacture, and distribute solar-powered electric bicycles in the Territory as provided under the terms of this agreement (the "**Joint Venture**").

If only one party is performing under the performative provision, then it is usually followed with a reciprocating performance or promise from the other party. For example, a party receiving a license to manufacture, use, and market products will promise to pay fees or royalties for this right.

10.1.2 Exchanging primary obligations

Aside from any primary performative provision, the core provisions will often start with an exchange of basic promises establishing the *consideration* for the contract. For example, purchase agreements are contracts that state the terms and conditions for the purchase of property, goods, or services. Let's say you're interested in purchasing a motor scooter. If you needed time to obtain financing to pay for the scooter, or perhaps the seller needs time to release any encumbrances on the title to the scooter, you and the seller might sign a purchase agreement, stating the terms and conditions of the purchase, which will take place at a future date. In this purchase agreement, the primary provision would be an exchange of promises to finalize the transaction at a future time and place.

Subject to the provisions of this agreement, Seller shall sell and Buyer shall purchase the Motor Scooter.

In this primary provision, the parties are promising a future action, and thus it differs from a performative where the *doing* takes place at the signing. For example, let's say that all conditions in the contract have been satisfied for the purchase of the motor scooter. When you finalize the sale, the seller gives to you a "bill of sale," a document stating, "Seller hereby sells and transfers ownership of the Motor Scooter to Buyer." This performative transfers ownership of the motor scooter from the seller to you at the time that the seller signs the document.

The exchange of promises can be stated in the same sentence, as in the motor scooter purchase agreement example above or as shown in the following examples.

Equipment lease agreement:
Subject to the provisions of this agreement, ABC Rental Company leases to TC Partnership and TC Partnership leases from ABC Rental Company the Equipment.

Independent contractor agreement:
Subject to the provisions of this agreement, Company shall engage Contractor and Contractor shall provide the work described in **Schedule A**.

Not all primary exchanges of obligations, however, are stated in the same sentence. When the respective obligations are more complex, they can be expressed in different provisions and typically are stated in separate paragraphs. Assume, for example, that a company and its executive sign a noncompetition and employment severance agreement. Here, the first section of the core provisions might state the company's obligations to pay monies and specific benefits when the executive leaves the company's employ. In exchange for these promises, the executive in a separate provision promises not to compete with the company's business or reveal the company's confidential information.

In a revolving loan, the borrower can withdraw, repay, and redraw monies as often as it desires for a designated period of time so long as it does not exceed the maximum amount of the loan.

Another example is a revolving credit loan. In this agreement, the primary obligation of the lender would be to promise to loan money from time to time to the borrower. A provision or series of provisions might set out the restrictions for lending the money, and a separate provision would specify that the borrower promises to follow a stated process for withdrawing money and will pay any borrowed money according to a certain schedule and with interest.

10.2 Term of the contract

Provisions relating to the term of the contract can include any or all of the following:

- The contract's effective date.
- The contract's duration.
- The process for the contract's renewal.

10.2.1 Effective date

The **effective date** of a contract is the date on which the contract provisions go into operation. Typically, the effective date is the same date that the parties sign the contract. In those instances where the effective date is different from the signing of the contract, then the effective date should be explicitly stated, preferably in one of the contract's core provisions.

> The effective date of this agreement is June 22, 20XX.

Warranties and obligations will begin on the effective date. Therefore, if the parties sign the contract but they have already begun performance under the agreement, then the effective date should be the date on which performance began. If the parties sign the contract, but performance will not begin until a future date, then the effective date is the date on which performance will begin.

The effective date also affects representations. See the discussion in section 10.5.4.

10.2.2 Duration

If the contract will extend over a period of time, the contract should explicitly state the time period during which the contract will remain in effect. For clarity and conciseness, state the month, day, and year for the effective date and the ending date (see Example 1), though this might not always be possible (see Example 2). Use the word choice tips for expressing time and duration discussed in Chapter 8, section 8.2.2. For additional clarity, state that the duration of the contract is subject to earlier termination as provided under the other provisions of the contract (see Examples 1 and 2).

> *Example 1:*
> This agreement begins on March 6, 20XX, and ends on March 5, 20XX, subject to earlier termination under the provisions of this agreement.
>
> *Example 2:*
> This agreement begins on the date the last party signs the agreement, and ends on the day preceding the second anniversary of the date the last party signs this agreement, subject to earlier termination under the provisions of this agreement.

10.2.3 Renewal

Sometimes parties want the option to extend the contract's duration. The most common renewal provision requires one or both parties exercise an option to renew. (See Example 1.) If this option is not exercised, then the agreement ends at the end of the current contract term. Another, less common type of renewal provision provides for the automatic renewal of the contract. In this situation, one or both parties are given the option to not renew the contract. (See Example 2.)

List of Drafting Guidelines

When drafting a renewal provision, explicitly address the following concerns:

♦ State the duration of the renewal period.

♦ If a party or parties have the option to renew, then identify
  • the party or parties who have the option to exercise the renewal option,
  • when the party or parties must exercise the option to renew, and
  • the procedure for exercising the option to renew.

♦ If the contract is automatically renewed, then identify
  • the party or parties who have the option to end the contract,
  • when the party or parties must exercise the option to terminate, and
  • the procedure for exercising the option to terminate.

Example 1:
This agreement begins on July 1, 2014, and ends on June 30, 2018. Despite the preceding sentence, either party may renew this agreement for an additional two years if the party exercising the renew option sends written notice to the other party no later than thirty days before June 30, 2018. Notwithstanding anything in this paragraph to the contrary, the initial term and renewal term of this agreement are subject to earlier termination under the provisions of this agreement.

Example 2:
This agreement begins on July 1, 2014, and ends on June 30, 2018. This agreement will automatically renew for an additional two years, unless one of the parties elects to end this agreement by sending written notice to the other party no later than thirty days before June 30, 2018. Notwithstanding anything in this paragraph to the contrary, the initial term or renewal term of this agreement is subject to earlier termination under the provisions of this agreement.

10.3 Monetary provisions

Contracts commonly provide for the payment of money for services rendered or for property purchased. Sometimes there are several different types of payments provided for in a contract. For example, an employee might be paid a percentage commission additional to a base salary. Or, a party receiving a license might pay an initial fee in addition to periodic royalties for the sale of the licensed product. Note the different types of payments that will be made in the contract (e.g., base salary and percentage commission; initial fee and periodic royalties).

List of Drafting Guidelines

For each type of payment, ensure that the provisions identify the following:

- The party making payment. Use the operative word for an obligation (e.g., *shall*).
- The party receiving payment.
- When payment(s) will be made.
- What the payment is for.
- Any formula for calculating payments.
- The procedure for tendering payment.
- The currency to be used for payment, if the parties or subject of the agreement are multinational.

Figure 10-1 shows an example of monetary provisions involving two types of payments. It is an executive employment agreement where the executive will be marketing software outside the United States.

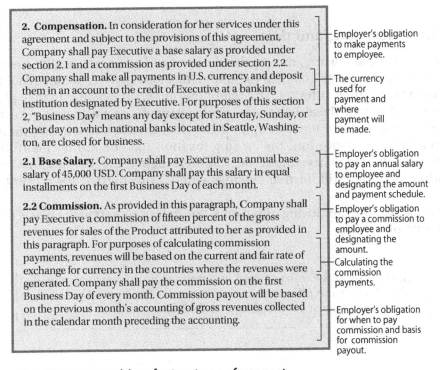

2. Compensation. In consideration for her services under this agreement and subject to the provisions of this agreement, Company shall pay Executive a base salary as provided under section 2.1 and a commission as provided under section 2.2.
— Employer's obligation to make payments to employee.

Company shall make all payments in U.S. currency and deposit them in an account to the credit of Executive at a banking institution designated by Executive. For purposes of this section 2, "Business Day" means any day except for Saturday, Sunday, or other day on which national banks located in Seattle, Washington, are closed for business.
— The currency used for payment and where payment will be made.

2.1 Base Salary. Company shall pay Executive an annual base salary of 45,000 USD. Company shall pay this salary in equal installments on the first Business Day of each month.
— Employer's obligation to pay an annual salary to employee and designating the amount and payment schedule.

2.2 Commission. As provided in this paragraph, Company shall pay Executive a commission of fifteen percent of the gross revenues for sales of the Product attributed to her as provided in this paragraph.
— Employer's obligation to pay a commission to employee and designating the amount.

For purposes of calculating commission payments, revenues will be based on the current and fair rate of exchange for currency in the countries where the revenues were generated.
— Calculating the commission payments.

Company shall pay the commission on the first Business Day of every month. Commission payout will be based on the previous month's accounting of gross revenues collected in the calendar month preceding the accounting.
— Employer's obligation for when to pay commission and basis for commission payout.

Figure 10-1 Monetary provisions for two types of payment

10.4 Closing provisions

> A **lien** is a creditor's legal interest in property (usually belonging to the debtor), which remains until either (i) the debt is paid, or (ii) the property is sold and the debt is paid from the proceeds of the sale.

Many transactions have no formal closing. The parties simply sign the contract and any related documentation. A formal closing, for example, would not take place for an agreement for distribution of goods. Even in simple transactions involving the transfer of property, a formal closing is not required; money is given in return for title to the property. Remember the example of the motor scooter discussed in section 10.1.2. This would likely be a simple transaction, involving the payment of money in return for title to the motor scooter. But other deals can be far more complicated. For instance, a contract for the purchase of business assets or an agreement to merge one company into another can involve complex financing and require multiple documents to complete the transaction. These transactions require time to obtain the financing and prepare the documentation as well as complete other actions, such as inspections or removing liens. Therefore, the closing will likely be delayed. In these situations, the parties sign a contract expressing their intent to complete the transaction if certain terms and conditions are satisfied. These contracts include provisions stating the place, date and time of the closing, and the items each party will be responsible for delivering at the closing.

10.4.1 Place, date, and time

Even in a formal closing, the parties do not need to be physically present. A party may designate an agent to handle the closing on its behalf. Also, the use of fax machines, Internet, and telephone allow for closings to take place remotely. Even in these instances, designating a central location for the closing makes sense. For example, if the deal involves borrowing money from a lending institution, the closing location may be at that institution even though one party might be remotely delivering documents from another location. Still, formal closings where both parties are present do occur.

When drafting the closing provisions, you can simply state the place, date, and time of closing.

> The closing of the transaction contemplated by this agreement will take place at the offices of ABC Abstract & Title Co. in Lawrence, Kansas, on August 17, 20XX, at 1:00 P.M. local time.

List of Drafting Guidelines

Sometimes there is much to do before the closing can take place, and the parties may want to leave open the particulars of the date and time and sometimes even the place of closing. In this situation, consider including the following:

◆ A deadline when the party or parties must designate the place, date, and time of the closing. Here, the date is often linked to satisfaction of stated conditions.

◆ A **drop-dead date** when the parties must close or the transaction is terminated. This is important so that the closing is not delayed for an unreasonable period of time.

◆ An option for the parties to change any deadlines or drop-dead dates.

The following is an example of an open-ended provision with a drop-dead date.

4.1. Closing. The closing of the transaction contemplated by this agreement will take place on the first business day occurring ten days after the date on which all of the conditions precedent stated in paragraphs 5 and 6 of this agreement have been satisfied (the "**Closing**"). Notwithstanding the preceding sentence, the Closing will take place no later than three months after the date Seller signs this agreement, unless extended by mutual agreement of Seller and Buyer. The Closing will take place at 10:00 A.M. Chicago time at the offices of Sharpe & Edwards, Chicago, Illinois, unless otherwise agreed in writing by the parties.

10.4.2 Deliveries

The drafter of the contract is typically responsible for making a list of items that the respective parties will deliver at closing. Therefore, you should create a list of the deliveries, stating who is responsible for preparing certain documents. Confirm this list with the counsel for the other contracting party. In the contract, list the deliveries for which the stated party is responsible to bring to the closing and express these deliveries as an obligation.

4.2 Seller's Deliveries. At the Closing Seller shall deliver or shall cause to be delivered to the Buyer all of the following items (all documents will be duly executed and acknowledged where required):

(a) A warranty deed in substantially the form of **Exhibit 2**.
(b) The Easement Agreement described in Section 9.2.

Continued

> (c) Additional documents as might be reasonably required by Buyer to consummate the sale of the Property to Buyer.
>
> **4.3 Buyer's Deliveries.** At the Closing Buyer shall deliver or cause to be delivered to Seller all of the following items and all documents will be duly executed and acknowledged where required:
>
> (a) The cash payment described in Section 2.2.
> (b) The Note and Mortgage described in Section 2.3.
> (c) The Easement Agreement described in Section 9.2.
> (d) Such other documents as might be reasonably required by the Seller to consummate the sale of the Property to the Buyer.

10.5 Representations and risk-shifting

Chapter 7, section 7.5.1, introduced you to representations and basic drafting tips. Recall that representations are statements made by a party regarding present or past facts, or both, made to induce the other party to enter into the contract.

Chapter 8, section 8.6, discussed how the use of qualifying words or phrases in a representation can shift risk from one party to the other party. A representing party will always want the representations drafted as narrowly as possible to limit its risk, whereas the party receiving the representation will want them stated as broadly as possible. For this reason, the precise wording of a representation will be intensely negotiated. Some common ways to shift risk or otherwise reduce the scope of a representation are to use (1) knowledge qualifiers, (2) materiality qualifiers, (3) exceptions, and (4) time limitations.

10.5.1 Knowledge qualifiers

Constructive knowledge means "knowledge that one using reasonable care and diligence should have and therefore that is attributed by law. . . ." Black's Law Dictionary 950 (Bryn A. Garner, ed., 9th ed., West 2011).

A **knowledge qualifier** limits the representation to the representing party's awareness of the facts. The representing party will want "knowledge" limited to what it actually knows so that it will not have to spend time and money conducting an investigation (see Example 3). If the representing party is an entity, it may want to further reduce its risk by limiting the knowledge to a certain group of people within the entity (see Example 4). On the other hand, the party receiving the representation will not want any knowledge qualifier (see Example 1). But, if a knowledge qualifier is included, the party receiving the representation will favor broadening the definition of "knowledge" to include the representing party's *constructive knowledge* in addition to its actual knowledge (see Example 2).

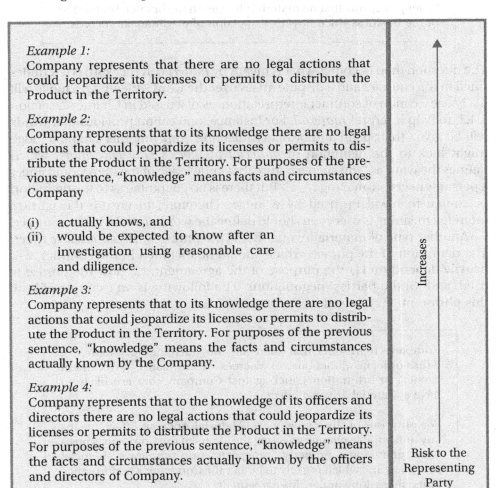

> *Example 1:*
> Company represents that there are no legal actions that could jeopardize its licenses or permits to distribute the Product in the Territory.
>
> *Example 2:*
> Company represents that to its knowledge there are no legal actions that could jeopardize its licenses or permits to distribute the Product in the Territory. For purposes of the previous sentence, "knowledge" means facts and circumstances Company
>
> (i)   actually knows, and
> (ii) would be expected to know after an investigation using reasonable care and diligence.
>
> *Example 3:*
> Company represents that to its knowledge there are no legal actions that could jeopardize its licenses or permits to distribute the Product in the Territory. For purposes of the previous sentence, "knowledge" means the facts and circumstances actually known by the Company.
>
> *Example 4:*
> Company represents that to the knowledge of its officers and directors there are no legal actions that could jeopardize its licenses or permits to distribute the Product in the Territory. For purposes of the previous sentence, "knowledge" means the facts and circumstances actually known by the officers and directors of Company.

Figure 10-2 Representations—shifting risk in knowledge qualifiers

10.5.2 Materiality qualifiers

A **materiality qualifier** usually reduces the risk of the representing party. The word *material* might be used as an adjective as shown in Examples 1 and 2.

> *Example 1:*
> License Owner represents that its performance under this agreement will not conflict with any material agreement to which it is a party.

Continued

> *Example 2:*
> Seller represents that no material changes in the financial condition of the Business since Buyer's inspection of the financial records.

The question then becomes what is meant by *material*. If the word is left undefined in the contract and a dispute arises over the word's meaning, a judge will likely use a canon of contract interpretation, as discussed in Chapter 2, section 2.4.2, to help interpret *material*. For instance, one canon provides that words will be given their plain and ordinary meaning. Applying this canon, a judge might look to the definition of *material* in *Black's Law Dictionary*, which defines the word as "[o]f such a nature that knowledge of the item would affect a person's decision-making . . . ."[3] But there is no guarantee as to the definition or source that will be used by a judge. Therefore, to ensure the parties' intended meaning is used, you should define the word *material* in the contract.

Another type of materiality qualifier is the phrase *material adverse effect*. The definition of the phrase, which should be included in the contract, will heavily depend on (1) the purpose of the agreement, (2) how the phrase is used, and (3) the parties' negotiations. The following is an example of how this phrase might be used in a representation.

> Company represents that there are no outstanding judgments, writs, orders, injunctions, or decrees of any court, government agency, or arbitration panel against Company that are likely to have a Material Adverse Effect.
>
> For purposes of this agreement, "**Material Adverse Effect**" means any unfavorable change affecting the affairs of the Company's business, operations, property, prospects, or Company's financial condition and which is likely to hinder the Company's performance of its obligations under this agreement.

10.5.3 Exclusions

In addition to "knowledge" and "materiality" qualifiers, the representing party may want to limit the scope of its representation by carving out exceptions. The scope of the exceptions will depend on the nature of the representations and the parties' negotiations. Exceptions can be either incorporated into the representation statement (see Example 1), or referenced and listed in an attached schedule (see Example 2). If the exceptions are listed in a schedule, be mindful that it is common for parties to prepare schedules

---

3. *Black's Law Dictionary* 1066 (Bryan A. Garner, ed., 9th ed., West 2011).

shortly before a contract is signed. If the other party is preparing the schedule, you will want sufficient time for your client and you to review carefully the exceptions listed in the schedule to ensure that they are acceptable. The following are examples of exclusionary language in a representation.

Example 1:
Seller represents that it is not a party to an oral or written contact cancelable with penalty upon less than thirty days notice except for the equipment lease with OP Rentals, Inc., dated March 20, 20XX, attached as **Exhibit D**.

Example 2:
Seller represents that the Assets are not subject to any lien, encumbrance, impairment, or charge, except for the liabilities listed in **Schedule 4**.

10.5.4 Timing

Timing considerations are extremely important for purposes of risk allocation. The representing party must ensure that the statements are correct as of that date it is making the representations. In addition, some contracts, particularly those involving purchases, might include provisions requiring the representing party restate its representations made at an earlier date (often referred to as *bring-down provisions*) and, in some cases, provide for the survival of representations beyond closing.

a. When the accuracy of a representation is determined

The accuracy of a representation is determined at the time it is made. For representations in a written contract the statements must be accurate at the time the representing party signs the contract, unless otherwise expressly stated. This can be a problem if the parties begin performing their obligations before signing a written contract. Let's say that on August 3 a seller of a convenience store represents to the buyer that there are no liabilities, liens, or encumbrances on the business assets. Based on this and other representations, the buyer agrees to purchase the convenience store. The parties are impatient to begin working toward the closing, which will take place on September 15, and begin performance without waiting on a written purchase contract. (This is not an advisable course of action, but it does happen.) The purchase contract memorializing their agreement

> *A convenience store is a small retail shop that sells basic groceries, such as milk and bread, along with snacks and household products.*

is eventually drafted and the parties sign it on August 15. In the purchase contract, the parties will likely want the representations made as of the contract's effective date (August 3) rather than the date when the contract was actually signed (August 15). If this is the case, then the introductory clause to the Representations and Warranties should explicitly state this (see Example 1). Thus, in this instance, the Representations and Warranties must be accurate on the effective date. Alternatively, the introductory clause could state that representations were made as of the contract's effective date and then restated ("brought down") as at the signing of the agreement (see Example 2). Here, the representing parties will need to ensure that the representations were accurate not only on the effective date but also on the signing date.

Example 1:
Seller represents as of the Effective Date: . . .

Example 2:
Company represents as of its signing this agreement and as of the Effective Date: . . .
NOTE: For purposes of these examples, "Effective Date" was defined elsewhere in the contract.

---

b. "Bring-down" provisions

Provisions requiring that representations made on the effective date of a purchase contract are still true at the time of closing are commonly referred to as bring-down provisions.

Certificates reaffirming that the facts of the representations made on the effective date of a contract are still true at the time of closing are commonly referred to as bring-down certificates.

Example 2 in section 10.5.4(a) above is one example of a "bring-down" provision. Another example of a bring-down provision can be found in certain types of loan agreements. For example, in a revolving loan, the borrower will make representations as of the date the loan documents are signed but the lender might also require the borrower to restate the representations each time that the borrower withdraws money. Still another example of a bring-down provision can be found in purchase contracts where the parties make representations but also promise to restate these representations at the closing. Recall the convenience store purchase from above. Let's say the seller represented on the day it signed the contract (August 15) that there were no liabilities, liens, or encumbrances on the business assets. However, this might change during the gap period (see Figure 10-3) between August 15 and the closing (September 15).

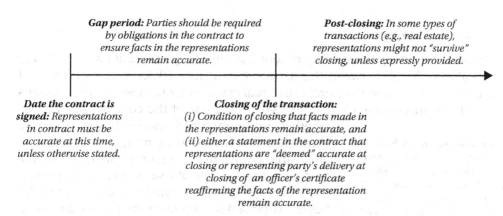

Figure 10-3 Representations—timing issues in transactions with closings

So to protect the buyer's interests, the contract could include

(1) the seller's obligation to keep the assets free from liabilities, liens, or encumbrances prior to closing (see Example 1);

(2) conditions of closing that the seller's representations must be accurate at the time of the signing of the contract and at the time of closing (Example 2); and

(3) a statement that the seller's representations will be deemed restated at closing (Example 3) or delivery at closing of a certificate signed by seller's authorized officer that the representations remain accurate.

> *Example 1:*
> Prior to the Closing, Seller shall keep the Business Assets free of liabilities, liens, and encumbrances.
>
> *Example 2:*
> Buyer's obligation to make the deliveries required at Closing is subject to the satisfaction or waiver by Buyer of each of the following conditions:
> (a) Seller's representations in Section 3 must be accurate as of the date of this agreement and must be accurate as of the Closing.
> (b) Seller must have performed all covenants of this agreement that are required to be performed on or before the Closing.
>
> *Example 3:*
> Seller's representations in Section 3 will be deemed restated at Closing.

Therefore, if the seller breaches the obligation, the buyer has a right to seek damages, subject to any applicable indemnification provisions (see section 10.10). And, if the seller fails to satisfy the conditions of closing, the buyer has the right to walk away from the deal.

c. Survival clause

Clauses addressing the survival or termination of representations after closing can also shift risk between the parties. (See Figure 10-4.) In certain types of transactions, such as the purchase of real estate or a business, representations might not survive the closing. The governing law of the contract determines whether representations made in the purchase contract are superseded or merged into the sale at closing. For example, under the *merger doctrine* as it relates to the sale of real estate,[4] a deed transferring title to the real estate from the seller to the buyer supersedes representations made in a purchase contract. The rationale for this rule is that the deed represents the final terms of the agreement between the parties; therefore, representations made in the earlier purchase contract do not survive. Exceptions to this rule include fraud or mistake; also, the parties can expressly agree that representations will survive the closing.

> A **statute of limitations** is a statute that imposes a time limit for suing on a claim. The permitted time period mandated by a statute of limitations will vary depending on the nature of the claim. The time period usually begins at the time the injury occurred, but in some instances, the time period will not begin until the injury is, or should have been, discovered.

Therefore, in situations where some or all representations do not survive closing under law, the buyer will likely want to include a **survival clause** in the purchase contract. The clause will provide for a time period during which the buyer may recover damages from the seller for misrepresentations discovered after closing. The clause can also apply to representations that would otherwise survive closing under law, extending the time available under statute to bring a claim (*statute of limitations*). Obviously, the buyer would prefer a survival clause that provides an unlimited time in which to bring a claim even for those representations that survive closing. Because this places a heavy risk on the seller (see Figure 10-4), the seller will resist this, though it might be willing to provide an unlimited survival period for a few representations (see example below). The parties, however, are more likely to negotiate a limited survival period for all or at least some of the representations (see example below), which reduces the seller's risk (see Figure 10-4).

> *Example providing for a limited survival period for some representations and an unlimited survival period for another representation (Section 3.3):*
>
> The parties' representations will survive the Closing until the day immediately preceding the eighteen-month anniversary of the Closing Date, except that representations made in Section 3.3 (Corporate Authority) will indefinitely survive the Closing.

Continued

---

4. For a discussion of the law relating to the general concept of merger, see the discussion in Chapter 13, section 13.8.

NOTE: If the survival clause extends the period to bring a claim than otherwise provided under applicable statutes of limitations, then consider adding the following statement: "This clause is intended to lengthen the period to bring a claim otherwise provided under applicable statutes of limitations." Nevertheless, inserting this statement does not guarantee that the governing law will permit a longer time period.

A survival clause is not always for the benefit of a buyer. Governing law might mandate that certain representations survive the closing and permit the buyer to bring a claim for misrepresentation within a statutorily designated time period. In this case, the seller might want to want to limit its continuing risk by shortening the time to bring a claim. Ideally, a seller may strive to include a provision in the purchase contract that terminates representations at closing (see Example 1). This would place the risk burden entirely on the buyer after closing (see Figure 10-4). Understandably, the buyer will want to resist this harsh provision. Therefore, the parties might negotiate a compromise for a survival clause that shortens the applicable statute of limitations—the time period provided under law to bring a claim (see Example 2)—though it still increases the buyer's risk (see Figure 10-4).

Example 1 (representations terminating at closing):
The parties' representations in Sections 3 and 4 will terminate at Closing and the representing party's liability for its representations in these sections will cease at that time. This clause is intended to limit the period to bring a claim otherwise provided under applicable statutes of limitations.

Example 2 (representations surviving closing but terminating before the expiration of applicable statutes of limitations):
The parties' representations will survive the Closing until the day immediately preceding the twelve-month anniversary of the Closing Date. This clause is intended to limit the period to bring a claim otherwise provided under applicable statutes of limitations.

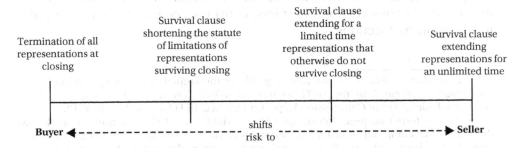

Figure 10-4 Representations—shifting risk in survival clauses

Alternatively, in more complex negotiations, the parties might agree that some representations will survive beyond closing or applicable statutes of limitations while others have an indefinite survival period and still others remain subject to applicable statute of limitations (see example below).

Example providing for mixed survival/termination periods:
Seller's representations will survive the Closing until the day immediately preceding the twelve-month anniversary of the Closing Date, except

(a) representations made in Section 3.3 (Corporate Authority) will indefinitely survive the Closing, and

(b) representations in Sections 3.5 (Employees and Employee Benefits) and Section 3.9 (Payment of Taxes) will survive until the expiration of the applicable statutes of limitations.

Buyer's representations in Section 4 will terminate at Closing and any liability for its representations in this section will cease at that time.

Whether a survival clause extends or shortens the time for bringing a claim for misrepresentations, the length of the survival period and the representations subject to the time period will depend, in part, on the nature of the representations and the parties' negotiations. Keep in mind, though, that governing law can override attempts by the parties to shorten statutes of limitations or to extend the time in which to bring a claim beyond statutes of limitations. You must research the governing law to identify issues in interpreting survival clauses and ensure that your draft complies with any requirements or limitations.

10.6 Warranties

A **warranty** is an express or implied promise that the matter covered by the warranty is as stated and will continue to remain so. This section provides a brief introduction to U.S. warranty law for goods and services found in commercial contracts. Keep in mind, however, that there is additional warranty law not discussed here that applies to particular transactions, such as in the case of construction contracts, consumer contracts,[5] and computer information transactions.[6]

---

5. Consumer contracts for the sale of goods in the United States are governed by the state-enacted Article 2 of the UCC, as well as federal law under The Magnuson-Moss Warranty–Federal Trade Commission Improvement Act, 15 U.S.C. §§ 2301 to 2312.

6. The Uniform Computer Information Transactions Act (UCITA) is a uniform model law that applies to computer information transactions, such as software licenses and development. In the drafting stages, UCITA started out as a part of the UCC and became a separate

Express warranties for goods or services can be found in a wide variety of contracts. For **implied warranties,** which can arise particularly in transactions for goods, governing law assumes that a warranty is given even though no explicit language in the contract provides for the warranty. For instance, Article 2 of the Uniform Commercial Code (UCC)[7] implies warranties of merchantability and warranties of fitness for a particular purpose in certain contracts for the sale of goods.[8]

10.6.1 Express warranties

Express warranties for goods or services were introduced in Chapter 7, section 7.6. Express warranties can be oral or written. Under the UCC, express warranties for goods can even arise from such things as illustrations, brochures, advertisements, and samples or models of goods.[9] The following discussion, however, focuses exclusively on express warranties found in written commercial contracts.

No special word or phrase is required to invoke a warranty.[10] Further, under the UCC, the seller doesn't even have to intend to create a warranty.[11] In particular, the UCC states:

> **Any affirmation of fact or promise made by the seller to the buyer which relates to the goods and becomes part of the basis of the bargain creates an express warranty that the goods shall conform to the affirmation or promise.**[12]

Therefore, a key requirement for an express warranty for goods is that it must be "part of the basis for the [parties'] bargain." To show that it was part of the basis for the bargain in a written contract, the affirmation or promise should be explicitly stated in the contract. Place the warranty in the middle part of the contract with the other core provisions. Including the express warranty in a written contract is critically important if the contract includes a merger clause stating that the contract is a complete, exclusive, and final expression of the parties' agreement.[13] In a contract containing an enforceable merger clause, an express warranty made during negotiations will not be

---

model law when it drew controversy, particularly from consumer groups, on numerous matters, including its default warranty provisions. As of this writing, only two states—Maryland and Virginia—have enacted the UCITA into law.

7. As explained in Chapter 2, the UCC, governing the sale of goods, has been adopted in some form in every state.

8. *See* UCC §§ 2-314(1) & 2-315. Article 2 also provides for implied warranties arising from trade usage or course of dealing. UCC § 2-314(2).

9. *See* UCC § 2-313(1)(b) & (c).

10. UCC § 2-313(2) states: "It is not necessary to the creation of an express warranty that the seller use formal words such as 'warrant' or 'guarantee' . . . ."

11. *Id.*

12. UCC § 2-313(1)(a).

13. See Chapter 13, section 13.8, for a discussion of merger clauses.

considered a basis of the bargain if it is not included in the final written contract. To further support that the warranty was a basis of the bargain, you can also explicitly state this in the recitals.

List of Drafting Guidelines

As a general rule, when drafting express warranties you will want to draft the warranty statement as narrowly as possible if your client is making the warranty, and as broadly as possible if the other party is making the warranty. When drafting an express warranty, also consider the following *in light of governing law*:

♦ Describe as specifically as possible what goods or services are being warranted.

♦ Carefully word statements regarding the quality of goods or services to reflect the parties' intent.

♦ For a warranty extending to future performance limit the warranty to a specified time period.

♦ Consider limiting the buyer's available remedies under the warranty. UCC § 2-714(2) and (3), *which is applicable to both express and implied warranties*, states the remedies available to the buyer *unless otherwise limited by the seller*:

> (2) The measure of damages for breach of warranty is the difference at the time and place of acceptance between the value of the goods accepted and the value they would have had if they had been as warranted, unless special circumstances show proximate damages of a different amount.
> (3) In a proper case any incidental and consequential damages[14] under the next section may also be recovered.[15]

The seller's power to limit remedies, however, is restricted by UCC § 2-719. Subject to specific exceptions, section 2-719(1)(a) does permit limiting remedies to reimbursement, repair, or replacement of the nonconforming good.[16] If reimbursement, repair, or replacement is provided, consider stating a process for accomplishing this as a condition to reimbursement, repair, or replacement. The process might include a requirement for written notice to the warranting party within a specific period of time. In addition, the seller may limit the amount of damages recoverable, including limiting or barring consequential damages unless deemed unconscionable under the

---

14. *See generally* the discussion in Chapter 11, section 11.4.3 regarding consequential and incidental damages.

15. UCC § 2-714.

16. UCC § 2-719(1)(a).

circumstances.[17] See also the general discussion in Chapter 11, section 11.4.3 on remedies and limiting damages.

♦ If there are any exclusions, ensure that these are explicitly stated in the warranty clause. Typical exclusions include goods that have been modified, damaged, or misused.

♦ Include clauses disclaiming other warranties (see Section 10.7).

The following is an example of a simple warranty clause:

Supplier warrants that the Product

(a) will be materially free from defects in material and workmanship and

(b) will function and perform according to Supplier's specifications as stated in Schedule B for a period of one year, beginning on the date of shipment to Distributor. Despite the previous sentence, Supplier's warranty does not apply to any Product that has been modified, improperly repaired, damaged by accident, or misused. Supplier's obligation for failing to meet its warranty is to replace or repair a nonconforming Product if within the warranty period

(i) Supplier has received notice of the nonconformity,

(ii) the nonconforming Product has been returned to Supplier, and

(iii) Supplier has determined that the Product is nonconforming and that the nonconformity was not the result of modification, improper repair, damaged by accident, or misuse.

[Add provisions disclaiming other warranties and limiting damages, if applicable.]

10.6.2 Implied warranty of merchantability

UCC § 2-314 recognizes an implied warranty of merchantability for goods if the seller is a merchant who commonly sells goods of that kind:

> **Unless excluded or modified (Section 2-316), a warranty that the goods shall be merchantable is implied in a contract for their sale if the seller is a merchant with respect to good of that kind.[18]**

---

17. UCC § 2-719(3).

18. UCC § 2-314(1). *See also* article 35(2) of the United Nations Convention on Contracts for the International Sale of Goods (the CISG) (Apr. 11, 1980), providing an implied warranty somewhat similar to the UCC's warranty of merchantability: "Except where the parties have agreed otherwise, the goods do not conform with the contract unless they are (a) fit for the purposes for which goods of the same description would ordinarily be used . . . ." As of

Subsection (2) of section 2-314 describes what is considered *merchantable*. At a minimum, goods must

(a) pass without objection in the trade under the contract description; and

(b) in the case of fungible goods, [be] of fair average quality within the description; and

(c) [be] fit for the ordinary purposes for which such goods are used; and

(d) run, within the variations permitted by the agreement, of even kind, quality and quantity within each unit and among all units involved; and

(e) [be] adequately contained, packaged, and labeled as the agreement may require; and

(f) conform to the promise or affirmations of fact made on the container or label if any.[19]

10.6.3 Implied warranty for a particular purpose

The UCC also implies a warranty for a particular purpose in the following circumstances:

> **Where the seller at the time of contracting has reason to know any particular purpose for which the goods are required and that the buyer is relying on the seller's skill or judgment to select or furnish suitable goods, there is unless excluded or modified under the next section an implied warranty that the goods shall be fit for such purpose.[20]**

Unlike in the instance of an implied warranty for merchantability, the seller does not need to be a merchant in an implied warranty for a particular purpose. Nevertheless, the UCC does indicate that the seller must have some level of expertise or skill, because the buyer is relying on "the seller's skill or judgment to select or furnish suitable goods . . . ."[21]

10.7 Warranty disclaimer clauses

The purpose of warranty disclaimer clauses is to exclude or modify warranties, express or implied. Governing law will mandate specific requirements

---

August 1, 2011, 77 countries have adopted the CISG. The CISG automatically governs a contract for the sale of goods between parties residing in countries that have adopted the CISG, unless the parties have expressly opted out of the CISG. *See* CISG arts. 1(1)(a), 6. Under the U.S. Constitution's Supremacy Clause, the CISG substantially supplants state sales law, including a state's version of UCC Article 2.

19. UCC § 2-314(2).

20. UCC § 2-315. *See also* CISG art. 35(2), which implies fitness for a particular purpose.

21. UCC § 2-315.

for making disclaimers and might even impose limitations on what or how much can be disclaimed.

10.7.1 Disclaimers of express warranties

Once an express warranty is given in a contract, it is extremely difficult to disclaim all or any part of it. Under the UCC, a disclaimer that conflicts with an express warranty will not be given effect to the extent it is inconsistent with the express warranty.[22] The rationale behind this is that an express warranty was particularly negotiated between the parties and thus goes to the essence of the parties' bargain.

Disputes between parties sometimes arise when the contract disclaims express warranties, but the buyer argues that the seller made oral or written affirmations or promises about the quality of the goods prior to signing the contract.

List of Drafting Guidelines

In an attempt to limit disputes, you should consider including in the contract the following, as appropriate:

♦ An express warranty clause, if any, specifically stating the extent of the warranty (see section 10.6.1).

♦ An explicit disclaimer that there are no express or implied warranties, written or oral, in the contract. If there is an express warranty in the contract, make a specific exception for this warranty and ensure that the disclaimer language does not conflict with the express warranty. For special rules relating to disclaimers of implied warranties, see section 10.7.2.

♦ The disclaimer should be conspicuous. See the discussion in section 10.7.3.

♦ A merger clause stating that the contract is a complete, exclusive, and final expression of the parties' agreement.[23]

---

22. UCC § 2-316(1) states:

Words or conduct relevant to the creation of an express warranty and words or conduct tending to negate or limit warranty shall be construed wherever reasonable as consistent with each other; but subject to the provisions of this Article on parol or extrinsic evidence (Section 2-202) negation or limitation is inoperative to the extent that such construction is unreasonable.

23. See Chapter 13, section 13.8, for a discussion of merger clauses.

10.7.2 Disclaimers of implied warranties

Implied warranties are easier to disclaim than express warranties because they are implied by law and thus are less likely to be the basis of the parties' bargain. Under the UCC, implied warranties can be explicitly disclaimed so long as the buyer is made aware of the disclaimer.[24] For disclaimers governed by the UCC, this can be achieved by making the disclaimer conspicuous in the contract and, in the case of an implied warranty of merchantability, using the word *merchantability* in the disclaimer.[25]

List of Drafting Guidelines

When drafting disclaimers of implied warranties, consider the following:

♦ For a disclaimer of an implied warranty of merchantability governed by the UCC, include the word *merchantability* in the disclaimer.

♦ Although the UCC does not require specific wording for a disclaimer of an implied warranty of fitness, the disclaimer is deemed sufficient if it states that "[t]here are no warranties which extend beyond the description on the face [of this agreement.]"[26]

♦ In addition to implied warranties of merchantability and for a particular purpose, implied warranties can arise from usage of trade or the parties' course of dealing. Therefore, you should consider making a disclaimer *all implied warranties, including those arising from trade usage or course of dealing*.

♦ UCC § 2-316(3)(a) provides for a general disclaimer of all implied warranties and does not require that the disclaimer be conspicuous:

> [U]nless the circumstances indicate otherwise, all implied warranties are excluded by expressions like 'as is', 'with all faults' or other language which in common understanding calls the buyer's attention to the exclusion of warranties and makes plain that there is no implied warranty[.][27]

---

24. In addition to disclaimers in writing, implied warranties can be disclaimed

    (i) by course of dealing, course of performance, or usage of trade (UCC § 2-316(2)(c)), or

    (ii) when the buyer before entering into the contract has examined the goods or the sample or model as fully as he desired or has refused to examine the goods there is no implied warranty with regard to defects which an examination ought in the circumstances to have revealed to him (UCC § 2-316(2)(b)).

25. UCC § 2-316(2).

26. *Id.*

27. UCC § 2-316(3)(a).

While you might think this is the simplest way to disclaim all warranties, it does raise enforceability issues, especially in consumer transactions, as to whether the buyer understands the import of the general disclaimer. It is strongly recommended that you draft a more explicit disclaimer, complying with the other UCC disclaimer restrictions and satisfy the conspicuous requirement for disclaimers.

♦ All disclaimers should be conspicuous. See the discussion in section 10.7.3.

10.7.3 "Conspicuous" requirement

UCC § 2-316(2) requires that a disclaimer in writing must be conspicuous. What satisfies "conspicuous" will depend on the requirements mandated by the governing law. The UCC defines "conspicuous" as meaning

. . . so written displayed, or presented that a reasonable person against which it is to operate ought to have noticed it. Whether a term is "conspicuous" or not is a decision for the court. Conspicuous terms include the following:

(A) a heading in capitals equal to or greater in size than the surrounding text, or in contrasting type, font, or color to the surrounding text of the same or lesser size; and

(B) language in the body of a record or display in larger type than the surrounding text, or in contrasting type, font, or color to the surrounding text of the same size, or set off from surrounding text of the same size by symbols or other marks that call attention to the language.[28]

10.8 Non-competition clauses

Non-competition clauses can be difficult to negotiate. These clauses restrain one or both parties from competing with the other party's business, which can include working with competitors of the other party and hiring personnel from the other party. The restriction covers a geographical area and is in effect during the term of the contract and often stays in effect for a period after the contract ends.

Most states disfavor non-competition clauses because they restrain free trade, especially when the parties had unequal bargaining power when entering into the contract. Therefore, when a dispute arises over the enforcement of a non-competition clause, U.S. courts will take note of the parties' relative bargaining power. One party might have more extensive business experience, better information, and valuable resources as compared to the other party. Thus, for example, in an employment agreement between a large

---

28. UCC § 2-201(10).

corporation and a person hired to work as its sales representative, a court may find that the individual was in a weaker position to bargain with the corporation for terms of employment.

There's nothing wrong with a powerful party, like a corporation, using its expertise, knowledge, and other resources to an advantage over a weaker party, such as the sales representative, in a business deal. Contracts between stronger and weaker parties in the United States are enforced so long as the provisions are reasonable. Courts, however, will not enforce oppressive provisions where the stronger party exploited the other party's weakness. Therefore, in a dispute over the reasonableness of a non-competition clause, a court will look more critically at a clause in an employment contract than a clause, for example, in a contract for the purchase of a business between parties with relatively equal bargaining power.

Non-competition clauses—even those involving parties with unequal bargaining power—are enforceable in most states if the non-competition clause is necessary for the protection of the promisee's business, is reasonable it in its restriction of the promisor's rights, and does not adversely affect the public's interest. When making these determinations, a court will look at three factors:

(1) the scope of the business sought to be restrained,

(2) the geographic area covered by the restriction, and

(3) the duration of the restriction.

If a term of the non-competition clause is found to be unreasonable, what will be enforced depends on the governing law of the contract. Depending on the governing law, a judge could (a) strike the entire non-competition clause, (b) "**blue-line**" the clause—striking out the unreasonable terms but not adding anything—or (c) modify the clause. Chapter 2, section 2.5, discussed the options of "blue-lining" or modifying a non-competition clause in an example employment agreement, and how this can result in an unsatisfactory outcome for one or both parties. Your responsibility as drafter is to draft a reasonable clause so that it will not be left for a judge to decide. Therefore, before drafting a non-competition clause, you must research the governing law of the contract to determine what are considered reasonable restrictions under your client's circumstances.

List of Drafting Guidelines

When drafting a non-competition clause, include the following components and ensure these components satisfy the governing law of the contract:

◆ A legitimate business reason or reasons for the restriction, as recognized under governing law, which might be the protection of customer relationships, confidential information, or trade secrets.

◆ The activities that are restricted.

♦ The geographic area where the activities are restricted

♦ The duration of the restriction.

♦ The consideration for the promise not to compete, if it is not evident elsewhere in the contract.

When drafting these components, the nature of the business and the scope of the restricted party's performance under the contract are also important considerations.

Let's say, for example, that you have been asked to draft an employment agreement between a health club, Bella Fitness, and a fitness trainer, who will be responsible for designing fitness programs and working with club members to become physically fit. The employment agreement will include a non-competition clause. Bella Fitness's membership is comprised entirely of Green City residents. Club members commit to a one-year membership, which can be renewed for successive one-year periods. Bella Fitness also has facilities in nearby towns, though members of these facilities are residents in those towns. During her employment, the fitness trainer will be expected to build a group of clients who will work exclusively with her. Therefore, Bella Fitness does not want the trainer leaving its employ to start her own competing fitness facility or to join another fitness facility that draws Bella Fitness members away from its business.

The non-competition clause should acknowledge that the trainer will have access to information regarding Bella Fitness members, which is valuable to the club's business. Perhaps this information is also confidential. The membership information might be deemed confidential if only a select group of Bella Fitness employees, who are also subject to non-competition clauses in their employment agreements, have access to it.

The trainer's non-competition clause should also include a statement restricting her from engaging in explicitly identified activities that would compete with the club's business.

The geographic area subject to the noncompetition restriction should not be overly inclusive. Although Bella Fitness has facilities in neighboring towns, the club members at the Green City facility do not frequent those facilities. Recall that Bella Fitness is only concerned about the personal relationships that the fitness trainer will develop with its clients at the Green City facility. Therefore, to expand the clause to include areas beyond Green City might be too broad, unless the fitness trainer had access to confidential information about Bella Fitness clients or business operations from other Bella Fitness facilities.

The duration of the non-competition restriction should not last too long. Let's say you've discovered in your research that non-competition clauses with three-year durations in employment agreements have been upheld under the governing law. However, in those instances, clients of those businesses often stayed with the businesses for a two- or three-year period, or at least this period gave businesses sufficient time to train new employees and allow these employees to create a relationship with its clients. Bella Fitness membership only runs for one year, and these members are free to move on to other competing facilities after that time period. Therefore, a non-competition restriction of one year might be reasonable, or perhaps a few months longer if it can be shown that this extra time period is needed to train new employees and allow them sufficient time to establish a relationship with the clients.

Because the non-competition clause is part of the employment agreement, which the trainer will sign before beginning work, there is probably sufficient consideration[29] for the clause. If the non-competition promise is a separate, standalone agreement or if the trainer had already begun working at the facility, you will need to research the governing law to ensure that there is sufficient consideration provided for the clause. Applicable law will determine whether mere continuation of employment, a monetary payment, or something else that has economic value will serve as consideration for the clause.

Considering all the previously discussed factors, you might draft the non-competition clause between Bella Fitness and the trainer as follows.

> Employee acknowledges the highly competitive nature of the business conducted by Bella Fitness and the need to protect Bella Fitness's Confidential Information. Therefore, the Employee shall not directly or indirectly
>
> > (a) own,
> > (b) manage,
> > (c) advise,
> > (d) invest in,
> > (e) be employed by, or
> > (f) perform services for
>
> any business that provides services similar to those performed by Bella Fitness's business in the area of Green City during the term of this agreement and for a period of one year after the voluntary or involuntary termination of this agreement.

10.9 Confidentiality clauses

Sometimes during the performance of a contract a party will receive from the other contracting party information that is not public knowledge or that is not readily available through other sources. Perhaps this information is important

29. See the discussion of consideration in section 10.1.

to the business livelihood of the party providing the information (called the *holding party*, for purposes of this discussion). For example, under contracts for employment, consultancy, licensing, or product distribution, the receiving party might be given the holding party's confidential customer lists, marketing plans, or perhaps research and development (R&D) information. Or, in a business acquisition, merger, or joint venture, the receiving party will have access to the holding party's financial information and business plans, perhaps in addition to client lists, marketing plans, and R&D information. In these instances, the holding party will likely want to restrict the receiving party from disclosing the information to others, except in limited circumstances. Confidentiality clauses can serve to safeguard this information.

Confidentiality clauses are found in many commercial contracts, but similar to promises not to compete (see section 10.8) or indemnifications (see section 10.10), the promise to keep information confidential can be a separate, standalone agreement. This discussion, however, focuses on a confidentiality clause included in a larger contract between the parties.

10.9.1 Confidential information: trade secrets versus non-trade secrets

One of the first issues that might arise when drafting a confidentiality clause is what information will be restricted by the clause. Much has been written about what constitutes confidential information, and this complex subject is far beyond the scope of this book. Therefore, the intent of this discussion is merely to introduce you to issues that you should consider when drafting a Confidentiality clause.

At the writing of this book, 47 states and the District of Columbia have adopted the UTSA, each with some modifications. Massachusetts, New York, and Texas have their own statutes or common law for the protection of trade secrets.

In the United States, distinctions are drawn between different types of confidential information. *Trade secrets*, one type of confidential information, are protected by state statutes or common law. The definition of trade secrets can vary from state to state, but the Uniform Trade Secrets Act (UTSA) defines **trade secret** as

> . . . information, including a formula, pattern, compilation, program, device, method, technique, or process, that:
> (i) derives independent economic value, actual or potential, from not being generally known to, and not being readily ascertainable by proper means by, other persons who can obtain economic value from its disclosure or use, and
> (ii) is the subject of efforts that are reasonable under the circumstances to maintain its secrecy.[30]

---

30. UTSA § 1(4) (1985).

Some state courts also use the following six factors, or a variation of these factors, to help guide them in determining what qualifies as a trade secret:

(1) the extent to which the information is known outside of [the holding party's] business;

(2) the extent to which it is known by employees and others involved in [the holding party's] business;

(3) the extent of measures taken by [the holding party] to guard the secrecy of the information;

(4) the value of the information to [the holding party] and to [its] competitors;

(5) the amount of effort or money expended by [the holding party] in developing the information; [and]

(6) the ease or difficulty with which the information could be properly acquired or duplicated by others.[31]

Examples of information that are protected trade secrets include the formula for Coca-Cola[32] and the recipe for the herbs and spices that go into the recipes for KFC (Kentucky Fried Chicken).[33] If information meets the governing state's definition of a trade secret, then that state's law provides protections against revealing trade secrets and allows for remedies when trade secrets are improperly acquired, or used or disclosed without authorization. Remedies for misappropriation of trade secrets can include actual losses or unjust enrichment resulting from the misappropriation; exemplary damages if the misappropriation was willful or malicious; and an injunction (provided by court order) to prevent threatened or ongoing misappropriations.

Besides trade secrets, the holding party may want to protect information that does not meet the governing law's definition of a trade secret. Trade secrets are protected by governing statutes and common law for trade secrets, but other confidential information can be protected by the contract's governing law. Therefore, the purpose of including a confidentiality clause in a contract is to protect against misappropriation of non-trade secret information. Although a confidentiality clause will not transform non-trade secret information into a trade secret, it allows for remedies for breaching the contractual promise not to misappropriate the information. Remedies for breaching the promise of confidentiality should be expressly stated in the contract. Remedies might include permissible monetary damages (e.g.,

---

31. Restatement (First) of Torts § 757 cmt. b (1939).

32. *Coca-Cola Bottling Co. of Shreveport, Inc. v. Coca-Cola Co.*, 107 F.R.D. 288, 289 (D. Del. 1985).

33. *See* KFC History: The Secret Recipe, http://www.kfc.com/about/secret.asp.

consequential damages, punitive damages, attorney's fees, litigation costs) and an injunction.[34]

10.9.2 Basic components of a confidentiality clause

List of Drafting Guidelines

Consider including the following components when drafting a confidentiality clause. Additional requirements can be added, depending on the parties' negotiations and the nature of the transaction.

- A clear and precise definition of confidential information.

- A list of information excepted from confidential information.

- Receiving party's standard of conduct in preventing misappropriation or impermissible disclosures of confidential information, which might include an absolute obligation without any risk-shifting qualifiers or with risk-shifting qualifiers (e.g., best efforts, reasonable efforts).

- When the confidential information can be shared and with whom.

- A requirement that the receiving party report unauthorized uses or disclosures of confidential information.

- When and how information will be returned to the holding party.

- The holding party's remedies if the receiving party breaches its obligations

- The duration, if any, of the confidentiality obligation.

10.9.3 Defining confidential information

The confidentiality clause typically begins with the definition of what is "confidential information," followed by what is excluded from that definition. Because a confidentiality clause is restricting the receiving party from revealing "confidential information," the main focus of negotiations will be on the definition of that term. Calling something *confidential information* does not necessarily make it so. More particularly, what the holding party may consider confidential information might, in fact, not be confidential because the information is too widely known or available.

You must take great care in drafting the definition for *confidential information*. If the definition is drafted too broadly, a court could find the clause unreasonably restrictive on the receiving party and refuse to enforce it.

---

34. *See* the general discussion of remedies in Chapter 11, section 11.4.3.

What is included in the definition of *confidential information* will depend, in part, on the underlying business transaction and the purpose of the transaction. A definition of *confidential information* will typically include information beyond just trade secrets. Trade secrets should be excluded from the definition of *confidential information* if trade secrets will be addressed separately. Why would you want to exclude trade secrets from the definition of confidential information? There are two reasons. First, trade secrets might have broader protections available under the governing trade secret law than under governing contract law. For example, under UTSA, as adopted in most states, the holding party has a right under certain circumstances to *enjoin* third parties who innocently acquire the trade secret from using the trade secret. Second, trade secrets are protected as long as the information remains a trade secret. Conversely, the restriction for use or disclosure of non-trade secrets can only last for a reasonable period of time under the circumstances. If the duration of the restriction for non-trade secret information is too long, a judge will find the clause to be unreasonable. In this event, the judge may refuse to enforce it or "blue-line" it by striking out the unreasonable parts of the clause and not adding anything. Blue-lining, as discussed in relation to non-competition clauses, can result in striking out the most important parts of a clause and thus wiping out the purpose for the clause.

> *To enjoin means to prohibit action by court order. The court order prohibiting the action is called an* injunction.

Therefore, consider one of the following options for defining confidential information and the duration of the restrictive obligation. Unfortunately, none of these options are without flaws, as stated.

Option 1: Make no distinction between trade secrets and non-trade secret confidential information (see Example 1 below) and do not include a duration period for the restrictive obligation (see Example 1 in section 10.9.4). The problem here is that non-trade confidential information could be excluded from the clause because there is no duration period for the restrictive obligation.

Option 2: Make no distinction between trade secrets and non-trade secrets in the definition of confidential information (see Example 1 below) and state a reasonable duration period for the restrictive obligation (see Example 2 in section 10.9.4). Because the duration period arguably also applies to trade secrets, these trade secrets could lose their status as well as any protections and remedies provided under trade secret law.

Option 3: Provide a definition for non-trade secret confidential information and a separate definition for trade secrets (using the definition recognized by the governing law) (see Example 2 below). For the duration of the restrictive obligation, state a time period for trade secrets, and state a time period, reasonable under the circumstances, for non-trade secret confidential information. (See Example 3 in section 10.9.4.) The only problem with this option is in the application of the provisions. Despite trade secret law providing definitions and factor tests, courts can still struggle with determining what information is a trade secret. In these instances, the contracting parties will likely struggle, as well, when deciding what information is a trade secret and what information is non-trade secret confidential information.

Definitions in an employment agreement:

Example 1:
"Confidential Information" means information, business practices, records, processes, and data of Company or its operations, including but not limited to information related to employees, suppliers, customers, sales, financial affairs, pricing, product information and research and development,
  (a) that has been or will be disclosed to Employee, or
  (b) of which Employee has become or will become aware as a consequence of or through his employment with Company
and is not generally known to the public, the industry, or Company's competitors.

> The definition will depend, in part, on the business underlying the transaction, the purpose of the transaction, and the parties' negotiations.

Example 2:
"Confidential Information" means information, business practices, records, processes, and data of Company or its operations, including but not limited to information related to employees, suppliers, customers, sales, financial affairs, pricing, product information and research and development,
  (1) that has been or will be disclosed to Employee, or
  (2) of which Employee has become or will become aware as a consequence of or through his employment with Company
and is not generally known to the public, the industry, or Company's competitors. Despite the preceding sentence, Confidential Information does not include Trade Secrets. **"Trade Secrets"** means information, including a formula, pattern, compilation, program device, method, technique, or process of Company or its operations that

> The definition will depend, in part, on the business underlying the transaction, the purpose of the transaction, and the parties' negotiations.

  (i) derives independent economic value, actual or potential, from not being generally known to, and not being readily ascertainable by proper means by, other persons who can obtain economic value from its disclosure or use, and
  (ii) is the subject of efforts that are reasonable under the circumstances to maintain its secrecy.

> The definition should reflect governing law. For example purposes only, the definition here was derived from the UTSA

Standard exceptions to the definition of *confidential information* include information already publicly known, or already possessed by or known to the receiving party through other means. See the example below. Additional exceptions might be added depending on the circumstances.

> *Example of exclusions to the definition of "confidential information":*
> Despite the preceding sentence, Confidential Information does not include information or data that
> > (i) was or becomes available to the public, except as a result of Employee's action in violation of this Section XX or by unlawful means,
> >
> > (ii) was in Employee's possession at the time he received the information from Company and was not acquired, directly or indirectly, from Company, or
> >
> > (iii) becomes available to Employee on a non-confidential basis from a source other than Company having a legal right to transmit the information or data

Exceptions will depend, in part, on the business underlying the transaction, the purpose of the transaction, and the parties' negotiations.

10.9.4 The receiving party's restrictive obligation

The receiving party's nondisclosure obligation follows. This can be prefaced by the receiving party's acknowledgements that it has or will receive confidential information and that violating the confidentiality clause might result in damages to the holding party. How broadly or narrowly the nondisclosure obligation is expressed depends on the parties' negotiations. Each of the following examples begins with two acknowledgements and then expresses a strict obligation that has not been moderated by qualifiers such as *best efforts* or *reasonable efforts*. Note that no duration period is included in the restrictive obligation in Example 1; a duration period is included in the restrictive obligation in Example 2; and duration periods for confidential information and trade secrets, respectively, are included in Example 3. The duration language used will depend on the factors discussed previously in section 10.9.3.

Receiving party's acknowledgements and nondisclosure obligation:

Example 1:

Employee acknowledges that during the term of this agreement he will have access to or become aware of Confidential Information. Executive also acknowledges that Company's business depends to a significant degree upon possessing Confidential Information and unauthorized use or disclosure of Confidential Information could — Acknowledgements

place Company at a competitive disadvantage and result in damages or losses to Company. Therefore, Employee shall keep in strictest confidence all Confidential Information and not use, disseminate, or disclose any Confidential Information to any person, firm, corporation, business or other entity.

— Receiving party's restrictive obligation

Example of risk-shifting language: "Employee shall use its best efforts to keep in strictest confidence . . . ."

Example 2:

Employee acknowledges that during the term of this agreement he will have access to or become aware of Confidential Information. Executive also acknowledges that Company's business depends to a significant degree upon possessing Confidential Information and unauthorized use or disclosure of Confidential Information could place Company at a competitive disadvantage and result in damages — Acknowledgements

or losses to Company. Therefore, during the term of this agreement and for two years after voluntary or involuntary termination of this agreement, Employee shall keep in strictest confidence all Confidential Information and not use, disseminate, or disclose any Confidential Information to any person, firm, corporation, business or other entity.

— Duration of restrictive obligation

Example 3:

Employee acknowledges that during the term of this agreement he will have access to or become aware of Confidential Information and Trade Secrets. Executive also acknowledges that — Acknowledgements

Company's business depends to a significant degree upon possessing Confidential Information and Trade Secrets, and that unauthorized use or disclosure of Confidential Information and Trade Secrets could place Company at a competitive disadvantage and result in damages or losses to Company. Therefore, Employee shall keep in strictest confidence all Confidential Information and Trade Secrets, and Employee shall not use, disseminate, or disclose any Confidential Information and Trade Secrets to any person, firm, corporation, business or other entity.

— Receiving party's restrictive obligation

The obligations under this Section XX for Confidential Information will be performed by Employee during the term of this agreement and for a period of two years after the voluntary or involuntary termination of this agreement. The obligations under this Section XX for Trade Secrets will be performed by Employee

— Duration of restrictive obligations for confidential information

    (i) during the term of this agreement; and
    (ii) for a period of two years after the voluntary or involuntary termination of this agreement or until the time when the information is no longer a Trade Secret, whichever period is longer

— Duration of restrictive obligations for trade secrets

Following the nondisclosure obligation, state any exceptions to the obligation, including when disclosure is permissible and to whom the information can be revealed. If disclosure is required by law, the holding party may want the right to raise an objection to the disclosure (as shown in the following example).

> ***Example of exceptions to the nondisclosure obligation:***
> Despite the preceding sentence, Employee may use or disclose Confidential Information [and Trade Secrets]
> > (1) to the extent he reasonably believes necessary in Company's best interests to perform his obligations under this agreement,
> > (2) if Company gives Employee its prior written consent, or
> > (3) to the extent necessary if
> > > (i) required by any court, government agency, or regulatory body,
> > > (ii) Employee gives reasonable advance written notice of the proceeding or law to Company so that Company may seek a protective order or other appropriate remedy, and
> > > (iii) Company waives seeking a protective order or other appropriate remedy.

10.9.5 The receiving party's duty to notify of unauthorized use or disclosure

Typically, the confidentiality provision will also include the receiving party's obligation to notify the holding party of any unauthorized use or disclosure of the confidential information that comes to the receiving party's attention. The receiving party may also be required to help retrieve the confidential information or help remedy the harm caused by the unauthorized use or disclosure.

> ***Example of receiving party's obligations to notify the holding party of any unauthorized use or disclosure and to assist in remedying the harm:***
> Employee shall promptly notify Company of any unauthorized use or disclosure of Confidential Information [and Trade Secrets], or any breach of this Section XX. Employee shall assist Company in retrieving any Confidential Information [and Trade Secrets] and taking any other reasonable action to mitigate the harm caused by the unauthorized use or disclosure. Employee's notification and assistance does not waive any breach or any rights of Company to seek a remedy for a breach of Employee's obligations in this Section XX.

10.9.6 The receiving party's duty to return information

Confidentiality clauses should also include the receiving party's obligation to return or destroy all information upon termination of the agreement or at the holding party's request.

> *Example of receiving party's obligation to return information:*
> Upon termination of this agreement or upon Company's request, Employee shall promptly deliver to Company all property, including but not limited to Confidential Information [and Trade Secrets] (whether in written, electronic, or other medium format) in Employee's possession or under his control. For purposes of the preceding sentence, "property" includes but is not limited to
> (A) computers, software, keys, entry cards, identification badges, and
> (B) originals and copies, whether created by Employee or provided by Company, of documents, materials, records, notes, client files, prototypes, drawings, computer media, and electronic or non-electronic data.

10.9.7 The holding party's remedies

The holding party's remedies for the receiving party breaching an obligation as to non-trade secret confidential information can be included as part of the confidentiality clause. Alternatively, the applicable remedies provision is included in the exit provisions section of the contract, especially if the remedies not only apply to breaches of the confidentiality clause but also to breaches of other obligations in the agreement. Typically, equitable remedies are made available to the holding party in addition to monetary damages. In this event, consider including a provision that expressly states that holding party's pursuit of equitable remedies are in addition to other remedies at law.

Equitable remedies include an injunction (a court order requiring a party to perform or forebear from performing) or specific performance (see definition in Chapter 7, section 7.1.1).

> *Example of a remedies provision included as part of the confidentiality clause:*
> Employee acknowledges that the remedy at law for any breach of Employee's obligations under this Section XX would be inadequate and would cause Company irreparable harm. Therefore, in the event of any breach or threatened breach of Employee's obligations under this Section XX, Company is entitled to injunctive or other equitable relief (without posting bond or other security) in any

Continued

> proceeding brought to enforce the provisions in this Section XX. Company's resort to equitable relief is not a waiver of any of its other available rights or remedies.

10.9.8 Summary

The example provisions you have seen throughout this section are not perfect and precise terms will depend on the transaction, the nature of the business, and the parties' negotiations. Above all, though, you must research the governing law of the contract to ensure that the confidentiality clause is reasonable and enforceable under the circumstances.

10.10 Indemnifications

10.10.1 Indemnification clauses

Indemnifications shift the risk of loss from one party to another by assuming the duty to pay for losses or claims of a party and, in some instances, to defend a party against particular actions brought by third parties. The party assuming these duties is the **indemnitor**. The protected party is the **indemnitee**. Sometimes only one party will indemnify the other party. Many commercial contracts, however, include mutual indemnifications. Take, for example, a license agreement where a license owner is giving a company the exclusive right to use its patents and trademarks to develop, manufacture, and market products. The license owner represents that no other entity or person has been given the right to use the patents and trademarks. Here, the license owner might be required to indemnify the company in the event that representation proves untrue and claims arise against the company for infringement of a third party's rights to those same patents and trademarks. In turn, the company might indemnify the license owner for any claims arising out of the license owner's use of the patents and trademarks or its products that use those patents and trademarks.

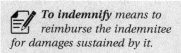 *To indemnify means to reimburse the indemnitee for damages sustained by it.*

Sometimes indemnifications can be separate, standalone agreements between the parties. More often, though, indemnifications appear in clauses as part of a larger contract between the parties.

Indemnification clauses are complex. Therefore, the contracting parties should carefully negotiate these clauses, and in turn, you, as the drafter, should give close attention to the details in the provision. Resist the urge to merely copy an indemnification provision from one contract and paste it into the present draft. As with other clauses discussed in this chapter, you must be mindful of the parties' intent and research the governing law of the contract to determine any mandated requirements (including any operative language) to ensure the indemnification is effective.

List of Drafting Guidelines

In addition to any legal requirements, include the following when drafting an Indemnification clause, though this is not intended to be a complete list for every situation:

◆ Identify the indemnitor.

◆ Identify the indemnitee.

◆ State whether the indemnitor assumes the duty to defend the indemnitee.

◆ List what the indemnification will cover (e.g., threats of claims, lawsuits, and legal actions). Be extremely specific here or you risk that the indemnification will not cover what has not been listed.

◆ List what the indemnitor will pay (e.g., damages, losses, liabilities, costs of defending, including attorney's fees, court costs, and expenses). Again, be explicit here or you risk that some items will not be included in the indemnification.

◆ In a cross-border agreement, state whether the indemnification will be limited to to certain countries (such as the countries where performance of the agreement will take place). If not explicitly stated, it could be assumed to apply globally.

◆ Identify the actions that are subject to indemnification (e.g., misrepresentations, breaches of warranties, breaches of other obligations, payment of taxes). Almost all indemnifications cover the indemnitor's negligence. Some jurisdictions, however, might allow for indemnifications of the indemnitee's negligence in limited circumstances. Again, you will need to research the governing law to determine the permissible scope of the indemnification.

A court may award an injured party punitive damages in addition to actual damages. Punitive damages are not always permitted under law, though. For example, punitive damages are not permitted in contract actions. But in circumstances where they are available and awarded, they are intended to punish the wrongdoer for reckless or malicious conduct.

◆ State what will not be covered by the indemnification (commonly referred to as *carve-outs*), including anything that is illegal or impermissible by law. For example, an indemnification might include a carve-out for punitive damages, if attributable to the indemnitee's misconduct; others might exclude any losses attributed to the indemnitee's gross negligence or willful misconduct.

♦ State whether the indemnity will be limited to certain monetary amounts. Sometimes the indemnitor will be responsible for losses exceeding a certain amount (often referred to as a **basket**). A basket can simulate an insurance deductible or it can be a **tipping basket**: When the basket simulates an insurance deductible, the indemnitor is responsible for amounts exceeding the basket. For instance, if the basket was $100,000, and the indemnitee incurred a loss of $150,000, then the indemnitor would only be responsible for paying the $50,000. If the indemnification provides for a tipping basket, then the indemnitor is responsible for all losses, if the losses exceed the basket. Thus, if the tipping basket was $100,000 and the indemnitee incurred a loss of $150,000, then the indemnitor would be responsible for the entire $150,000. An indemnification can also provide for a **cap**, which limits the indemnitor's responsibility to losses under a certain amount. Thus, if the indemnification has a cap of $100,000 and the indemnitee incurs a loss of $150,000, the indemnitor is only responsible for paying $100,000.

♦ State the timing and process for giving notice of a claim to the indemnitor and whether this will include giving notice of threatened claims.

♦ State who has control over the defense of a claim. Usually the indemnitor has sole control, though the parties may negotiate exceptions to when the indemnitee may participate.

♦ State whether the indemnification will be the sole remedy and whether the indemnitee will still be able to seek equitable remedies.

♦ State the duration of the indemnification, if any, including, if relevant, the time limit for survival after the end of the contract.

The breadth of the Indemnification clause will likely depend on the relative bargaining power of the parties. If the indemnitor is in a stronger bargaining position, then it is likely that the indemnification will not be as broad as in those instances where the indemnitor is in a less powerful bargaining position. The following is an example of an indemnification provision. Each indemnification provision that you draft should be tailored to address the particular transaction.

TSK's Indemnification and Insurance

Example 1:

9.1 Indemnification. Except as provided in Section 9.2 and conditioned upon the satisfaction of the requirements in Section 9.3, TSK shall indemnify and defend Jason Enterprises, its officers, directors, employees, and agents (**"Indemnitees"**) against

    (a) all actual and threatened claims, actions, investigations, proceedings, and suits in the United States and Canada (the "Indemnified Claims"), and

    (b) pay all damages, losses, liabilities, judgments, penalties, costs, expenses, and reasonable attorney's fees

arising out of or related to

    (i) TSK's breach of any representation, warranty, or obligation in this agreement, or

    (ii) the manufacture, use, service, sale, offer for sale, or import of Products into the Territory.

TSK's indemnification obligation will remain in effect for the duration of this agreement and for at least a period of three years after termination of this agreement or for as long as the statute of limitations remains in effect for any Indemnified Claim, whichever is the longer period.

9.2 Exceptions. Notwithstanding the indemnification in Section 9.1, TSK shall not have any obligation to indemnify Indemnitees based on [list the exceptions].

9.3 Notice. Eligibility for the indemnification provided in Section 9.1 is contingent upon the satisfaction of all the following conditions:

    (a) Indemnitees must give TSK prompt written notice of the Indemnified Claim but in no event later than five days after Indemnitees becomes aware of its existence of the Indemnified Claim asserted.

    (b) TSK must have sole control of the defense and settlement negotiations of the Indemnified Liabilities.

    (c) Indemnitees must cooperate with TSK in the defense and settlement negotiations of the Indemnified Claim.

Annotations (right margin):

- Cross-reference to exceptions and conditions
- Indemnification obligation
- Coverage of indemnification
- Duration of indemnification
- Exceptions to indemnification obligation (exceptions are listed here)
- Conditions for indemnification obligation

10.10.2 Escrow or insurance clauses

Escrow is an arrangement in which a neutral third person holds money, documents, or property in trust and delivers the items to a designated party upon the occurrence of an event or satisfaction of a condition.

The value of the indemnification is equal to the indemnitor's financial ability to make good its promise. If there is any question about the financial strength of the indemnitor either at the time of contracting or in the future, then the indemnitee should either require the indemnitor

(1) to place money in escrow to cover any possible losses, or

(2) to maintain an insurance policy to cover the indemnitor's obligations under the indemnification provision and name the indemnitee as an insured.

If the indemnitor opts to put money in escrow to cover its obligations, you should draft the escrow agreement, reference it in the contract that contains the indemnification clause, and attach a copy as an exhibit to the contract. On the other hand, if the indemnitor is concerned about tying up money in escrow, it might opt to take out an insurance policy to cover its obligations.

List of Drafting Guidelines

In the event an insurance policy is used to cover the indemnitor's obligations, the insurance provision in the contract should include the following:

♦ The indemnitor's obligation to maintain the insurance and to name the indemnitee as an insured.

♦ Identification of the types of insurance required and monetary limits for each policy. Types of insurance and limits will depend on the nature of the deal and the scope of what is being indemnified.

♦ The time period for maintaining the insurance.

♦ Whether the insurance limits the indemnitor's indemnification obligation.

♦ Provision for notice in the event of cancellation, nonrenewal, or material change that reduces the indemnitee's coverage or benefits.

♦ The indemnitor's obligation to present a certificate of insurance for each policy to the indemnitee and when this will occur.

The following is an example of an insurance provision related to an indemnification in a contract.

9.4 Insurance. For the duration of the indemnification obligation provided in Section 9.1, TSK shall obtain and keep in force, at its expense, commercial general liability insurance

(a) from a recognized, creditworthy insurance company
(b) on an occurrence basis,
(c) that includes contractual liability, completed operation, and products liability,
(d) with coverage limits of at least One Million USD per occurrence and Two Million USD annual aggregate.

This insurance does not limit TSK's indemnification obligations under this Article 9. Within thirty days after the effective date of this agreement, TSK shall submit to Jason Enterprises a certificate of insurance naming Indemnitees as additional insureds. Thereafter, TSK shall submit to Jason Enterprises a certificate of renewal ten days prior to the effective date of renewal. Each certificate will include an endorsement stating that the insurance company will give Jason Enterprises at least ten days prior written notice in the event of a cancellation, nonrenewal, or material change that reduces coverage or any benefits accruing to Indemnitees.

Despite including an insurance provision in the contract, the indemnitee must ensure that the policy includes the proper coverage and must do so by carefully reviewing the policy and any endorsements.

Exercises

▶ **Exercise 10-1   Performatives**

By using the FIND function of your word processing program, find ten examples[35] of the use of the word *hereby* in the "Contract Database" file on the companion website (www.aspenlawschool.com/books/Adams). Are they all used as performatives? Rephrase sentences containing *hereby* if *hereby* is used incorrectly.

---

35. Try to get examples from several contracts and do not always search in sequential order—e.g., rather than examples from DA#1, DA#2, DA#3, etc., choose examples in the middle as well as the end of the contract collection.

▶ **Exercise 10-2   Exchanging primary obligations**

Go over 15 contracts in the distribution contract collection in the "Contract Database" file on the companion website and find examples of the introductory reciprocal exchange of primary obligations. Where in the contract and under which heading(s) did you find the exchange of primary obligations?

> *Example:*
> **Supplier appoints** Distributor as its exclusive sub-distributor of the Products within the Territory during the Term of this Agreement, and **Distributor accepts** such **appointment**. [DA#12]

Follow-up #1:

Now, create an introductory reciprocal exchange of primary obligations between a company and a consultant based on your insights from the distribution agreements in the "Contract Database" file on the companion website. When you are done, look for introductory reciprocal exchanges in consulting contracts and compare with your document.

Follow-up #2:

To find more examples of primary obligations after the introductory obligations, search for the word *duty* or *duties*.

▶ **Exercise 10-3   Term—effective date**

Search for the use of the word *effective* in the "Contract Database" file on the companion website. What is the most common word combination or collocation you can find? (See Chapter 1, section 1.4.) How else is the word *effective* used in the contracts?

What does the word *commence* mean in various Term-of-the-Contract clauses and Termination clauses?

Find the word *commence* in a Term-of-the-Contract clause and a Termination clause first and compare to other Term-of-the-Contract clauses and Termination clauses that use a synonym for *commence*. How many synonyms for *commence* can you find?

▶ **Exercise 10-4   Analyzing effective date and duration clauses**

Compare the three clauses below. Which of these would you choose as having the best wording? Explain why. Which of the three clauses is the most ambiguous one? Explain why.

Clause 1:

> The Agreement shall commence upon the date first set forth above and shall continue for a term of three (3) years unless it is sooner terminated as provided for herein or by the mutual written agreement of the parties. [DA#35]

Clause 2:

> This Agreement shall be effective on the Effective Date and shall remain in effect for an initial term of 10 Contract Years, unless sooner terminated according to the terms set forth in this Agreement. [DA#3]

Clause 3:

> This Agreement shall come into effect on signature and, subject to earlier termination pursuant to this Clause 9, shall continue for as long as the Distribution Agreement continues in force. [DA#14]

▶ **Exercise 10-5   Term renewal**

Look up forms of the word *renew* in the "Contract Database" file on the companion website (www.aspenlawschool.com/books/Adams). Then pick two or three Renewal clauses and use the list provided in this chapter to analyze the completeness of the clause. What synonyms for the word *renew* are used in renewal clauses?

▶ **Exercise 10-6   Analyzing renewal clauses**

Analyze the following Renewal clauses:

> At the end of the tenth Contract Year and each succeeding anniversary of the Effective Date, this Agreement shall renew automatically for a successive one-year term **unless one party gives the other party written notice of termination at least 12 months in advance of the renewal date.** [DA#3]

> The license and distributorship granted hereunder by this Agreement shall be for an initial term of two (2) years from the Effective Date and shall automatically renew for subsequent one (1) year periods (each a "Renewal Term"), **unless earlier terminated in accordance with this section.** [DA#13]

> Renewal of Agreement. This Agreement shall thereafter be renewed for successive periods of one year (each a "Renewal Term"), **unless terminated by either party pursuant to the provisions of Section 15 ("Termination") below, or by notice, in writing, addressed to the other party, no less than 3 months prior to the expiration of the term, and no more than six (6) months prior to the expiration of the Initial term or Renewal Term as the case may be.** [DA#16]

Follow-up #1:

Look into the consulting contract collection in the "Contract Database" file on the companion website and find Renewal clauses. To what extent do they differ from Renewal clauses in distribution agreements?

Follow-up #2:

Which kinds of contracts are more likely to have an automatic Renewal clause?

▶ **Exercise 10-7   Effective date—duration—renewal**

Your supervising attorney has sent you the following email asking you to draft a preliminary Term-of-Contract clause. Draft the clause.

From: Tony Wallace
Sent: Monday, August 06, 2012 9:34 PM
To: Jeff Rogers
Subject: Term of the Contract—Beringer Deal

Jeff,

I have just finished a meeting with the client, and I think we can finalize the term and termination terms. I'd like you to give me a first draft from my notes by 3pm tomorrow. Let me summarize where we stand now. And let me know if you have any questions.

Duration: From effective date until March 31 (whole day should be included) 2016. That's the initial term.

Agreement can be terminated before. I have a list of causes that I will send you tomorrow, but this isn't important for clause. Just make a general reference that the duration is subject to early termination

Agreement can be renewed automatically for five years following the initial term. Exception: if either party notifies the other one of intent to terminate, but it can't be before 180 days before the end of the initial term or if it is terminated because of the reasons from the list I am going to send you.

Terms for Renewal period are the same as current terms unless, of course, otherwise negotiated.

Best,
Tony

▶ **Exercise 10-8   Monetary provisions**

By looking for key words such as *payment* or *pay* in the "Contract Database" file on the companion website (www.aspenlawschool.com/books/Adams), find monetary provisions.

In the consultation contract, you may also look for key words such as *salary, compensation,* or *commission.*

Use the checklist given below to assess the completeness of the monetary provision for Example 1. When you are done, analyze Example 2 and compare to Example 1.

	Terms	Exceptions/Comments
Party making payment		
Party receiving payment		
Payment schedule		
Purpose of payment		
Any formula for calculating payments (including late payments)		
Payment procedure		
Currency used for payment		

Example 1:

> 7.9 PAYMENT TERMS. Distributor will pay for the initial order 90 days after shipment. Subsequent orders will be paid on a net 30 days basis unless Supplier and Distributor agree on alternate terms for payment.
>
> 8.5 PAYMENT. Full payment of the Distributor's Purchase Price for the Products (including any freight, taxes or other applicable costs initially paid by the Supplier but to be borne by the Distributor) will be made by the Distributor to the Supplier according to the terms in Section 7.9. and payment will be made by wire transfer, check or other instrument approved by the Supplier. Payment will be in United States dollars and will be in an amount equal to the Distributor's Purchase Price for the Products plus all applicable taxes, shipping charges, and other charges to be borne by the Distributor. All exchange, interest, banking, collection, and other charges will be at the Distributor's expense. The Distributor will pay all of the Supplier's costs and expenses (including reasonable attorneys' fees) to enforce and preserve the Supplier's rights. [DA#11]

Example 2:

> Invoice and Payment Terms. All Products sold by the Company to Distributor under this Agreement shall be sold in accordance with the pricing schedule set forth in Exhibit "A." The Company reserves the right, from time-to-time and in its sole discretion, to increase or decrease the prices set forth in Exhibit "A," and shall provide Distributor ninety (90) days prior written notice of any pricing changes. The Company shall invoice Distributor for each purchase order submitted to the Company for the Products at the prices set forth in Exhibit "A." Payment for each invoice shall be due to the Company in the amount of fifty percent (50%) of the total invoice upon receipt of order by the Company and the remaining fifty percent (50%) shall be due to the Company upon shipment of the Product (each a "Due Date"). If Distributor fails to pay any amount due to the Company on or before a Due Date, interest shall accrue at the rate of one-half percent (0.5%) per month on all past due amounts until paid in full. [DA#13]

▶ **Exercise 10-9   Closing provisions**

Compare the use of the words *delivery*, *deliver*, and *deliveries* in distribution and asset purchase agreements from the "Contract Database" file on the companion website.

There are at least two very different meanings of the word *deliver*. Give a definition and example for each.

▶ **Exercise 10-10   Representations: knowledge shifting**

1. Why did the drafter in Example 1 state *Supplier's knowledge* and *best of Supplier's knowledge?*
2. What does the pronoun **its** in *As of the date of this Agreement, and to the best of its knowledge and belief,* in the provision refer to? Is it used correctly?

   Go back to the original contract clause in DA#3 to get more clues from the context.

Example 1:

> 8.1.3 As of the date of this Agreement, and **to the best of its knowledge** and belief, neither the manufacture, nor the use, nor the sale of the Products in the Territory constitutes a misuse or misappropriation of confidential information or trade secrets or a breach of confidence, and does not infringe or violate any valid patent, trademark, or copyright or any other intellectual property rights of any third party. Supplier has disclosed to Distributor all patents and other intellectual property rights which, to **Supplier's knowledge**, may have a material effect on Distributor's ability to market the Products.
> 8.1.7 **To the best of Supplier's knowledge** and belief, Supplier possesses all governmental and other approvals required for the collection and processing of donor allograft tissue, . . . [DA#3]

3. What does the expression *no actual knowledge* in Example 2 imply?

   Could you delete *actual* from the sentence without changing the meaning?

Example 2:

> 8.2 Non-Infringement. Supplier represents and warrants that it has **no actual knowledge** that the Product infringes any valid copyright or other proprietary rights of any third party. [DA#22]

4. Can the nominalization *to enter into this Consulting Agreement* in the first line of the example below be reduced to a verb? What does the pronoun *its* in subsection (c) refer to?

> As an inducement to the parties to enter into this Consulting Agreement, each party hereto represent to the other as of the date hereof

Continued

> as follows: (c) Absence of Litigation. As of the date of this Consulting Agreement, there is no action pending or, to **its** knowledge, threatened, before any governmental entity or tribunal that seeks to delay or prevent the consummation of the transactions contemplated by this Consulting Agreement. [CA#15]

▶ **Exercise 10-11   Representations: "material"**

Look for the words *material* or *material adverse* or *materially adverse* in the "Contract Database" file on the companion website (www.aspenlawschool. com/books/Adams)and analyze how they are defined.

▶ **Exercise 10-12   Warranties: disclaimer/disclaim**

Using the FIND function of your word processing program, look for words such as *disclaim* or *disclaimer*. Make a list of commonly used phrases that use the words *disclaim* or *disclaims*. Can these words be found in other contexts than in warranty clauses?

▶ **Exercise 10-13   Non-competition clauses**

Reduce the following non-competition clause from an asset purchase agreement into shorter sentences.

> 7.4 Non-Competition and Non-Solicitation; No-Hire. For a period commencing on the Closing Date and ending on the three year anniversary thereof (the "Restricted Period"), S shall not directly or indirectly own, manage, operate, control, enable (whether by license, sublicense, assignment or otherwise) or otherwise be affiliated in any manner with or engage or participate in (which shall include, without limitation, marketing of any of S's current products or services) any business or activity whose services or activities compete in whole or in part with the Business as it related to the Products in the places in which it is being conducted or proposed to be conducted as of the Closing Date, unless otherwise approved in writing by Buyer in its sole discretion. [APA#1]

Follow-up:

If possible, choose the law of a specific state, research the law, and determine whether this provision meets the requirements of the law.

▶ **Exercise 10-14   Confidentiality clauses**

Analyze the confidentiality clause provided below as to completeness, accuracy, and implications for both sides. Use the confidentiality clause checklist below for guidance.

Confidentiality

From and after the date hereof, Consultant shall maintain the confidentiality of any confidential information concerning the Company, its subsidiaries or their respective businesses, including, without limitation, any such information that may hereafter be received by Consultant in connection with Consultant's provision of Services or otherwise pursuant to this Agreement (the "Confidential Information"); provided, however, that this Section 10 shall not restrict: (a) any disclosure by Consultant of any Confidential Information required by applicable law or regulation, or any securities exchange (but only such portion of the Confidential Information that Consultant is legally required to disclose), but if permitted by applicable law or regulation, Consultant shall give the Company notice and a reasonable opportunity to contest such disclosure or seek an appropriate protective order; (b) any disclosure by Consultant of any Confidential Information in connection with the exercise of his rights and obligations as a member of the Board of Directors of the Company (or any committee thereof); (c) any disclosure on a confidential basis to Consultant's attorneys, accountants and other advisors; and (d) any disclosure of information that: (i) is publicly available as of the date of this Agreement; (ii) after the date of this Agreement, becomes publicly available through no fault of Consultant; or (iii) is received by the Company from a third party not, to Consultant's knowledge, subject to any obligation of confidentiality with respect to such information. [CA#2]

Confidentiality Clause Checklist

	Term provision	Implications for parties
Clear and precise definition		
Exceptions for use		
Standard of conduct (e.g., best efforts)		
Permissibility of sharing		
Report of unauthorized uses or disclosures		
Time and mode of return of confidential information		
Remedies for breach		
Duration of obligation		

▶ **Exercise 10-15   Indemnification**

Compare the three indemnification clauses below by cutting the relevant passages and pasting them in the following grid:

	Who	Indemnifies	Whom	From what	How	Exceptions
CA#8						
CA#12						
CA#13						

When you are finished, answer the following questions:

1. **Who:** Who is indemnifying in each clause (e.g., both parties in the same sentence, in separate sentences, only one party in the entire clause)? Why do you think the drafter did this?
2. **Indemnifies:** Is there a difference between *indemnifies* and *hold harmless*? Do the sentences containing the indemnification verb also include another verb or verbs that are coupled synonyms. How would you redraft to fix the coupled synonyms?
3. **Whom:** Same as in #1
4. **From what:** Are the indemnification events similar or different?
5. **How:** Why do some drafters give more attention to detail on procedure? Is this necessary?
6. **Exceptions:** Do the exceptions favor any specific party?
7. **Comments (not in grid):** Are there any extra clauses added? If so, how do they modify the indemnification process? Are indemnification clauses phrased identically for each party? If not, what are the differences, and why is the wording different?

Indemnification

8.01. Each party hereto indemnifies and agrees to hold the other harmless from and against any and all claims, demands, and actions, and any liabilities, damages, or expenses resulting therefrom, including court costs and reasonable attorney fees, arising out of or relating to the breach of its obligations and warranties set forth herein. Each party's obligations under this Section 8.01 shall survive the termination of this Agreement for any reason. Each party agrees to give the other prompt notice of any such claim, demand, or action and shall, to the extent it is not adversely affected, cooperate fully with the indemnifying party in the defense and settlement of the claim, demand, or action. [CA#8]

═══════

7.3. Indemnification. Company agrees to defend, indemnify and hold harmless Consultant from and against any and all claims,

Continued

losses, liabilities or expenses (including attorney's fees) which may arise, in whole or in part, out of a material breach by Company of its obligations under this Agreement. Consultant agrees to defend, indemnify and hold harmless Company from and against any and all claims, losses, liabilities or expenses (including attorney's fees) which may arise, in whole or in part, out of a material breach by Consultant of his obligations under this Agreement. In addition, Company shall indemnify, defend and hold Consultant harmless from any and all liability, loss, damage, cost or expense (including reasonable attorneys' fees) incurred by Consultant in defending or responding to any claim arising out of or related to the Transaction except to the extent that such claim arises out of the willful misconduct or gross negligence of Consultant. Likewise, Consultant shall indemnify, defend and hold Company harmless from any and all liability, loss, damage, cost or expense (including reasonable attorneys' fees) incurred by Company in defending or responding to any claim arising out of or related to the Transaction if the claims arise out of or are related to the Consultant's willful misconduct or gross negligence. [CA#12]

---

3. Indemnification. Except as provided below, the Parties shall indemnify each other, their parents, affiliates, and subsidiaries, and each of their directors, officers, employees, agents, representatives, investors, and Members (collectively, the "Indemnified Parties"), and hold them harmless from and against any and all claims, actions, damages, consequential damages, liabilities and expenses (collectively, "Losses") occasioned by any act or omission of the other Party, its parents, affiliates, and subsidiaries, and each of its directors, officers, employees, agents, representatives, investors, partners, or Members, relating to the performance of its obligations hereunder, provided such obligations arise after the execution of this Consulting Agreement. If the Indemnified Parties shall, without fault on their part, be made party to any litigation concerning the Indemnified Party or the Indemnified Party's performance hereof, or commenced by or against the Indemnified Party, then the other Party shall protect and hold the Indemnified Party harmless, and shall pay all costs, Losses, expenses, and reasonable attorney's fees incurred or paid by the Indemnified Party in connection with said litigation.

[Paragraph 4 omitted.]

5. In addition to the indemnification provisions above, the Indemnified Parties shall reimburse one another for any legal or other expenses reasonably incurred by them in connection with investigating, preparing, or preparing to defend or defending losses, lawsuits, claims, or other proceedings arising in any manner out of or in connection with the rendering of services to the Company hereunder, except for any losses or expenses arising out of a failure on the part of Consultant to procure or maintain any necessary

Continued

licenses or qualifications necessary to perform services under this Consulting Agreement

6. The Indemnified Parties agree that the indemnification and reimbursement commitments set forth in Sections 3, 5, and 6 in this Consulting Agreement shall apply whether or not any Indemnified Party is a formal party to any such lawsuit, claim, or other proceeding, and that each of the Indemnified Parties is entitled to retain separate legal counsel of its choice in connection with any of the matters to which such commitments relate and that such commitments shall extend beyond the Term of this Consulting Agreement.

7. The Consultant agrees that it will be liable for any costs, fees and expenses incurred under circumstances as outlined in Sections 3, 5, and 6 above, including without limitation those arising from the indemnity provisions hereof, even if the transactions contemplated hereby are not closed and irrespective of any reasons. [CA#13]

▶ **Exercise 10-16   Add to your vocabulary list**

Add at least ten new words to your vocabulary list from the "Contract Database" file on the companion website (www.aspenlawschool.com/books/Adams). Use the model from section 1.4 in Chapter 1 for guidance. Modify your old lists if you have new information regarding a word.

▶ **Exercise 10-17   Pegasus/Azteca deal—drafting the core provisions**

Using your draft of the provisions from the Pegasus/Azteca deal in Exercise 9-17 in Chapter 9, and the term sheet found in the materials section of Chapter 10 on the book's companion website (which provides additional agreed terms for this deal), do the following:

1. Identify the agreed terms that are core provisions.
2. For each identified terms that is a core provision:
   a. Identify the type of provision (see Chapter 7) that will best express the agreed term.
   b. Draft the agreed term into contract provisions applying the concepts discussed in this chapter and in Chapters 4, 6, 8, and 9.
   c. Determine the order in which these provisions should be presented in the contract.

Exit Provisions

Exit provisions address what happens when the contract ends (or **terminates**). Most contracts end naturally, as the parties had anticipated and hoped for when entering into the contract. However, contracts can end prematurely and sometimes unpleasantly. Premature endings can occur through (1) the mutual consent of both parties, (2) the actions of one party (e.g., a breach of an obligation or misrepresentation), or (3) by operation of law (e.g., business declared illegal, death, or legal incapacity). Exit provisions identify events that will result in a contract's premature ending as well as provide for appropriate remedies. Exit provisions might also provide for the survival of obligations in the event of either a natural ending or a premature ending.

> *Terminates (verb) or termination (noun) can refer to both natural endings to a contract as well as premature endings to a contract. Sometimes, though,* terminates *or* termination *is used more narrowly, to refer only to a premature ending. In these instances,* expires (verb) *or* expiration (noun) *is used to refer to a natural ending to the contract, as anticipated by the parties. The distinction can be helpful if the rights and obligations of the parties differ after the contract ends, depending on whether the contract ended naturally or prematurely.*

As legal counsel for your client, you will be primarily responsible for anticipating possible circumstances that ought to trigger a premature ending and identifying the parties' rights and remedies should an event arise. It can be an unpleasant task, and your client might not fully appreciate your efforts. You are giving thought to disagreeable outcomes while your client is excited at the prospect of entering into an advantageous business deal. No wonder attorneys are labeled by some people as *deal killers*! Nevertheless, your duty is to consider the possibilities and draft provisions that will protect your client's interests if an event arises that could result in a premature end of the contract.

11.1 Events triggering a premature ending

A contract can end prematurely upon mutual consent of the parties, an event caused by a change in law, or an event of default. As legal counsel for your client, you must consider the possible circumstances that should give rise to a termination in each of these situations. You will want to address these circumstances in the exit provision, along with providing appropriate remedies, post-termination obligations, and surviving obligations.

11.2 Premature ending by mutual consent

The *term-of-the-contract* clause (see Chapter 10, section 10.2) states the duration for the contract's performance. Nevertheless, the parties might want the option to end the contract earlier by mutual consent. Although the parties can accomplish an early ending without including an express provision in the contract, a provision to this effect makes the parties' intent clear to the reader.

> Notwithstanding the term of the contract provided in Section XX, the parties may terminate this agreement at any time by mutual written consent.

11.3 Premature ending by a change in law

A premature ending by an event caused by a change in law should be a change that materially or adversely impacts performance under the contract. In this situation both parties are blameless. Two common causes for termination resulting from a change in law are when the new law makes performance under the contract illegal or imposes taxes that adversely impacts the transaction intended by the parties. In the termination clause, specifically identify the change in law circumstances that will result in a premature ending to the contract.

> In the event that, by operation of law or governmental decree, it becomes illegal to market and sell the Product in the Territory, then this agreement will terminate.

11.4 Drafting "event of default" clauses

An **event of default** is an occurrence that gives rise to a non-defaulting party's right to seek remedies (e.g., termination, acceleration, liquidated damages, injunctive relief, or specific performance). Events of default might include a defaulting party's breach of an obligation, misrepresentation, merger, bankruptcy, death, or legal incapacity. When drafting an event of default clause, specify each circumstance that will constitute an event of default. In addition, you might need to distinguish between circumstances that will give rise to an *immediate event of default* and other circumstances that will merely give rise to a *potential event of default*.

11.4.1 Immediate event of default

Some occurrences so substantially disrupt performance or so significantly increase the non-defaulting party's risk that they should give rise to an immediate event of default. Immediate events of default result in the automatic termination of the contract and the non-defaulting party's right to exercise other remedies. What constitutes an immediate event of default will depend on the nature of the contract and the parties' negotiations. Examples of what might give rise to an immediate event of default include a party's bankruptcy, death, legal incapacity, or conviction of a crime. The following example focuses only on insolvency issues, though it could also include other circumstances.

> This agreement will automatically terminate in the event either party makes (i) an assignment for the benefit of creditors, or (ii) petitions, applies for, or permits, with or without its consent, the appointment of a custodian, receiver, trustee in bankruptcy, or similar officer for all or substantially all of its business or assets.

11.4.2 Potential event of default

Sometimes the circumstance is not deemed serious enough to call for an immediate event of default. In this situation, the occurrence merely gives rise to a potential event of default. The actual event of default occurs only if certain conditions are satisfied. These conditions vary, though they usually include written notice to the defaulting party of the non-defaulting party's intent to terminate the contract and exercise other remedies. Sometimes this notice will also give the defaulting party a **grace period**, a designated time for the defaulting party to **cure** (that is, to fix) the problem. If the defaulting party fails to cure the problem within the grace period, then the problem becomes an actual event of default, at which time remedies for the non-defaulting party arise.

List of Drafting Guidelines

When drafting a potential event of default clause, consider the following:

- Specify each circumstance that will give rise to a potential event of default.
- Require the non-defaulting party give written notice of a potential event of default to the defaulting party. Notice should include identifying the problem that gave rise to the potential event of default.

- ◆ State when the actual event of default will occur. The actual event of default can occur immediately after the non-defaulting party's notice (see Example 1) or after a defaulting party's failure to cure the problem within a designated grace period. In the latter situation, the actual event of default usually arises automatically at the end of the grace period without need for further action by the non-defaulting party (see Example 2).

- ◆ State the circumstances that will be subject to a grace period. The problem must be within the defaulting party's ability to cure. Examples of what might be considered potential events of default possibly curable within a given grace period include breaches of obligations, such as a failure to make payments or make deliveries when due.

- ◆ State when a grace period begins. Usually, a grace period doesn't begin until the non-defaulting party gives notice of the potential event of default to the defaulting party.

- ◆ State the duration of a grace period. Depending on the problem, the duration can be of varying length. A grace period should provide a reasonable time for the defaulting party to cure the problem but should not be so long that they materially increase the non-defaulting party's risk.

Example 1:
Either party may terminate this agreement upon giving written notice to the other party in the event that party makes (i) an assignment for the benefit of creditors, or (ii) petitions, applies for, or permits, with or without its consent, the appointment of a custodian, receiver, trustee in bankruptcy, or similar officer for all or substantially all of its business or assets.

Example 2:
If Employee breaches any material obligation under this agreement, Company will give written notice of the breach to Employee. If Employee fails to cure the breach on or before 30 days after receiving written notice from Company, then this agreement will terminate.

11.4.3 Remedies

The parties are not required to include remedial provisions in the contract. Parties might leave it to the courts to designate the appropriate remedies as provided under the governing law. Even so, rather than leaving it entirely to the courts to fashion a remedy appropriate for an event of default, the parties should consider designating in the exit provisions some, if not all, of the remedies available to the non-defaulting party. This does not, however, mean that the parties have unlimited control in deciding the appropriate remedies for an event of default. Governing law can still limit or prohibit remedies, such as in the case of liquidated damages, specific performance, attorneys' fees, or punitive damages.

A remedy does not have to be exclusive of other remedies. Often more than one remedy is available and can be in addition to those available under governing law. In these instances, the provision will list specific remedies and add a catch-all phrase that includes remedies available under governing law (e.g., "in addition to other remedies available under law or in equity"). Also, the stated remedies do not have to apply to all events of default. If appropriate, consider designating certain remedies for specific events of default.

a. Termination

Termination of the contract is a common remedy for an event of default. However, termination is typically in addition to other remedies available under the contract and under governing law. As discussed in sections 11.4.1 and 11.4.2, state whether termination is immediate upon an event of default or whether it occurs after the satisfaction of conditions (e.g., upon notice to the defaulting party or after the defaulting party's failure to cure).

b. Acceleration

Acceleration clauses are most commonly found in contracts for the payment of debt. The clause provides that in the event of a default, all sums payable by the defaulting party under the contract become immediately due. Usually the clause is drafted so that the non-defaulting party is given the discretionary power to invoke acceleration, rather than declaring acceleration automatic upon an event of default. If written notice to the defaulting party is a condition to acceleration, state this in the clause.

> In the event of a default as provided in Section XX, [non-defaulting party] may declare the total unpaid balance under this agreement immediately due and payable.

c. Money damages (and "limitation on damage" clauses)

Under common law in the United States, damages for breach of contract include damages that compensate the non-breaching party for losses directly resulting from the breach, as well as **consequential damages** (indirect losses) and **incidental damages** (costs incurred for dealing with the breach)[1] if the consequential and incidental damages were reasonably foreseeable. Nevertheless, parties who are of equal bargaining power can agree to limit available damages. In these instances, a *limitation on damage* clause is generally enforceable so long as the limitation is not so low, as compared to what could have been recovered, that it is declared to be unconscionable. Depending on governing law, other public policy exceptions can also prevent enforcing a limitation on damage clause.[2]

> Notwithstanding anything in this agreement to the contrary, neither party will be liable to the other party for consequential, incidental, or special damages for any claim arising from or related to this agreement.

d. Indemnifications

See Chapter 10 for a discussion of the purpose of indemnifications and drafting concerns relating to indemnifications.

e. Liquidated damages

If the parties are concerned that there could be difficulty assessing damages in an event of default, they might agree to include in the contract a **liquidated damages** clause, which sets in advance a damage amount that will be paid by the defaulting party in an event of default. With the exception of consumer contracts and some real property contracts, liquidated damage clauses are valid. A court will enforce the damage amount so long as it merely compensates the non-defaulting party for its economic loss and is not an excessive amount that is intended to punish or deter the defaulting party. When drafting a liquidated damages clause, state the parties' acknowledgement of the

---

1. *See, e.g.,* UCC § 2-715:

(1) Incidental damages resulting from the seller's breach include expenses reasonably incurred in inspection, receipt, transportation and care and custody of goods rightfully rejected, any commercially reasonable charges, expenses or commissions in connection with effecting cover and any other reasonable expense incident to the delay or other breach.

(2) Consequential damages resulting from the seller's breach include

(a) any loss resulting from general or particular requirements and needs of which the seller at the time of contracting had reason to know and which could not reasonably be prevented by cover or otherwise; and

(b) injury to person or property proximately resulting from any breach of warranty.

2. *See, e.g., Global Crossing Telecommunications, Inc. v. CCT Communications, Inc.,* 464 B.R. 97 (Bankr. S.D.N.Y. 2011).

difficulty in assessing damages for the related event of default. Also, the parties should declare that the stated amount is a reasonable forecast of probable loss and is not a penalty. While these statements will not guarantee enforcement, they at least express the parties' intent.

f. Specific performance

Specific performance is a court-ordered remedy requiring performance of an obligation as promised under the contract. In the United States specific performance is an extraordinary remedy that is only permitted when damages would be inadequate. Damages might be deemed inadequate when the promised services or goods[3] are unique. Whether the services or goods are unique is left to the court to decide, though the parties could make statements in the contract that might assist the court in making a finding and ordering specific performance.

g. Attorneys' fees

In the United States, the prevailing party in a legal action or proceeding on a contract cannot recover attorneys' fees unless the contract explicitly provides for this or unless specifically provided by statute. Therefore, if the parties agree to a recovery of attorneys' fees for a prevailing party, include a provision for this.

h. Punitive damages

Punitive damages, awarded to the prevailing party, punish a wrongdoer for reckless or malicious conduct, and discourage future wrongful conduct. Punitive damages are available in tort actions where the defendant's conduct was reckless or malicious. In the United States, however, contract law is not based on punishing a wrongdoer's conduct but instead on compensating a party's economic loss. Therefore, punitive damages are not available for claims based solely on contract law.

11.5 Post-termination obligations and survival clauses

Explicitly state the obligations of each party to wind down the parties' business affairs after the contract ends. For example, clauses might provide for return of promotional or marketing materials; return of inventory; an orderly liquidation of inventory; the return of any **collateral** (property or goods held as security for a loan); the release of a mortgage; or the removal of trade

---

3. UCC § 2-716 (permitting specific performance for unique goods in addition to damages).

names, trademarks, and logos from promotions and websites. Also, if some representations or certain obligations (such as a non-competition restriction, a confidentiality restriction, or indemnification) are intended to survive the contract's end, ensure that the survival of these representations and obligations, along with any time limits for survival, are stated either in the clauses creating these representations or obligations[4] or in a general clause listing all surviving representations and obligations.

Exercises

▶ **Exercise 11-1   Comparing termination clauses**

Compare causes for termination given in the clause below with causes in other consulting agreements found on the website database (www.aspenlawschool.com/books/Adams) and make a list of all causes.

1. Before you look up the definition of *Good Reason* in CA#7 (in the "Contract Database" file on the companion website), identify what *good reason for termination* might include.
2. What should be the consequences for each reason you identify in question 1?

The Term of Agreement shall terminate upon the earliest to occur on (i) the Consultant's death, (ii) a termination by the Company by reason of the Consultant's Disability, (iii) a termination by the Company with or without Cause, or (iv) a termination by Consultant with or without Good Reason. Upon any termination of Consultant's services for any reason, except as may otherwise be requested by the Company in writing and agreed upon in writing by Consultant, the Consultant shall resign from any and all directorships, committee memberships or any other positions Consultant holds with the Company or any of its subsidiaries. [CA#7]

▶ **Exercise 11-2   Rewriting a termination clause**

Rewrite the termination clause below using shorter sentences.

1. Check in the contract collection on the web database whether *material breach* or *default* is defined in DA#8.
2. How would you define *reasonable judgement of the non-breaching party*?
3. What is a material breach?

---

4. See the discussion in Chapter 10, sections 10.5.4c., 10.8, 10.9, and 10.10.

(a) Upon the occurrence of a material breach or default as to any obligation hereunder by either party and the failure of the breaching party to promptly pursue (within thirty (30) days after receiving written notice thereof from the non-breaching party) a reasonable remedy designed to cure (in the reasonable judgment of the non-breaching party) such material breach or default, this Agreement may be terminated by the non-breaching party by giving written notice of termination to the breaching party, such termination being immediately effective upon the giving of such notice of termination. [DA#8]

▶ **Exercise 11-3   Comparing "right to cure" provisions**
Compare the cure provisions in the following termination clauses.

1. What is the most frequently stated cure period in the clauses below? In which situations are cure periods longer/shorter?
2. What do the clauses say about notice?
3. How can the breach be cured?
4. Are there situations that are not subject to a cure period?
5. Who decides whether the situation has been cured and how?
6. What does the expression *just cause* mean in the context of a termination clause?

Termination. This Agreement may be terminated at any time by the mutual written consent of the Parties evidenced by an agreement in writing signed by all Parties, and either Party may terminate this Agreement prior to its expiration or automatic termination on sixty (60) days' written notice to the other Party. Either Party may terminate this Agreement immediately (i) in the event a material breach of any term of this Agreement by the other Party continues uncured for a period of thirty (30) days after notice thereof is given in writing by the non-breaching Party to the breaching Party; (ii) upon a breach by the Distributor of the provisions of Section 9 (Confidential Information) or Section 10 (Compliance with Laws) hereof; (iii) upon the other's insolvency; or (iv) upon the other's filing of a voluntary or involuntary petition in bankruptcy, assignment for the benefit of creditors, or any comparable event or proceeding under the laws of the jurisdiction in which the other is located. [DA#12]

16.1 Termination (curable). If the Company or Distributor materially breaches this Agreement and if such breach remains uncured for thirty (30) days after written notice of such breach, the innocent party may terminate this Agreement for Cause by delivery of written

Continued

notice of termination, effective thirty (30) days after the date of such notice. The breaching party may avoid termination by curing its breach to the non-breaching party satisfaction within the thirty (30) day cure period. Distributor's material breach of this Agreement which the Company may find susceptible of cure include the following: If Distributor (1) fails to substantially comply with any of the terms and conditions of this Agreement, other related agreements and forms attached hereto and thereto; (2) fails, refuses or neglects to obtain the Company's prior written approval or consent as required in this Agreement; (3) fails, refuses, or neglects to promptly pay when due any amounts Distributor may owe to the Company hereunder; (4) fails to submit when due any reports, financial information, or any other information or documents required under this Agreement; (5) fails to observe or maintain any of the standards or procedures the Company prescribes herein or otherwise in writing; or (6) in the Company's sole discretion, Distributor engages or has engaged in any illegal, fraudulent, unfair or deceptive business practices. [DA#27]

12.3. DISTRIBUTOR shall have twenty (20) days after written notice specifying a breach of this Agreement to cure such breach. If, under the circumstances then current, it would appear that any breach is final, or cannot be cured, SUPPLIER may terminate the Agreement immediately for cause by giving notice to this effect.

12.4. Either SUPPLIER or DISTRIBUTOR may terminate this Agreement in the event that the other is dissolved, becomes insolvent, files a petition in bankruptcy, or is declared bankrupt, or makes an assignment for benefit of creditors, or there is reasonable evidence indicating the possibility of such filing or assignment during the term this Agreement is in effect. Termination under this provision shall be effective twenty (20) days following written notice to that effect.

12.5. DISTRIBUTOR may terminate this Agreement immediately for just cause should SUPPLIER breach any provision of this Agreement, provided that any such termination shall not take effect if SUPPLIER has cured such breach within twenty (20) days following written notice of DISTRIBUTOR's intention to terminate on account of such breach. [DA#30]

▶ **Exercise 11-4   Rewriting a "right to cure"/"correction of default" provision**
Based on your evaluation of right to cure/correction of default provisions, rewrite the following clause:

> Termination for Cause. If either party fails to perform any material obligation under this Agreement, including, in the case of Distributor, the failure to meet the Minimum Purchase Commitments set forth in Exhibit C, then upon thirty (30) days' written notice to the breaching party specifying such default, the non-breaching party may terminate this Agreement, without liability, unless: (i) the breach specified in the notice has been cured within the thirty (30) day period; or (ii) the default is not of an urgent nature in the sole discretion of the non-breaching party and reasonably requires more than thirty (30) days to correct (and specifically excluding any failure to Minimum Purchase Commitments or pay money), and the defaulting party has, in the reasonable judgment of the non-breaching party begun substantial corrective action to correct the default within such thirty (30) day period and diligently pursues such action, in which event, termination shall not be effective unless ninety (90) days has expired from the date of the notice without corrective action being completed and the default remedied. [DA#16]

▶ Exercise 11-5   Finding words relating to bankruptcy

Review several termination clauses in the contracts from the "Contract Database" file on the companion website (www.aspenlawschool.com/books/Adams) and look for the words *bankrupt* or *bankruptcy*. What other topics related to bankruptcy tend to appear in or near sentences that contain these words? Make a list of terms that commonly appear in these passages.

▶ Exercise 11-6   Finding termination causes

Find termination clauses within one contract category (DA, APA, CA) from the "Contract Database" file on the companion website, and make a list like the one shown below. State the clauses that could give rise to termination if violated, and identify which party would cause the termination.

Contract Categories	Caused by Party A	Caused by Party B
Warranties/ Representations		
Confidentiality		

▶ **Exercise 11-7   Questions**

1. What does the word *has* in subsection 17.2.2 below refer to?
2. What does *unethical conduct* in subsection 17.2.3 below refer to? Can you think of conduct that could arguably be termed unethical?

> 17.2 By Supplier. Supplier shall have the right to immediately terminate this Agreement and/or any Schedule by giving written notice to Distributor in the event that Distributor does any of the following: . . .
>
> 17.2.2 Makes any change in the current management of Distributor, which in the opinion of Supplier, substantially impairs Supplier's rights under this Agreement, or has or threatens to damage the reputation of ABCD, or the Licensed Product; . . .
>
> 17.2.3 Engages in any illegal, unfair, or deceptive business practices or unethical conduct whatsoever, whether or not related to the Licensed Product; . . .

▶ **Exercise 11-8   Finding effect of termination provisions**

Review termination clauses in the same category as in Exercise 11-6 and make a list like the one shown below. Fill in the effects of termination on each party with regards to selected contract provisions.

	Effect on Party A	**Effect on Party B**
Confidentiality		
Intellectual Property		
Delivery		
Payment		

▶ **Exercise 11-9   Comparing survival clauses**

Compare survival clauses in contracts CA#8 and CA#10 with survival clauses in contracts CA#15 and CA#16. Which system of stating survival clauses do you prefer and why?

▶ **Exercise 11-10   Revising a survival clause**

Rewrite the clause below by deleting any unnecessary wording and legalese.

> Consultant shall maintain accurate written records of contacts made pursuant to this Consulting Agreement, and agrees to give the Company copies of such records upon request. This duty to maintain said records referenced in the sentence immediately preceding and to provide such records upon request to the Company shall survive the termination of this Consulting Agreement. [DA#13]

▶ **Exercise 11-11   Add to your vocabulary list**

Add at least ten new words to your vocabulary list from the "Contract Database" file on the companion website (www.aspenlawschool.com/books/Adams). Use the model from section 1.4 in Chapter 1 for guidance. Modify your old lists if you have new information regarding a word.

▶ **Exercise 11-12   Pegasus/Azteca deal—drafting the exit provisions**

Using your draft of the provisions from the Pegasus/Azteca deal in Exercise 9-17 in Chapter 9 and the term sheet found in the materials section of Chapter 10 on the companion website (which provides additional agreed terms for this deal), do the following:

1. Identify the agreed terms that are exit provisions.
2. For each identified terms that is an exit provision:
   a. Identify the type of provision (see Chapter 7) that will best express the agreed term.
   b. Draft the agreed term into contract provisions applying the concepts discussed in this chapter and in Chapters 4, 6, 8, and 9.
   c. Determine the order in which these provisions should be presented in the contract.

Alternative Dispute Resolution Provisions

12.1 Overview

Litigating a contract dispute in court can be a lengthy, expensive, and public process. Adding to these concerns, a party to a cross-border agreement might find itself litigating in a foreign court with unfamiliar court procedures. Even if the dispute is litigated in a familiar court, the prevailing party could still face a challenge when attempting to enforce the judgment in a foreign court with personal jurisdiction over the losing party. Therefore, parties involved in contract disputes, especially those involving cross-border agreements, commonly resort to alternative dispute resolution (ADR) methods for resolving their differences.

Although not technically considered an ADR method, informal negotiations is a process the parties might undertake with each other before proceeding to other means for resolving the dispute. Also, mediation and arbitration are widely accepted means for resolving contract disputes in United States contracts. **Mediation** is a non-binding method of ADR where the parties seek to resolve their differences through mutual collaboration and problem-solving with an impartial third party (**mediator**) overseeing the process but not deciding the outcome. **Arbitration** is a more formal ADR method where parties choose one or more persons (**arbitrators**) to settle their dispute. In arbitration, the parties present their respective positions (including relevant witness testimony and evidence) to the arbitrator or panel of arbitrators. The arbitrator or panel, as the case may be, render a decision that settles the dispute (**arbitral award**). At the parties' option, the arbitral award can be binding on the parties; that is, the parties are required to adhere to the arbitral award (**binding arbitration**). Binding arbitration is common in commercial contract disputes.

Conciliation is an ADR method frequently used in civil law countries. **Conciliation** is similar to mediation in that it is a non-binding method for resolving disputes; but, unlike mediation where the mediator's role is to encourage discussion between the parties and guide them in their efforts to reach a resolution, the objective third-party facilitator in conciliation (**conciliator**) can make proposals to settle the dispute. Conciliation can also be less structured than mediation. Conciliation is not a common means to resolve disputes in the United States, and in fact, many confuse conciliation with mediation. Because this book focuses on drafting U.S. international contracts, the following discussion focuses on mediation, which is widely used in the United States. If the parties prefer conciliation, the basic considerations for drafting a mediation provision discussed below can also apply to a conciliation provision. Because of the confusion between mediation and conciliation, however, ensure that the contracting parties understand the difference between the two methods and agree on the preferred process before drafting the provision.

One of the benefits of informal negotiations and ADR is that the parties can decide which methods to employ and, as discussed in this chapter, can even shape the procedure for each method. Parties may choose to undertake any one or more of these methods in an effort to resolve their differences. If one method proves unsuccessful in resolving the dispute, parties can resort to another method for resolving the dispute. Figure 12-1 illustrates alternative steps the parties might undertake for resolving disputes.

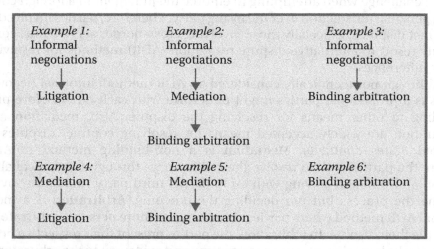

Figure 12-1 Alternative steps for resolving disputes

This freedom to custom design a process makes informal negotiations and ADR attractive options. Additionally, informal negotiations and ADR methods can save money and time, and ensure more privacy than litigating in court.

Major institutions provide ADR services for arbitration, mediation and, in some cases, conciliation, as well as other ADR processes. ADR institutions offer model procedural rules; model contract clauses; facilities; and lists of persons registered to serve as arbitrators, conciliators, or mediators (commonly referred to as *neutrals*). While parties are not required to use the services of an ADR institution in order to conduct ADR, many elect to use at least some of these offered services, despite the cost, because of the convenience and reliability of the services.

ADR institutions with international expertise include the International Institute for Conflict Prevention and Resolution (ICDR) (which is a division of the American Arbitration Association (AAA)), the International Chamber of Commerce (ICC), the Hong Kong International Arbitration Centre (HKIAC), the China International Economic and Trade Arbitration Commission, and the London Court of International Arbitration (LCIA).

Rather than waiting until a dispute arises, the parties should discuss the dispute resolution process as part of their contract negotiations. At this point, the parties are working towards finalizing the deal and can more objectively decide on the best course for resolving disputes. It could prove far more challenging for the parties to agree on a dispute resolution process when they are under pressure from an actual dispute.

Once the parties have negotiated a dispute resolution process, you should explicitly state that process in the contract. If the parties settle on one or more ADR options, include provisions detailing as much as possible of the agreed procedure for each option. Details of the ADR procedure are also best decided before a dispute arises.

The following discussion introduces you to drafting provisions for informal negotiation, mediation, and arbitration. Suggested considerations for drafting are provided, though these are not meant to be an exhaustive list of concerns. The example provisions show what might be included. The flexibility inherent in ADR, however, offers an abundance of options. The details of an ADR provision, whether a single ADR approach or a multi-step approach such as those shown in Figure 12-1, will heavily depend on, and should be tailored to, the parties' preferences.

Drafting ADR provisions can be challenging. While you want to ensure that important criteria are included in the provision, resist the urge to over-draft these provisions. Imposing too many requirements might make ADR difficult or nearly impossible to implement and defeat one of the advantages of ADR—flexibility. Also, take care to draft provisions that are fair to all contracting parties. ADR provisions that too heavily favor one party (e.g., requiring one party to submit to arbitration while the other party is free to seek litigation in court) might be found to be unenforceable.

12.2 Informal negotiation provisions

In informal negotiation, the parties typically designate officers or employees within their respective organizations to work on resolving issues. Unlike mediation or arbitration, informal negotiation does not usually involve outside persons. For this reason, informal negotiation is probably the simplest and cheapest dispute resolution method to implement.

List of Drafting Guidelines

When drafting an informal negotiation provision, consider the following:

♦ *Matters subject to informal negotiations.* Will all disputes or only some types of disputes (e.g., product sample approval, employee expense reimbursement) be subjected to this process? If only certain disputes are subject to informal negotiations, expressly state this in the provision.

♦ *Selecting the negotiators.* Who will represent each party in this process? Typically this is not addressed in the informal negotiation provision, thus leaving it to the parties to designate their respective negotiators when the dispute arises. However, in the interest of setting a procedure ahead of time, negotiation provisions can identify the position or job title of those who will negotiate on behalf of the respective parties. Will they be company officers, executive employees, or managers? For example, the negotiations might begin with the supervisors of the departments where the dispute originated. Whoever is designated must have the power to resolve disputes on behalf of their organization. Also, the negotiators should be on equal level of authority within their respective organizations. It is not an optimal negotiation experience, for instance, to have a mid-level manager negotiating with the other party's chief financial officer.

♦ *An appeal process.* If the initial negotiators are unable to reach a resolution, will the dispute be referred to someone higher in the organizational hierarchy for further negotiation? For instance, if there is a dispute over the marketing of a product, negotiations may begin with those in charge of marketing in the respective organizations. If they are unable to reach a resolution, the dispute could be referred to their supervisors for further negotiation. This type of appeal process can be effective in pushing the initial negotiators to find a resolution rather than bringing it to their busy supervisors, who will then need to deal with the problem.

♦ *Standard for negotiating conduct.* Parties should be required to negotiate for a resolution in "good faith."

♦ *Duration of the negotiation process.* The length of time spent on informal negotiations can be left open or the parties can agree on a specific time period. Designating a time period ensures that the negotiations do not continue for an unreasonably lengthy period. If the parties agree to impose a time limit on negotiations, you should include this in the contract. Consider adding an option for the parties to shorten or extend that time upon mutual consent.

> *Good faith* in contracts means that the parties will conduct themselves honestly and deal fairly with each other in keeping with the conduct standards of their trade.

♦ *The next step in resolving the dispute.* If the parties are unable to reach a resolution through informal negotiations, what will be the next step in the resolution process? Will it be mediation, arbitration, or litigation? Explicitly state this in the contract.

The following is an example of an informal negotiation provision. The details included in an informal negotiation provision will depend on the nature of the agreement and the parties' negotiations.

> In the event of any dispute arising under or related to this agreement, the parties shall initially attempt in good faith to resolve the dispute through informal negotiation. A party shall give written notice of the dispute to the other party (the "**Request to Negotiate**"). The Request to Negotiate will state the nature of the dispute and the requested relief.
>
> No later than five days after delivery of the Request to Negotiate, each party shall designate a representative to meet as often as the parties deem reasonably necessary to resolve the dispute. Notwithstanding the previous sentence, the parties shall submit the dispute to mediation if the parties are unable to resolve the dispute 60 days after delivery of the Request to Negotiate. The parties may shorten or extend the 60-day negotiation period by mutual written consent.
>
> If the parties are unable to reach a settlement of the dispute within the 60-day negotiation period, or as shorten or extended by the parties' mutual written consent, then the matter will be submitted to arbitration as provided in Section 10.1.

12.3 Mediation provisions

As noted earlier, mediation is a formal negotiation process supervised by an impartial, trained expert, called a *mediator*. Mediation can effectively resolve disputes in less time, with less expense, and with more privacy than arbitration or litigation. For this reason, mediation is becoming a more common ADR method used by U.S. parties involved in commercial contract disputes. Mediation can be especially helpful in disputes arising from cross-border agreements where the parties' language and cultural differences have led to miscommunication, misperceptions, or misinterpretation.

The objective of mediation is for the parties, under the guidance of a mediator, to work toward a settlement or resolution of the conflict. Mediation usually begins with the parties presenting to the mediator, orally or in writing, their respective positions in the disagreement. Thereafter, the mediator will work with the parties through a series of sessions, sometimes jointly and other times individually. In these sessions, the mediator's role is to support the parties' progress towards settlement. The mediator can facilitate the process, probe issues with the parties, ensure the parties understand the issues, and discuss settlement options with the parties.

The parties must agree on a mediator, preferably one with expertise in the area of the dispute (e.g., trademarks, copyright, oil and gas law, entertainment law) and, in the case of cross-cultural disputes, familiar with both cultures. Although not required, parties can chose a mediator from a list of mediators registered with an ADR institution. The parties can also elect to have the mediation process administered by an ADR institution, including using its rules and facilities. Alternatively, the parties may proceed with an **ad hoc mediation**, where the parties use their own facilities and create their own rules process, or adopt a modified ad hoc mediation that adapts an ADR institution's rules to suit their particular needs and goals. An attractive feature of mediation is that the parties have the power to determine all aspects of the mediation process, including the number of sessions, the duration of the sessions, and the scheduling of sessions.

Because the nature of the process requires each party to continue communication and to work together toward a common goal of settlement, the additional benefit of mediation is the preservation of goodwill between the disputing parties. Therefore, parties will want to consider mediation if they are interested in a continuing business relationship beyond the resolution of the dispute.

Nevertheless, mediation does have disadvantages that might convince parties to forego mediation and resort to arbitration or litigation, especially if the dispute has already caused a serious breakdown in communication and goodwill. One of the biggest disadvantages is there is no guarantee that, after all the time and effort invested by the parties and a mediator, a resolution will be reached. Also, one of the parties may decide at some point in the mediation to refuse to proceed with mediation. Furthermore, even if the parties reach a settlement and sign an agreement, one party could decide not to abide by that agreement. If this occurs, the other party would have to resort to a court with jurisdiction over the breaching party to seek enforcement of the agreement. Another concern of failed mediation is that the parties will move on to arbitration or litigation, a forum where the parties are no longer working together but are adversaries. This possibility could disrupt mediation efforts because parties might be reluctant in mediation to reveal sensitive information that could later be used against them in arbitration or in court.[1] Finally, if mediation fails, the parties are still faced with paying mediation costs, including mediator fees, legal fees, and travel costs.

---

1. Some jurisdictions have laws protecting certain information divulged during mediation (such as a party's willingness to settle or preferable settlement terms) from being admitted in a

List of Drafting Guidelines

If a Mediation clause is included in a contract, consider including provisions that address the following:

- *Defining mediation.* Include a definition of *mediation* if there are cultural differences as to what mediation entails or if there is a risk that the process will be confused with conciliation.

- *Scope of mediation.* Explicitly state whether all disputes or only certain types of disputes will be subject to mediation.

- *Duration of mediation.* Establish a time period for mediation.

- *Location of mediation.* Perhaps state where the negotiations will take place—for example, at one of the parties' offices, a lawyer's offices, at a neutral place such as an ADR institution's offices, or any combination of places.

- *Selecting a mediator.* Establish a procedure for selecting a mediator, such as selecting from a list of mediators registered with a designated ADR institution. If the mediator must have certain business or legal expertise, be careful not to make the criteria too detailed so that it becomes difficult to find a mediator.

- *Rules for mediation.* State whether the mediation will be administered under an institution's procedural rules or whether the parties may modify these rules or create their own mediation rules. Be mindful that creating mediation rules can be challenging. More often than not, parties would be better served by using institution's ready-made mediation rules that have been tried and proven effective and fair.

- *Standard for parties' mediation conduct.* Parties should be required to mediate in good faith.

- *Confidentiality.* If the parties are concerned about keeping mediation communications confidential in the event mediation fails, then address this issue in the provision. Either state that the mediation will be confidential, or attach as an exhibit to the contract a form of confidentiality agreement that will be used in the event of mediation.

---

later court proceeding. *See, e.g.,* European Union Draft Directive on Certain Aspects of Mediation in Civil and Commercial Matters, art. 6, http://eur-lex.europa.eu/LexUriServ/LexUriServ.do?uri=COM:2004:0718:FIN:EN:PDF. In jurisdictions without these laws, the parties should consider entering into a confidentiality agreement before engaging in mediation. The agreement's goal is to prevent confidential information learned in mediation from being admitted in a later court proceeding. Be mindful, however, that some jurisdictions could refuse to enforce the agreement and permit the admission of the confidential information anyway.

◆ *Costs, fees, and expenses.* Typically, both parties will share in paying the costs, fees, and expenses of mediation. For clarity, state how responsibility for payment will be apportioned between the parties.

◆ *Remedies for failure to mediate.* If a party fails to participate in mediation, perhaps provide a remedy for the other party, such as reimbursement for costs and attorneys' fees to enforce the mediation provision.

◆ *The next step in resolving the dispute.* State whether the parties may arbitrate the dispute or resort to litigation if the parties are unable to reach an agreement through mediation.

The following is an example of a simple mediation provision. The exact terms of a mediation provision, whether to exclude criteria or to include additional criteria, will depend on the nature of the contract and the parties' negotiations.

In the event of any dispute arising under or related to this agreement, the parties shall first try to settle the dispute through mediation as provided in this paragraph. A party shall give written notice to the other party requesting mediation (the "**Mediation Request**"). The Mediation Request will state the nature of the dispute and the requested relief.

The parties shall designate a mediator from a list of neutrals registered with [ADR institution]. Mediation sessions will be held at Manufacturer's offices in Houston, Texas. Unless otherwise provided in this section, mediation will be conducted according to the rules of [ADR institution]. Each party shall participate in good faith in the mediation sessions. If the dispute is not settled in 60 days after delivery of the Mediation Request, then the parties will submit to arbitration as provided in Section 12.2. Notwithstanding the previous sentence, the parties may shorten or extend the 60-day mediation period by mutual written consent.

Each party shall bear its own costs and expenses for the mediation and an equal share of the fees the mediator, except that a party refusing to submit to mediation under this section shall pay the costs and fees, including without limitation attorney's fees, incurred by the other party in an effort to compel compliance with this section.

12.4 Arbitration provisions

Unlike informal negotiations or mediation, arbitration is a formal dispute resolution process that is adversarial in nature. The parties present their respective positions, which might include witness testimony and evidence, at a hearing before a single arbitrator or panel of arbitrators.

Arbitration is promoted as being cheaper and quicker than litigating in court, though this is not always the case with international disputes. Nevertheless, arbitration is still more private than litigating in a public court. The disputing parties can even go a step further to ensure privacy by making the arbitration confidential, though the number of people usually involved in the process—not only the disputing parties and arbitrators but also any testifying witnesses—increases the risk that confidentiality could be broken.

For an interesting report on corporate views and practices related to the international arbitration of commercial disputes, see "2010 International Arbitration Survey: Choices in Arbitration," Queen Mary, University of London, available at http://www.arbitrationonline.org/research/2010/index.html.

The biggest advantages of arbitration over litigation are the ability of the parties (1) to select the arbitrators that are impartial and have expertise in the applicable business and law, (2) to fix the language and location of the arbitration, (3) to decide on procedural rules, and (4) to enforce arbitration awards in court.

By selecting the arbitrator or panel of arbitrators, the parties can help ensure that those making the arbitral award are objective and have the necessary expertise to make an informed decision. The latter can be crucial when the dispute involves highly technical or specialized areas, such as biotechnology or telecommunications.

When litigating a dispute, the parties may find themselves in a foreign court in an inconvenient location. In arbitration, the parties can agree on a mutually suitable location for arbitration. This can result in savings in travel cost and time. Also, neither party has the advantage of litigating in its local court, thus preventing concerns about partiality.

Avoiding litigation in court can also sidestep language issues. A court will use the national language for its proceedings. If a party is not fluent in the language, it will need to rely on an interpreter, which involves additional cost and possible problems with miscommunication. In arbitration the parties can agree on a language for arbitration.

Parties litigating a dispute must submit to the court's procedural rules. This becomes a problem when the case is litigated in a foreign court where a party is unfamiliar with the rules. Also, in some jurisdictions, such as the United States, litigation can involve a lengthy **discovery period**, where the parties seek additional information and evidence to assess the claims and prepare their positions. Motions filed by the parties can further delay the

UNCITRAL *stands for the* United Nations Commission on International Trade Law.

process. In arbitration, the parties are able to design their own procedural rules. Alternatively, they could use ready-made rules—for example, an ADR institution's rules or the UNCITRAL Arbitration Rules.[2] Therefore, arbitration allows the parties to streamline not only discovery, but also the hearing, by using procedural and evidence rules that are typically less stringent than court-promulgated rules. Of course, the parties must also keep in mind that streamlining rules can provide less protection to the parties. Also, limiting discovery can hinder a party's ability to prepare for the hearing.

Perhaps the most positive aspect of international arbitration is the ability to enforce an arbitral award. A foreign arbitral award can be easier to enforce than a foreign judgment. A party seeking enforcement of a foreign judgment must rely on international *comity* or a treaty with the foreign country providing for enforcement of judgments obtained in the other signatory country. Conversely, court enforcement of a foreign arbitral awards is more assured. Under the 1958 Convention on the Recognition of Enforcement of Foreign Arbitral Awards (commonly referred to as the *New York Convention*),[3] courts in countries that are signatories to the convention must enforce, with only limited exceptions, arbitral awards rendered in other signatory countries.[4] As of the writing of this book, 146 countries were signatories to the New York Convention, including all major trading nations.

> **Comity** *means "the recognition which one nation allows within its territory to the legislative, executive or judicial acts of another nation, having due regard both to international duty and convenience, and to the rights of its own citizens, or of other persons who are under the protections of its laws."* Hilton v. Guyot, *159 U.S. 113, 164 (1885).*

Arbitration, however, does have its disadvantages. As previously mentioned, international arbitration can be almost as expensive and lengthy as international litigation. There might be insufficient time for adequate discovery and fewer evidentiary rules designed for the parties' protection. Aside from these concerns, perhaps the most troubling aspect of arbitration is the lack of an appeals process. Although this is frequently promoted as a benefit of arbitration because it eliminates the time and expense of an appeal, a party is left with little recourse in the event of an adverse award. Courts are reluctant to review an arbitrator's decision, even if the arbitrator misapplied the governing law. Finally, because binding arbitration is consensual between the disputing parties, arbitrators have no power to compel third parties to participate in the arbitration. Nevertheless, despite these drawbacks, the flexibility of arbitration, the binding nature (in most instances)

---

2. The rules, designed for use by parties in civil law and common law countries, can be found at http://www.uncitral.org/uncitral/uncitral_texts/arbitration/2010 Arbitration_rules.html.

3. Convention on the Recognition of Enforcement of Foreign Arbitral Awards (New York, June 10, 1958), 330 U.N.T.S. 38 (1959), *entered into force* June 7, 1959 (the "New York Convention"); *see also* http://faculty.smu.edu/pwinship/arb-31.htm.

4. New York Convention, art. 5.

of the decision, and the degree of control given to the disputing parties make arbitration a favored ADR method for resolving contract disputes, especially international disputes.

List of Drafting Guidelines

When drafting an arbitration provision, consider addressing the following issues. As is the case with the considerations offered for informal negotiation and mediation, this is not meant to be an exhaustive list.[5]

♦ *Scope of arbitration.* State whether arbitration will be limited to certain types of disputes or whether it will apply to all disputes arising under or related to the contract.

♦ *Hybrid mediation–arbitration.* A mediator in an unsuccessful mediation could serve as an arbitral judge in the arbitration of the dispute. This arrangement saves time because the arbitrator would already be familiar with the issues. However, it could undermine mediation efforts if a party is reluctant to share information with the mediator out of concern that it might prejudice the mediator's decision-making in the arbitration.

♦ *Location of arbitration.* The parties will want to choose a place for arbitration that is relatively easy to reach. For this reason major cities are often the site for international arbitration. The arbitration can take place at an ADR institution's facilities or at some other neutral location.

♦ *The number of arbitrators.* Establish the number of arbitrators. For a simple, domestic dispute, one arbitrator is probably sufficient. However, for international arbitration a panel of arbitrators is more commonly used.

♦ *The process for selecting an arbitrator or panel of arbitrators.* State whether the parties will choose arbitrators from the registration roles of an ADR institution or whether they can choose anyone else with particular business or legal expertise. Be careful not to make the criteria too detailed so that it becomes difficult or impossible to satisfy (e.g., "The arbitrator will be an intellectual property lawyer who is fluent in Korean and English, holds a degree in Biomedical Engineering, and specializes in bioinfomatics issues.") For a panel of arbitrators, state the selection procedure. The procedure could simply reference an ADR institution's selection rules. Alternatively, the

---

5. For a detailed discussion of drafting international arbitration clauses, *see* Gary B. Born, *International Arbitration and Forum Selection Agreements: Drafting and Enforcing* (3d ed., Aspen 2010).

parties could state their own procedure. For example, when selecting a three-person arbitration panel, each party could choose an arbitrator and the two arbitrators could choose a third panelist.

♦ *Rules for arbitration.* Designate the rules that will be used for administering the arbitration. Parties may use the rules of an ADR institution or other procedural rules, such as the UNCITRAL Arbitration Rules for international arbitration. Parties may also modify the model rules or create their own rules (**ad hoc rules**) to suit their needs. Be mindful, though, that creating ad hoc rules can be time-consuming and expensive. Also, these ad hoc rules could create unanticipated procedural conflicts or issues. Therefore, the parties might be better served by using ready-made rules.

♦ *Governing law for the substantive issues.* The law governing the substantive issues should be stated in the general provisions section of the contract, rather than in the arbitration provision. (See Chapter 13, section 13.1.) If the governing law is only mentioned in the arbitration provision, then an ambiguity could arise as to whether the governing law requirement only applies to arbitrated disputes.

♦ *Confidentiality.* If the parties are concerned about keeping the arbitration confidential, then provide for this in the arbitration provision.

♦ *Language of arbitration proceedings.* In international arbitration, state the language that will be used for arbitration.

♦ *Arbitrator's written reasons for the award.* Arbitrators are not required to provide reasons for the award. If the parties want a written reason for the arbitrator's decision, they must ask for it. This should be included as a part of the arbitration provision.

♦ *Permitting punitive damages.* Whether arbitrators have the power to award punitive damages will depend on the governing law for the arbitration. Some legal systems, such as Germany, do not recognize punitive damages. Conversely, in the United States punitive damages are permitted in tort actions (e.g., fraud) or when specifically provided under statute. Even so, the arbitration laws in some states prohibit an arbitrator from awarding punitive damages, though arbitrators do have this power under the Federal Arbitration Act (FAA).[6]

---

6. 9 U.S.C. §§ 1-16.

- ◆ *Agreement to enter judgment.* Provide that the arbitral award can be filed with in a court with proper jurisdiction to enforce the award.[7]

- ◆ *Costs, fees, and expenses.* Designate whether both parties will share in the costs, fees, and expenses of arbitration. In some situations, the parties might agree that the losing party will be responsible for payment.

- ◆ *Remedies for failure to arbitrate.* If a party refuses to arbitrate, consider whether the other party should have a remedy, such as requiring the refusing party to pay the costs and attorneys' fees for court enforcement of this provision.

Whether an arbitration provision addresses all of the above considerations or includes additional considerations will depend on the nature of the deal and the parties' negotiations. The following is a sample arbitration provision.

In the event of any dispute arising under or related to this agreement, the parties shall submit the dispute to final and binding arbitration to be administered by [ADR institution] under the UNCITRAL Arbitration Rules. The dispute will be submitted to a panel of three arbitrators. Each party will choose one arbitrator from [ADR institution's] roster of arbitrators. The chosen arbitrators will choose a third arbitrator from the same roster. Arbitration will be conducted in English in Houston, Texas. Judgment on the award rendered by the arbitrators can be entered in any court having jurisdiction.

Each party shall bear its own costs and expenses for the arbitration and an equal share of the fees for arbitration, except that a party refusing to submit to arbitration under this section shall pay the costs and fees, including without limitation attorney's fees, incurred by the other party in an effort to compel compliance with this section.

Exercises

▶ **Exercise 12-1   Mediation clauses I**

Review the following Mediation clauses. For each clause, identify and make notes of the following:

1. What are the strengths?
2. What are the weaknesses? For example, is there too much detail or insufficient detail? Are there ambiguities?

---

7. *See, e.g.,* FAA § 9.

3. Redraft the two clauses so that the language is clear and concise.
4. Example A is taken from a distribution agreement, whereas Example B comes from a consulting agreement. Are any wording differences the result of the differing types of agreements?

Use the Mediation Checklist Worksheet below to establish where and how the clauses overlap and where there are gaps.

Example A:

17.4 Jurisdiction; Consent to Service of Process

(a) If any dispute arises between the parties regarding any matter under this Agreement, the parties will refer the dispute to senior executives of each party, who will attempt to resolve the dispute within ten (10) business days of the referral date. If the executives resolve the dispute, they will state the resolution in a writing provided to both parties. If the executives determine that they are unable to resolve the dispute (the date of such determination, the "Impasse Date"), the parties will seek to resolve the dispute through non-binding mediation conducted at a mutually agreeable location; if the parties are not able to agree on a mediator within ten (10) business days after the Impasse Date, the mediation will be conducted under the American Arbitration Association's ("AAA's") then-current mediation rules by a mediator selected at random from the AAA panel of mediators with property expertise. The mediation must be conducted within thirty (30) days after the Impasse Date, with each party to bear its own costs and to share equally in the cost of the mediation itself (including mediator's fees). No court action for damages may be commenced unless the parties have completed mediation without resolving the dispute. [DA#27]

Example B:

7.13. Mediation. Before either party may initiate any suit, arbitration or other proceeding the parties pledge to attempt first to resolve the controversy or claim arising out of or relating to this Consulting Agreement ("Dispute") by mediation before a mutually acceptable mediator within 30 days after either party first gives notice of mediation. Mediation shall be conducted in Los Angeles, California and shall be conducted and completed within 60 days following the date either party first gives notice of mediation. The fees and expenses of the mediator shall be shared equally by the parties. The mediator shall be disqualified as a witness, expert or

---

Continued

counsel for any party with respect to the Dispute and any related matter. Mediation is a compromise negotiation and shall constitute privileged communications. The entire mediation process shall be confidential and the conduct, statements, promises, offers, views and opinions of the mediator and the parties shall not be discoverable or admissible in any legal proceeding for any purpose; provided, however, that evidence which is otherwise discoverable or admissible shall not be excluded from discovery or admission as a result of its use in the mediation.

7.14. Attorneys' Fees. In any action at law (including arbitration proceedings), or in equity to enforce or construe any provisions or rights under this Consulting Agreement, or to enforce and arbitration award, the unsuccessful Party, as determined by a court or arbitrator, will pay the successful Party all costs, expenses, and reasonable attorneys' fees incurred.

7.15. Waiver of Jury Trial. Each Party acknowledges that by executing this Consulting Agreement, the Party waives any rights he or it may have to a trial by jury. [CA#12]

Mediation Checklist Worksheet

	DA#27	CA#12
Conditions leading up to mediation		
Defining mediation		
Scope of mediation		
Duration of mediation		
Location of mediation		
Selecting a mediator		
Rules for mediation		
Standard for parties' mediation conduct good faith		
Confidentiality		
Costs, fees, and expenses		
Remedies for failure to mediate		
Next step in dispute resolution		

▶ **Exercise 12-2   Mediation clauses II**

In the clause below, a comma has been omitted. How does the omission change the meaning of the clause?

> (a) If any dispute arises between the parties regarding any matter under this Agreement, the parties will refer the dispute to senior executives of each party who will attempt to resolve the dispute within ten (10) business days of the referral date. [DA#27]

▶ **Exercise 12-3   Mediation clauses III**

Which parties are referred to in the altered version of the Mediation clause below? Other than *Agreement*, are there any terms that should be defined?

> (a) If any dispute arises between parties regarding any matter under this Agreement, the parties will refer the dispute to senior executives of each party. [DA#27]

▶ **Exercise 12-4   Mediation clauses IV**

In the clause below, the original article *the* was changed to *a* in the phrase "resolving a dispute." Explain how the change affects the meaning.

> No court action for damages may be commenced unless the parties have completed mediation without resolving a dispute. [DA#27]

▶ **Exercise 12-5   Mediation clauses V**

1. Use the verbs in **bold** below in a sentence.
2. Then, look up their meaning in a regular non-law dictionary.
3. Next, look up these words in a legal dictionary.
4. Finally, find these words in the contract collection DA, CA, APA on the companion website (www.aspenlawschool.com/books/Adams) and note with which other words they commonly appear.

> 7.14. Attorneys' Fees. In any action at law (including arbitration proceedings), or in equity to **enforce** or **construe** any provisions or rights under this Consulting Agreement, or to **enforce** an arbitration award, the unsuccessful Party, as determined by a court or arbitrator, will pay the successful Party all costs, expenses, and reasonable attorneys' fees **incurred**. [CA#12]

▶ **Exercise 12-6   Arbitration clauses I**

Review the following Arbitration clauses. For each clause, identify and make notes of the following:

1. What are the strengths?
2. What are the weaknesses? For example, is there too much detail or insufficient detail? Are there ambiguities?
3. Choose Example A, B, or C and redraft so that the language is clear and concise.

Use the Arbitration Checklist Worksheet following the three examples to establish where and how the clauses overlap and where there are gaps.

Example A:

> Any disputes concerning questions of fact or law arising from or in connection with the interpretation, performance, non-performance, or termination of this Agreement, including the validity, scope, or enforceability of this Agreement to arbitrate, shall be settled by mutual consultation between the parties in good faith as promptly as possible, but if both parties fail to make an amicable settlement, such disputes shall be settled by arbitration in San Diego, California, in accordance with the Commercial Arbitration Rules of the Arbitration Association of America. The award of the arbitrators shall be final and binding upon the parties. [DA#10]

Example B:

> Arbitration. If a Dispute is not resolved by consultations within sixty (60) days after one Party has served written notice on the other Party for the commencement of such consultations, then such Dispute will be finally settled and determined by arbitration in Hong Kong under the Arbitration Rules of the United Nations Commission on

Continued

International Trade Law by arbitrators appointed in accordance with such Rules. The arbitration and appointing authority will be the Hong Kong International Arbitration Centre ("HKIAC"). The arbitration will be conducted by a panel of three arbitrators, one chosen by Supplier, one chosen by Distributor, and the third by agreement of the Parties; failing agreement within thirty (30) days of commencement of the arbitration proceeding, the HKIAC will appoint the third arbitrator. The proceedings will be confidential and conducted in English. The arbitral tribunal will have the authority to grant any equitable and legal remedies that would be available in any judicial proceeding instituted to resolve a disputed matter, and its award will be final and binding on the parties. The arbitral tribunal will determine how the parties will bear the costs of the arbitration. Notwithstanding the foregoing, each Party will have the right at any time to immediately seek injunctive relief, an award of specific performance or any other equitable relief against the other Party in any court or other tribunal of competent jurisdiction. During the pendency of any arbitration or other proceeding relating to a Dispute between the parties, the parties will continue to exercise their remaining respective rights and fulfill their remaining respective obligations under this Agreement, except with regard to the matters under dispute. [DA#12]

Example C:

9.9.1 In the event the Parties are unable to resolve any dispute or conflict arising from or relating to this Agreement within thirty (30) days after it is formally presented for resolution by written notice, any party may submit such conflict for resolution to the Chief Executive Officers of the parties.

9.9.2 In the event the Chief Executive Officers of the parties are unable to resolve such conflict within thirty (30) days after having such conflict submitted to them for resolution, the disputes shall be finally settled under the Rules of Conciliation and Arbitration of the International Chamber of Commerce in Paris ("Rules") by three arbitrators appointed in accordance with the Rules.

9.9.3 The place of arbitration shall be Zurich. The procedural law of this place shall apply where the Rules are silent.

9.9.4 The arbitral award shall be substantiated in writing. The arbitral tribunal shall decide on the matter of costs of the arbitration.

9.9.5 The language to be used in the arbitral proceedings shall be English. [DA#4]

Arbitration Checklist Worksheet

	Example A	Example B	Example C
Scope of arbitration	✓		
Location of arbitration	✓		
Number of arbitrators	✓		
Selection process/composition	✓		
Rules for arbitration (e.g., UNCITRAL)	✓		
Governing law for the substantive issues	✓		
Confidentiality			
Language of arbitration proceedings	✓		
Arbitrator's written reasons for the award			
Permitting punitive damages			
Agreement to enter judgment			
Costs, fees, and expenses	✓		
Remedies for failure to arbitrate			
Hybrid mediation–arbitration			
Additional points			

▶ **Exercise 12-7   Arbitration clauses II**

Exchange your Arbitration clause draft with that of a partner and review it according to content, organization, and style. Then return it to your partner.

▶ **Exercise 12-8   Arbitration clauses III**

The following subsection (c) follows a regular arbitration agreement between two parties with the establishment of an arbitral panel and binding nature of the arbitral award. What effect on the arbitration process may subsection (c) have?

> (c) Notwithstanding anything contained in Section 19 (b) to the contrary, each party shall have the right to institute judicial proceedings against the other party or anyone acting by, through or under such other party, in order to enforce the instituting party's rights hereunder through reformation of contract, specific performance, injunction or similar equitable relief. [DA#6]

▶ **Exercise 12-9   Arbitration clauses IV**

Use the Arbitration Checklist Worksheet to assess the detail of the following Arbitration clause. Is the clause succinctly written? Will it achieve its goal? Is it organized in a logical manner?

19.7 ARBITRATION. Except with respect to equitable remedies provided herein, including, without limitation, injunction relief, all claims, demands, disputes, controversies, differences or misunderstandings arising out of or relating to this Agreement, or the failure or refusal to perform the whole or any part thereof, shall be referred to and finally resolved by arbitration to be administered by the International Centre for Dispute Resolution, a division of the American Arbitration Association ("AAA"), in accordance with its International Arbitration Rules then obtaining (the "IA Rules"). The arbitration shall be conducted before one arbitrator to be selected by agreement of the parties or, if no agreement can be reached, in accordance with the IA Rules. The arbitration shall be conducted using the English language for all purposes. Either party hereto may initiate the arbitration by serving a written demand for arbitration on the other party, which demand shall contain a description of the nature of the dispute. All hearings of the arbitration shall take place in Orange County, California, United States of America.

The initial fees and costs of the arbitration shall be borne equally and paid timely by each party hereto. Failure by a party to pay said fees and costs to the AAA timely shall constitute a material default under this Agreement. The award shall be final and binding upon the parties, and the parties agree to be bound by the terms of the award and to act accordingly. The judgment upon any award may be entered in and enforceable by any court having jurisdiction over the party against whom the award has been rendered or wherever the assets of the party are located. Any award for costs shall include attorney fees and costs to the prevailing party, and attorney's fees and costs shall also be recoverable in any action to enforce the award.

The parties hereto, and each of them, hereby submit themselves to the jurisdiction of the state courts of the State of California and the United States Federal District Court in California in any proceeding for the enforcement of the award rendered by the arbitrator, and agree that judgment upon such award may be entered in any court, in or out of the State of California, having jurisdiction thereof. The arbitrator shall rule in accordance with the laws of California, without giving affect to the rules of conflict of laws thereof. The parties to the proceeding shall have reasonable rights of discovery in accordance with the Civil Rules of Federal Procedure used in the United States District Court.

Nothing contained herein shall prevent either party from applying to any court of law in order to obtain injunctions or any equivalent remedy, against any other party, in order to restrain the breach of any restrictive covenants pursuant to this Agreement. [DA#1]

▶ **Exercise 12-10   Arbitration clauses V**

In the following clause, some prepositions have been deleted. Before you fill in the correct preposition, follow the instructions in *a* and *b* below:

   a) Make a sentence using the boldfaced word, or a variation of the word. For example:

     arising/arise/arises

     in accordance/according

   b) Find examples of the word or its variation together with a preposition from the contract database.

> 13. ARBITRATION. The parties agree that any dispute or controversy **arising** . . . or in **connection** . . . this Consulting Agreement shall be **submitted** . . . and **determined** . . . arbitration in Denver, Colorado **in accordance** . . . the Commercial Arbitration Rules of the American Arbitration Association and agree **to be bound** . . . the decision in any such arbitration provision. [CA#20]

▶ **Exercise 12-11   Arbitration clauses VI**

Explain the difference in meaning between Version A and Version B of the following Arbitration clause:

Version A:

> The decision of the arbitrator shall be final and binding between the parties as to claims which were or could have been raised in connection with the dispute, to the full extent permitted by law. [CA#7, slightly altered]

Version B:

> The decision of the arbitrator shall be final and binding between the parties as to claims, which were or could have been raised in connection with the dispute, to the full extent permitted by law. [CA#7, slightly altered]

After your analysis, look up the original version of the Arbitration clause in contract CA#7.

▶ **Exercise 12-12   Add to your vocabulary list**

Add at least ten new words to your vocabulary list from the "Contract Database" file on the companion website (www.aspenlawschool.com/

books/Adams). Use the model from section 1.4 in Chapter 1 for guidance. Modify your old lists if you have new information regarding a word.

▶ **Exercise 12-13   Pegasus/Azteca deal—drafting the ADR provisions**
Using your draft of the provisions from the Pegasus/Azteca deal in Exercise 9-17 in Chapter 9 and the term sheet found in the materials section of Chapter 10 on the companion website (which provides additional agreed terms for this deal), do the following:

1. Identify the agreed terms that are ADR provisions.
2. For each identified terms that is an ADR provision:
   a. Identify the type of provision (see Chapter 7) that will best express the agreed term.
   b. Draft the agreed term into contract provisions applying the concepts discussed in this chapter and in Chapters 4, 6, 8, and 9.
   c. Determine the order in which these provisions should be presented in the contract.

Miscellaneous Provisions

After the exit provisions in a contract, you will find a group of provisions serving such a wide variety of purposes that they are often collectively referred to as *miscellaneous provisions*. In fact, lawyers can't seem to settle on just one label to identify this group. So in practice you might also hear them described as *general provisions, housekeeping provisions*, or *boilerplate provisions*. This book refers to them as miscellaneous provisions.

Though miscellaneous provisions appear near the end of a contract, this does not mean they are of lesser importance than other provisions. Indeed, they are of critical importance to the contract. These various provisions are placed at the end of the contract because they aren't core provisions, ADR provisions, or exit provisions. Depending on the nature of the contract, miscellaneous provisions might include the following:

1. The rules used to interpret the contract.
2. The circumstances, if any, under which a party's failure to perform obligations is excused.
3. The procedure used by the parties to communicate to each other about important matters related to the contract.
4. The circumstances, if any, under which the parties may assign their interests, delegate their duties, or change provisions.

Because some miscellaneous provisions are found in many different types of contracts, parties might assume these provisions must be included in all contracts and are non-negotiable, which is why they are sometimes referred to as *boilerplate*. But this is incorrect. Some provisions might be inappropriate to include in a contract, and miscellaneous provisions are always subject to the parties' negotiations.

> *Boilerplate means "ready-made or all-purpose language that will fit in a variety of documents."* Black's Law Dictionary 198 (Bryan A. Garner, ed., 9th ed., West 2011). Boilerplate *can also refer to the section of the contract containing these types of provisions. The term* boilerplate *originally referred to metal identification plates attached to engine boilers. In the late nineteenth century the term was used to describe steel plates stamped with text that were used repeatedly in printing newspapers.*

The first step in drafting miscellaneous provisions is deciding which ones should be included in the contract. The nature of the deal and the parties' negotiations will help determine this. For instance, if the parties are signing the contract at the same time and place, a **counterparts clause**, which addresses what happens when the parties sign the contract at different times and places, is unnecessary.

Once you've decided to include a provision in your draft, the next step is to draft the provision. You should not simply "cut and paste" a similar provision found in a form or another contract. The terms of the precedent provision might differ from the negotiated terms of the present deal. Aside from this, the provision might be poorly worded, containing legalese and ambiguities. Therefore, you must give the language careful thought and edit to concisely reflect the parties' intent.

Miscellaneous provisions found in contracts are numerous and varied. A discussion of these provisions could fill an entire book. Indeed, there are books devoted solely to this topic.[1] This chapter only introduces you to selected miscellaneous provisions. Not all provisions discussed in this chapter should be included in every contract, and some provisions (e.g., waiver of jury trials, "time is of the essence" clauses) not discussed here might be appropriate for certain contracts. Suggested considerations for drafting provisions as discussed in this chapter are not intended to be comprehensive lists. And, of course, what you ultimately include in your draft will depend on the nature of the transaction, the parties' negotiations, and governing law.

13.1 Governing law clause

A governing law clause stipulates the rules that will be used for interpreting contract provisions and filling in gaps left in contract provisions. In the United States, contract law is generally a matter of state law.[2] Therefore, governing law clauses in U.S. contracts will typically reference the law of a particular state. If the contract stipulates a particular state's law but does not mention U.S. federal law, U.S. courts will nevertheless apply relevant federal law,[3] even to the exclusion of chosen state law where required by the federal law. Conversely, parties can *exclude* federal law only if (1) the

---

1. *See, e.g.,* Tina L. Stark, ed., *Negotiating and Drafting Contract Boilerplate* (ALM Publg. 2003); Giuditta Cordero-Moss, ed., *Boilerplate Clauses, International Commercial Contracts and the Applicable Law* (Cambridge Univ. Press 2011).

2. See the discussion in Chapter 2, section 2.4.1.

3. This is required under the Supremacy Clause of the U.S. Constitution. *See* U.S. Const. art. VI, cl. 2. *See also Volt Info. Sci., Inc. v. Bd. of Trustees of Leland Stanford Junior U.,* 489 U.S. 468, 490-501 (1989); *Fidelity Fed. Sav. & Loan Assn. v. De la Cuesta,* 458 U.S. 141, 157 n.12 (1981).

law permits voluntary exclusion of its application and (2) the parties expressly state in the contract their intent to exclude the federal law's application.[4] Although most governing law provisions stipulate the law of a particular state or country, the parties could choose other rule sources. For example, if parties to a cross-border contract object to applying the local rules of the other party, they may agree to use the UNIDROIT Principles of International Commercial Law (UNIDROIT Principles)[5] or, perhaps for shipping rules, the International Chamber of Commerce Incoterms®.

Although the parties may stipulate the governing law in the contract, this is no guarantee that the clause will be enforced. To determine whether the clause itself is enforceable, a court will use the law of its own jurisdiction, which might be different than the stipulated law. For example, let's say that the governing law clause in a contract stipulates New York law, but the suit is brought in a California court. A California court will use its own conflicts of law rules to decide whether the governing law clause is enforceable. Like many other state courts in the United States, California courts follow the Restatement (Second) of Conflict of Laws (Restatement) sections 187 and 188 to resolve these issues.[6] In contracts for the sale of goods where the Uniform Commercial Code (UCC) applies, courts will apply a "reasonable relation" standard similar to the Restatement.[7]

The UNIDROIT Principles, drafted by a group of international experts, is a model set of contract rules for all types of international transactions. These rules are not based on the rules of a particular country. When drafting these rules, the experts looked at contract principles commonly recognized in various countries, taking into consideration the appropriateness of the rules' application to cross-border transactions.

Incoterms® "provide internationally accepted definitions and rules of interpretation for most common commercial terms." ICC: The New Incoterms® 2010 Rules; http://www.iccwbo.org/products-and-services/trade-facilitation/incoterms-2010.

For purposes of the present example, let's assume the Restatement applies to the contract. Using section 187(2), a California court will not enforce a governing law provision if

(a) the chosen state [law] has no substantial relationship to the parties or the transaction and there is no other reasonable basis for the parties' choice, or

---

4. *See, e.g., UHC Mgt. Co., Inc. v. Computer Sci. Corp.,* 148 F.3d 992, 997 (8th Cir. 1998) (holding that the Federal Arbitration Act [the Act] applied when the contract's governing law clause stipulated that state law applied and failed to make "abundantly clear" that the parties intended to exclude the Act).

5. *See* http://www.unidroit.org/english/principles/contracts/main.htm.

6. Restatement (Second) of Conflict of Laws §§ 187 & 188 (1971). Be mindful, however, that some states follow other conflicts of law rules. *See, e.g., Convergys Corp. v. Keener,* 582 S.E.2d 84, 87 (Ga. 2003) (rejecting Restatement sections 187(2) and 188 and retaining the "traditional rule" of *lex loci contractus,* meaning the law of the jurisdiction where the contract was made applies unless performance under the contract takes place in another state).

7. UCC § 1-105(1).

(b) application of the law of the chosen state would be contrary to a fundamental policy of a state which has a materially greater interest than the chosen state and which, under the rules of § 188, would be the state of the applicable law in the absence of an effective choice of law by the parties.[8]

First, under section 187(2)(a), the California court must determine whether there is either (1) a substantial relationship between New York law and the parties or the transaction, or (2) a reasonable basis for the parties choosing New York law.[9] If the parties or transaction do not bear a substantial relationship with the chosen state law or if there was no reasonable basis for choosing that state law, then the court's inquiry ends, and it will refuse to enforce the contract's governing law provision. Let's say, however, that in our example the California court finds there is a reasonable basis for choosing New York law because one of the contracting parties is a New York corporation with principal offices in New York City. So section 187(2)(a) is not satisfied. Next, the court will look at the criteria under section 187(2)(b). In our example, the court finds that California has "a materially greater interest" in the case because most of the parties' performance took place in California, and California law would have applied if the governing law provision had been absent from the agreement.[10] This does not end the analysis, however. Despite the heavy leaning to California law, the California court will *still enforce* the governing law provision, *unless* applying New York law to the substantive issues would be contrary to fundamental policy of a state with a materially greater interest—in this instance, perhaps California. If the court determines that California meets this requirement,

---

8. Restatement § 187(2). *See, e.g., Washington Mutual Bank v. Superior Court*, 15 P.3d 1071 (Cal. 2001); *Nedlloyd Lines B.V. v. Superior Court*, 834 P.2d 1148 (Cal. 1992).

9. Comment f to Restatement section 187 suggests factors that could show a substantial relationship or reasonable basis for the parties' choice, including where the parties are domiciled, where a party has its principal place of business, where performance occurred or, unless it was "wholly fortuitous and bears no real relation either to the contract or to the parties," where the negotiations or signing of the contract took place. Regarding cross-border contracts, comment f suggests:

> The parties may have a reasonable basis for choosing a state with which the contract has no substantial relationship. For example, when contracting in countries whose legal systems are strange to them as well as relatively immature, the parties should be able to choose a law on the ground that they know it well and that it is sufficiently developed. For only in this way can they be sure of knowing accurately the extent of their rights and duties under the contract. So parties to a contract for the transportation of goods by sea between two countries with relatively undeveloped legal systems should be permitted to submit their contract to some well-known and highly elaborated commercial law.

10. Under Restatement section 188, factors to consider include "(a) the place of contracting, (b) the place of negotiation of the contract, (c) the place of performance, (d) the location of the subject matter of the contract, and (e) the domicile, residence, nationality, place of incorporation and place of business of the parties."

then it will apply California law, instead.[11] Conversely, if the California court decides the requirements of both (a) and (b) of section 187(2) are not satisfied, it will apply New York law to the substantive issues raised in the case.

List of Drafting Guidelines

When drafting the governing law provision, consider the following:

- ◆ The law that will be used. Factors to take into account include:
  - *Familiarity with the law.* For an international contract, the choices for governing law are typically narrowed to the law of the jurisdictions where each party resides.[12] Understandably, a party is likely to prefer the familiarity of the law where it is domiciled while the other party will likely be reluctant to submit to unknown foreign law. Familiarity with the law is a crucial factor in choosing governing law. If you are not familiar with the law under consideration, you will want to consult with an expert in that law before making a decision.
  - *Well-developed contract law.* Another factor to consider when choosing governing law is whether the prospective jurisdiction's contract law is well developed, meaning contract issues have been adequately addressed by statutes or common law and tested by litigation. If the jurisdiction has well-developed law, the parties are better able to anticipate how disputes might be decided. In the United States, California, New York, and Texas are examples of states with well-developed contract law.
  - *Protecting your client's interests.* Ensure that the chosen law will protect your client's interests and provide adequate remedies in the event of another party's breach. For example, California will not enforce Non-competition clauses in employment agreements, except in limited circumstances.[13] California finds that an employee's "mobility and betterment are . . . paramount to the competitive business interests of employers . . . ."[14] Therefore, where the parties or the employment relationship has contacts with both California

---

11. *See, e.g., Application Group, Inc. v. Hunter Group, Inc.*, 61 Cal. App. 4th 881 (1st Dist. 1998). The California Court of Appeals refused to enforce a non-competition clause in an employment agreement between a California employer and a Maryland employee, even though the non-competition clause would have been enforceable under Maryland law, the parties chosen law governing the contract. *Id.* at 899-902. The court found that the non-competition clause violated a fundamental public policy of the state as expressed in Cal. Bus. & Professions Code § 16600, which prohibits enforcing these clauses except to protect an employer's trade secrets. *Id.* at 900-901.

12. *But see supra* n. 10.

13. *See supra* n. 12.

14. *Metro Traffic Control, Inc. v. Shadow Traffic Network*, 22 Cal. App. 4th 853, 860 (2d Dist. 1994).

and another state that enforces reasonable Non-competition clauses, an employer will want to choose the law of the other state to protect its interests. Furthermore, as will be discussed in section 13.2, ensure that the court or courts, designated in the forum selection clause, will enforce the chosen law. A California court, for example, will refuse to enforce most Non-competition clauses in employment agreements because this type of restriction is contrary to the state's fundamental public policy.[15]

- *Model rules or the law of a neutral jurisdiction.* Sometimes parties are unwilling to stipulate the law of another party's local law, they might consider choosing model rules, such as the UNIDROIT Principles, or the law of another jurisdiction unconnected to either party. Be aware, however, that these choices can raise their own set of problems. If the model rules have not been sufficiently litigated and the law remains unsettled in its application, the parties should be reluctant to choose these rules. Choosing a neutral jurisdiction's law also can present problems. Even assuming that the law of the neutral jurisdiction is well-developed, a court might refuse to enforce the provision if the circumstances surrounding the contract (e.g., parties' domiciles, the signing of the contract, or contract performance) bear no connection to the neutral jurisdiction.[16]

♦ Opting out of or into the Convention on the International Sale of Goods (CISG).[17] The United States and most trading countries in the world are signatories to the CISG. With only limited exceptions,[18] the CISG governs the international sale of goods between parties whose two countries are signatories to the agreement. Under the Supremacy Clause of the U.S. Constitution, the CISG supersedes any state laws governing the contract, including any state-adopted UCC rules. Thus, if the parties from different signatory countries choose New York law, the CISG will automatically apply if the contract involves the international sale of certain goods. If the parties do not want the CISG to apply, they can "opt out" of the CISG by expressly stating this in the contract and, perhaps to avoid any ambiguity, state that New York's enacted UCC law will apply instead. Alternatively, the

---

15. *See supra* n. 12 and accompanying text.

16. *See, e.g., supra* nn. 9 & 10. *But see* N.Y. Gen. Oblig. L. 5-1401(1). New York, although following a modified version of section 187, is one of a few jurisdictions in the United States that has special conflicts of law statutes that will permit the use of its own law even though the parties or the contract lack a substantial relationship to New York so long as the transaction involves at least $250,000 and is not one of the expressly stated exceptions.

17. See Chapter 2, section 2.4.1.

18. *See* CISG art. 2 (not applicable to sales of goods for personal, family or household use; by auction; on execution of law; of investment securities; of ships, vessels, hovercraft or aircraft; or of electricity).

parties could choose governing law of a country that is not a signatory to the CISG. Thus, an American party and a German party might choose the laws of England to govern the contract.[19] Conversely, if the CISG does not automatically apply (e.g., one or both parties are from countries that are not signatories to the convention), the parties can opt in to the CISG. To do this, the parties must expressly state this in the contract. Of course, when deciding whether to opt out of or opt into the CISG, the parties should compare the advantages and disadvantages of using the CISG over other law.

♦ State what issues are subject to the governing law provision. In the United States courts differ as to whether stating "arising under" also includes other types of disputes, such as torts or disputes relating to other instruments that relate to the contract.[20] If the intent is to include non-contractual claims or other matters, including the relationship of the parties, you should use broad language to indicate this (e.g., "arising under or relating to this agreement").

> ⚖ *The* renvoi doctrine *provides that "a court resorting to foreign law adopts as well the foreign law's conflict-of-law principles," which could result in the forum court using the choice of law rules of the foreign state, the forum state, or another state.* Black's Law Dictionary *1412 (Bryan A. Garner, ed., 9th ed., West 2011).*

♦ As previously mentioned, a court will usually apply its own conflicts of law rules when determining whether to enforce a governing law clause. However, under the doctrine of *renvoi* (a French word meaning "sending back"), the court might apply the law of the chosen state's conflicts of law rules. The Restatement section 187 rejects applying *renvoi* to the issue of enforceability of the clause and will only apply the chosen law's conflicts of law rules if it is shown that the parties intended to do so.[21] If there is any question as to whether a court will apply *renvoi*, you should expressly state in the governing law clause that the chosen law's conflicts of law rules either will apply or will not apply, as the case may be.

♦ Because conflicts of law rules can vary from state to state and from country to country, it is important that the parties also decide on a forum where disputes will be litigated when they are choosing the governing law. You want to ensure that the selected forum will

---

19. At the time of this writing, England is not a signatory to CISG. But, again, you must ensure that the court or courts designated in the forum selection clause will enforce the parties' chosen law.

20. *See, e.g., Phillips v. Audio Active Ltd.*, 494 F.3d 378, 389 (N.Y. 2007).

21. Restatement § 187, cmt. h.

enforce the governing law clause. For example, a California court may refuse to enforce the parties' choice of New York law if enforcing that law will conflict with a fundamental public policy of California. Thus, if the dispute involves the enforceability of a Non-competition clause in an employment agreement, the court might reject New York law because California statutory law prohibits enforcing Non-competition clauses in these instances.[22]

The following is an example of a simple governing law provision.

> New York law governs this agreement and all matters arising under or relating to this agreement.

13.2 Forum selection clause

Subject matter jurisdiction means the power of a court to hear and decide a claim; jurisdiction depends on the nature of the claim and the amount or type of relief requested.

A forum selection clause is often grouped with a governing law clause in a contract. Although these two clauses bear a close relationship with each other, they serve different purposes. A forum selection clause designates the court or courts where a dispute will be heard and decided. In the United States, these clauses are generally enforceable if they are just and reasonable,[23] and, particularly in the case of consumer transactions, if they are conspicuously placed in the contract to give the non-drafting party notice of the provision.[24] Even if the clause is reasonable and sufficiently conspicuous under the law, you also must ensure that the designated court will have *subject matter jurisdiction* over the dispute.[25] In addition, choose a forum that will give effect to the governing law clause. Recall from the governing law discussion in 13.1 that a court usually will look at the conflicts of law rules of its own jurisdiction to determine whether a governing law clause is enforceable.

---

22. *See Frame v. Merrill Lynch, Pierce, Fenner & Smith, Inc.*, 97 Cal. Rptr. 811 (Cal. App. 1st Dist. 1971). *See also supra* n. 12.

23. *See M/S Bremen v. Zapata Off-shore Co.*, 407 U.S. 1, 12-13 (1972) (holding that "freely negotiated international agreement[s], unaffected by fraud, undue influence, or overweening bargaining power . . . should be given full effect.").

24. *Carnival Cruise Lines, Inc. v. Shute*, 499 U.S. 585, 596 (1991).

25. In the United States, a court must have jurisdiction over the parties as well as jurisdiction over the subject of the suit.

List of Drafting Guidelines

Considerations for drafting a forum selection clause include the following:

- Explicitly state that the parties consent to the jurisdiction of the chosen court.

- Clearly state what types of disputes are subject to the clause. Ideally, forum selection clauses should be drafted broadly to include not only those claims arising under the contract, such as claims for breach of an obligation, but also include matters relating to the contract, such as tort claims (e.g., "all disputes arising under or related to this agreement").[26] This will help prevent litigators from artfully drafting complaints in order to avoid application of the forum selection clause.

- State as specifically as possible the designated court or courts.

- State whether the forum selected is permissive or mandatory. In a permissive clause one or both parties consent to litigate in the designated court. Even so, a party is not required to bring a claim in the designated court. The purpose of a permissive clause is to stipulate the consenting party's voluntary submission to the jurisdiction of the designated court that might not otherwise have authority over that party. A permissive clause can be a problem when it comes to enforcing a governing law clause. A party could bring an action in another jurisdiction (other than the one consented to by the parties) where the court, applying its conflicts of law rules, could refuse to enforce the governing law clause. See the discussion in section 13.1.

  This problem could be avoided by using a mandatory clause, where the designated court has exclusive jurisdiction over the litigation. Thus the parties must litigate in the designated court. Here, you want to ensure that the designated court would enforce the governing law clause. When drafting a mandatory clause, explicitly state that the designated court has exclusive jurisdiction. Otherwise, a court may construe the clause to be merely permissive. Also, be mindful that statutes might void mandatory clauses in certain types of agreements. For example, mandatory forum selection clauses for litigation in franchise agreements are void under some state laws.[27]

- The designated forum should have some connection to the parties or performance to avoid objections based on unreasonableness or discouraging litigation because of the remote location.

---

26. *See, e.g., Phillips,* 494 F.3d at 389.

27. *See, e.g.,* Calif. Bus. & Prof. Code § 20040.5; 815 Ill. Comp. Stat. 705/4 § 4; Ind. Code § 23-2-2.7-1(10); Mich. Comp. Laws § 445.1527.

◆ The parties should expressly waive their right to challenge the jurisdiction of the chosen court on the basis of *forum non conveniens.* The doctrine of **forum non conveniens** permits courts—although having personal jurisdiction over the parties and subject matter jurisdiction over the dispute—to decline exercising jurisdiction over a case if it determines that another court is a more appropriate forum. The defendant may raise the issue of forum non conveniens on a motion to dismiss the case or motion to transfer the case, though courts in the United States can raise the issue on their own. To prevent a defendant from raising the argument, the forum selection clause should include a waiver of a jurisdictional challenge based on forum non conveniens.

◆ If there is a question about proper service on a party of a writ or summons to make an appearance in and response to a complaint, the forum selection clause should detail the process for service. The clause includes how service will be made and the identity of any agent authorized to receive service on behalf of a party.

The following is an example of a simple, mandatory forum selection clause.

A party shall bring any suit arising out of or relating to this agreement in the United States District Court for the Southern District of Florida, in Miami, Florida, or if that court lacks jurisdiction to hear the claim, then in a state court in Miami-Dade County, Florida. Each party consents to the exclusive jurisdiction and venue of those courts for any suit. Each party waives asserting a claim that any of those courts in which any suit has been brought is an inconvenient forum.

13.3 "Choice of language" clause

A *choice of language* clause is important when the parties speak different languages. The primary purpose of this clause is to identify the languages used for the contract and which language is controlling in the event of a discrepancy or dispute. When drafting this clause, consider the following:

List of Drafting Guidelines

◆ Identify the language that will control the contract and that will be used by courts, arbitrators, and others for interpreting the contract and resolving disputes. Ideally, the contract should only be drafted in one language to avoid any misunderstandings or ambiguities. Sometimes, though, to promote goodwill, the parties may insist drafting and signing the contract in more than one language. In this instance, the language clause should acknowledge all languages used for the contract but explicitly state which language version controls in the case of a discrepancy or dispute.

◆ If possible, the choice of language clause should also provide that the controlling language will be used in all communications and documents relating to the contract.

◆ In situations where the governing law is available in more than one language,[28] state the language version that will be used, preferably the same one chosen to control the contract.

The following is an example of a choice of language clause.

> This agreement is written in American English, which is the official language of this agreement. All communications and documents relating to this agreement will be written in American English. American English will control in any interpretation or dispute arising under this agreement or other writings between the parties.

13.4 Force majeure clause

When performance under the contract will take place over an extended period of time, the parties should consider including a *force majeure* clause. One of the clause's primary purposes is to state the events (*force majeure events*) that can excuse a party's inability to perform as promised under the contract. Another purpose of the clause is to allocate the risk of non-performance between the parties. Generally, a party's non-performance is excused if it is caused by a force majeure event as defined in the clause. In this situation, the other party bears the risk of loss resulting from the affected party's non-performance. Conversely, if a party's non-performance is not due to a force majeure event as defined in the clause, then that party will bear the risk of its own non-performance. Here, the non-performing party might pay damages to the other party for its breach of an obligation.[29] Therefore, defining the force majeure event is extremely important. The more narrowly defined the force majeure event, the greater the risk on the non-performing party. The more broadly defined the force majeure event, the greater the risk on the other party.

---

28. For example, the UNIDROIT Principles are available in English and French.
29. One way parties might be able to reduce their risk is to obtain insurance to cover these events.

Much has been written about drafting force majeure clauses in international contracts, and there can be significant differences in interpreting and enforcing these clauses depending on the law applied.[30] Therefore, you will want to research the governing law before drafting a force majeure clause to ensure that you draft language that gives effect to the intent of the parties and prevents the application of any unwanted default rules.[31]

When drafting a force majeure clause, consider the matters discussed in sections 13.4.1 to 13.4.9.

13.4.1 Defining the force majeure event

In the United States, some states have codified definitions of force majeure that can apply to a wide variety of contracts or to only special types of contracts.[32] Even in the case where force majeure is codified under the governing law, courts will still look to the definition provided by the parties in the contract. Courts tend to narrowly interpret force majeure clauses, so you must give particular attention to drafting the definition.

Drafting a definition of a force majeure event can prove challenging. Excusing a party's non-performance can adversely affect the other party's business and result in unexpected costs. Therefore, you will not want to draft the definition too broadly. At the same time, it is unrealistic to expect that the force majeure clause can be drafted to anticipate and address every possible event that could give rise to an excused performance.

List of Drafting Guidelines

The following are considerations for drafting the definition of a force majeure event.

♦ *A general statement serving as the definition.* To qualify as a force majeure event, the event should always be beyond the non-

---

30. *See generally* Jennifer M. Bund, *Force Majeure Clauses: Drafting Advice for the CISG Practitioner*, 17 J.L. & Com. 381(1998); Catherine Kessedjian, *Competing Approaches to Force Majeure and Hardship*, 25 Intl. Rev. L. & Econ. 415 (2005); Joseph Lookofsky, *Impediments and Hardship in International Sales: A Commentary on Catherine Kessedjian's "Competing Approaches to Force Majeure and Hardship"*, 25 Intl. Rev. L. & Econ. 434 (2005).

31. Default rules, such as physical impossibility, commercial impracticability, or frustration of purpose, might offer broader or narrower rights and remedies than the parties' desire for an event that hinders performance under the contract. Absent an enforceable force majeure clause, courts in the U.S. apply the common law rule of commercial impracticability, excusing a party for its non-performance if an unforeseen event not caused by that party prevents its performance and creates a significant burden on that party beyond what it had impliedly or expressly assumed in the contract. *See also* UCC § 2-615, recognizing the defense of impracticability in contracts for the sale of goods.

32. *See, e.g.,* Colo. Rev. Stat. § 43-1-1402; Hawii Rev. Stat. § 182-1; and Tex. Util. Code Ann. § 39.055.

performing party's ability to control. Sometimes a definition for force majeure also includes the requirement that the event must have been unforeseeable by the non-performing party at the time it signed the contract.[33] The rationale for including this requirement is that the parties would have addressed foreseeable contingencies in the contract and, by failing to do so, assumed the risk.[34] The problem with limiting force majeure to foreseeable events is the uncertainty of whether the court will make a broad or narrow inquiry into whether the event was foreseeable. Using a broad inquiry, many events could be considered foreseeable, while using a narrow inquiry into the specific causes of the event could lead to a conclusion that the event was unforeseeable.[35] To avoid the uncertainty of a court inquiry, consider excluding the requirement of foreseeability from the definition. One drafting scholar proposes to include the language "whether foreseen or unforeseen" to express the parties' intent to exclude foreseeability.[36]

Another consideration when drafting a general definition is whether to include a requirement that the party could have avoided non-performance resulting from the force majeure event through the exercise of due diligence. The following example incorporates the considerations discussed here, though exactly what will be included in the listed criteria will depend on the parties' negotiations.

"**Force Majeure Event**" means any occurrence after the parties' signing the contract that

(a) was foreseeable or unforeseeable by the parties at the time of signing the contract,
(b) is beyond the non-performing party's control,
(c) is beyond the non-performing party's ability to avert through its exercise of due diligence, and
(d) prevents or delays the non-performing party's performance under this agreement.

---

33. This "unforeseeability" requirement, if included, is undoubtedly influenced by a similar requirement found in the default rule of commercial impracticability (see *supra* n. 31), which courts might apply to excuse non-performance, absent an enforceable force majeure clause.

34. Wm. Cary Wright, *Force Majeure Clauses and the Insurability of Force Majeure Risks*, 23 Const. L. 16, 17 (2003).

35. *Id.*

36. Nancy M. Persechino, "Force Majeure" in *Negotiating and Drafting Contract Boilerplate*, *supra* n. 1, at 330.

♦ *A list serving as the definition.* Sometimes the definition for force majeure events does not include a general definition but merely lists the events. Most of the time, however, lists are not used as the sole definition but are used to provide examples for the general definition. When drafting a list of events, whether it serves as the sole definition for a force majeure event or serves only as an example of an event, give careful consideration to the unique environment (political, weather, etc.) where the respective parties are located. For example, a party located on an island that is seasonally hit by typhoons or hurricanes should be prepared for disruptions caused by these events and plan accordingly. In this instance, perhaps typhoons or hurricanes should not be listed as a force majeure event for this party.

Events listed are typically disastrous or extraordinarily disruptive and are always beyond the control of the non-performing party. The parties may also limit the list to events that are unforeseeable or could have been avoided by due diligence, or both.

Events that are commonly included are those caused by nature, armed conflicts, labor disputes, and government action. Sometimes you will want to be specific as possible. Take the example again of the party located on an island that experiences seasonal hurricanes or typhoons and thus should assume the risk for these events. You might want to specifically list the natural causes that will constitute a force majeure event rather than generally referring to "disasters caused by forces of nature." Of course, if you do elect to generally refer to natural causes, you can explicitly make an exception for hurricanes or typhoons (e.g., "disasters caused by forces of nature, except for hurricanes or typhoons").

Another general phrase often used in force majeure definitions is "acts of God." This phrase was probably influenced by *force majeure*, a French expression that translates into English as "a superior force."[37] "Acts of God" usually refers to events caused by natural forces, such as floods, tornadoes, hurricanes, typhoons, tsunamis, lightening, earthquakes, and storms. However, it is not uncommon to find "acts of God" listed in addition to a listing of specifically named natural forces (e.g., "hurricanes, tornadoes, and acts of God"). In this instance, the reference to *acts of God* perhaps is intended to serve as a catch-all for any natural occurrences not specifically listed. Additional general phrases might be used to avoid providing an exhaustive list (e.g., "acts of government," "legislative, judicial, or government action," "government order or regulation").[38] Nevertheless, if your

---

37. *Black's Law Dictionary* 718 (Bryan A. Garner, ed., 9th ed., West 2011).
38. *See* Marcel Fontaine & Filip de Ly, *Drafting International Contracts: An Analysis of Contract Clauses* 411 (Transnational Pub. 2006).

parties want particular events included in the definition, you should specifically list those events to avoid questions as to whether they were intended to be included.

The following is a list of events that could be expanded, modified, or limited depending on the nature of the contract and the parties' particular circumstances.

> "**Force Majeure Event**" means any earthquakes, fire, landslides, tsunamis, epidemics, quarantines, acts of war, revolutions, acts of terrorism (whether actual or threatened), strikes, lockouts, explosions, interruption of transportation, action of the government or public authority. . . .

◆ *Combining a general definition with a list.* Sometimes a general definition of a force majeure event is followed by a list of events. The challenge here is to be clear about whether the events listed will constitute force majeure events despite not meeting the general definition or whether they constitute examples of force majeure events if they satisfy the criteria stated in the general definition of force majeure. To clarify the intent, precisely draft the words or phrases that connect the list to the general definition.[39] The following is an example of a combined definition where the list provides examples of force majeure events only if they satisfy the criteria of the general definition.

> "**Force Majeure Event**" means any occurrence after the parties' signing the contract that
>
> (a) was foreseeable or unforeseeable by the parties at the time of signing the contract,
> (b) is beyond the non-performing party's control,
> (c) is beyond the non-performing party's ability to avert through its exercise of due diligence, and
> (d) prevents or delays the non-performing party's performance under this agreement.
>
> Force Majeure Event includes, but is not limited to, each of the following so long as it satisfies (a) through (d): [list the examples].

◆ *Specific exclusions from the definition.* Sometimes the parties want a broad definition for what constitutes a force majeure event. In these

---

39. *See id.* at 414-415.

instances, consider listing specific events that are excepted from the broad definition: "Despite the occurrences listed in the previous sentence, a Force Majeure Event excludes hurricanes and floods."

13.4.2 Exceptions to excusing non-performance

In light of the parties' particular circumstances and the nature of the transaction, consider whether exceptions should be made to the force majeure clause so that some performances are not excused. For example, the parties might not want performance under the monetary provisions excused.

13.4.3 Giving notice of the force majeure event

Designate a procedure for a party affected by the force majeure event to invoke the clause. Consider including (1) when notice must be given, (2) the method for giving notice, (3) what information must be included in a notice, and (4) what happens if the affected party fails to satisfy the notice requirements.

List of Drafting Guidelines

The following are considerations for drafting a procedure for giving notice:

♦ *Time limitations for giving notice.* Sometimes the non-performing party must give notice within a designated time period, though sometimes the consequences of the force majeure event could make this impossible to satisfy. Therefore, the clause might require notice "as soon as practicable" under the circumstances.

♦ *The method for giving notice.* The method of giving notice could be oral or written. The manner of delivery might also be included in the clause, though drafting this requirement too narrowly (e.g., limiting to telephone, email, or facsimile) could make delivery impossible if the force majeure event has disrupted communication lines.

♦ *Information to include in a notice.* The notice should identify the nature of the force majeure event and the expected duration of the event.

♦ *Consequences for failure to satisfy the notice requirements.* If the non-performing party fails to give timely notice, the clause might provide that the party will only be excused beginning at the time it actually complied with the notice requirements. In this event, the non-performing party might be liable to pay any damages incurred by the other party up to the time late notice was given. Alternatively, the consequence for failure to satisfy the requirement could be that the party will not be excused from its non-performance.

13.4.4 Giving proof of the force majeure event

Sometimes the non-performing party is required to provide evidence of a force majeure event. This might require certification of the event's occurrence by local, national, or international institutions, or perhaps a certification from an unbiased third party. If this evidence is required in addition to notice, consider providing a slightly longer time period for the affected party to provide evidence of the event as it will likely involve additional effort to obtain the required evidence.

13.4.5 Overcoming the force majeure event

During the time the force majeure clause is invoked, the non-performing party or perhaps both parties should be required to exercise reasonable efforts or due diligence to overcome the event as quickly as possible.

13.4.6 Update reports

Sometimes a party will want periodic updates from the non-performing party as to its progress in overcoming the event. In this instance, consider including a requirement of periodic reports, state the frequency of these reports, whether they should be written or oral, and what information should be included in the reports.

13.4.7 Notice of the end of a force majeure event

Designate a procedure giving notice of the end of a force majeure event, including when notice must be given and when performance will recommence.

13.4.8 Termination or renegotiation of the contract

Perhaps include the ability to terminate the agreement or at least renegotiate provisions adversely affected by the non-performance (e.g., product pricing) if the force majeure event continues for a long period of time. This provision should designate the period of time that must elapse before a party can exercise the power to terminate or renegotiate. State whether one party (typically, this is the party not affected by the event) or both parties can exercise the power. In the case of renegotiation, specify the process for renegotiation, such as informal negotiations or mediation.

13.4.9 Remedies

State whether the force majeure clause is the exclusive remedy for either or both parties. Reflect on the effect delay or suspension of the affected party's performance has on the other party. This is particularly important when timely performance is critical. The party not affected by a force majeure event must carefully consider the consequences of assuming the risk of the other party's non-performance. Should the party not affected by the event have the ability to reduce any incurred costs? For example, under a supply contract, the supplier has promised to timely deliver parts that will be used in the manufacturer's production of widgets. Thereafter, an earthquake (a force majeure event as defined in the supply contract) severely damages the supplier's factory. The supplier cannot provide the parts in time for the manufacturer to meet its commitment to ship widgets to a distributor by a promised delivery date. Should the manufacturer have the right to find another supplier? If so, then distributor's option to mitigate its expenses caused by the other party's non-performance should be included in the Force Majeure clause.

13.4.10 Example force majeure provision

A "**Force Majeure Event**" means [list circumstances relevant to the parties' deal].

If a party is unable to perform any obligation under this agreement due to a Force Majeure Event, the party is excused from any delay or failure to perform its obligations under this agreement during the duration of a Force Majeure Event so long as the party

(i) provides notice of the Force Majeure Event, including its nature and expected duration, as soon as practicable after it knows or should have known of the Force Majeure Event giving rise to or appearing likely to give rise to a delay or failure to perform its obligations, and

(ii) continues to use its best efforts to recommence performance to whatever extent possible without delay.

Notwithstanding the previous sentence, a Force Majeure Event will not excuse the parties' obligations under [cross-reference to sections that are not excused].

The non-performing party shall resume performance of its obligations under this agreement as soon as reasonably possible after termination of the excused Force Majeure Event and notify the other party of the termination of the event.

If the non-performing party's delay or suspension of performance due to a Force Majeure Event lasts more than [state time period], the other party may terminate this agreement by giving written notice to the non-performing party.

This section is the non-performing party's exclusive remedy for a Force Majeure Event.

13.5 Notice clause

During the term of the contract, the parties will be communicating with each other for purposes of administering the contract. More particularly, some contract provisions might require a party to give notice to the other party. Notices—whether for the purpose of making a request or a demand, or providing a waiver, a consent, or an approval—can be found in provisions throughout a contract. In a licensing contract, for example, the license owner might be required to give notice to the licensee that it is rejecting a product sample. In many contacts, it is a common exit provision to require that a non-breaching party give notice of a potential event of default to a breaching party, triggering a grace period during which the breaching party has an opportunity to cure the default. As another example, some contracts provide an election to extend the term of a contract, which usually requires the electing party to give notice of its intent to renew several days or weeks before the present term ends. Therefore, the purpose of a notice clause is to establish the method for communicating notices and stipulates when notice will be deemed received.

List of Drafting Guidelines

When drafting a notice clause, consider the following:

- Designate that all notices must be in writing. In addition, if the notice clause states it applies to all notices required under the contract, this will eliminate the need to cross-reference to this clause in the provisions requiring notice.

- State the parties' respective addresses, including a fax number if notice will be permitted through facsimile. If the notice must be delivered to the attention of a particular department or person associated with the party, also include this information. Sometimes a party might want a copy of the notice delivered to its agent, such as its attorney. In this case, include the agent's contact information in addition to the party's contact information and explicitly state that the agent will be receiving a copy.

- State that notices of changes in contact information should be given in the same manner provided for other notices.

- Specify the method(s) of notice delivery, which might include personal delivery, postal services, express or overnight delivery services, or facsimile.

- Designate when notice will be deemed received. This can vary depending on the method(s) used. Sometimes a party, especially if it anticipates that it will be giving the notices, will push for a designation that receipt is deemed upon dispatch. While this might avoid problems arising from a recipient purposely evading delivery or might steer clear of questions as to when notice was actually received, it creates other significant problems. Unanticipated intervening events could prevent actual delivery to the recipient. Also, deeming delivery upon dispatch will shorten any time period for performance triggered by a notice. For example, if notice triggers a 30-day period during which a breaching party can cure its default, the breaching party may not receive actual notice for several days. When they finally receive the notice, the time period for curing the default has already started running, thus giving it less actual time to cure the default. Therefore, the parties might consider designating that notice is given upon receipt. Of course, the problem with this designation is establishing proof of when notice was actually given to the recipient, and giving notice when the recipient is avoiding receipt. While the following suggestions are not perfect solutions to the receipt problem, they are workable compromises often used in notice provisions.

- *Personal delivery.* Personal delivery is one of the surest methods of actual receipt. Here, notice can be deemed received on the day and time it was personally given to the recipient. Of course, if the intended recipient is located a long distance away, the party giving notice may need to hire an agent to deliver notice. This can be costly, especially if the recipient purposely attempts to evade receiving notice, requiring repeated attempts at delivery.
- *Postal services.* The U.S. Postal Service offers delivery by certified or registered mail with a receipt to be signed by the recipient and returned to the sender together with a stamp of the delivery date. The problem with this service is that the recipient, or its designated agent, must be present to sign the receipt. The recipient might purposely evade signing the receipt or might be unavailable to do so, resulting in no delivery. The best way to resolve this problem is to designate a reasonable number of days from dispatch when notice will be deemed received. If designating days, consider using "business days," instead of "calendar days," so that receipt is not deemed given on a holiday or non-business day when the recipient may not be in the office or may not be able to respond to the notice. As discussed in Chapter 8, you will want to define "business days" to clarify its meaning.
- *Express and overnight delivery services.* Express and overnight services track the delivery process and record the date the item was received. While these services are considered highly reliable, problems can arise with an unexpected disruption of service or lost packages. Therefore, as in the case of postal services, consider designating a reasonable number of business days from dispatch when notice will be deemed received.

- *Facsimile.* Facsimile is a common method for business communications. Successful delivery of a document is typically confirmed on the sender's machine, but this is not a reliable means of confirmation. The recipient may not receive the faxed document due to mechanical problems with its machine. Therefore, it is common to designate receipt of notice one business day or 24 business hours after dispatch.
- *Email.* Although email is often used for less formal day-to-day business communications, it is not a recommended method for communicating notices. Unless a recipient confirms receipt of the email, it is difficult, if not impossible, to confirm actual delivery to the recipient.

The following is an example of a simple notice provision.

The parties shall send any notice or other communication required by this agreement in writing and by a nationally recognized express courier. Notices and communications will be sent

(a) to Supplier at the following address:
   [insert information], and
(b) to Distributor at the following address:
   [insert information].

Notices and communications will be deemed received [insert time period] after the day of dispatch. A party may change its address for notice at any time upon written notice to the other party as provided in this paragraph.

13.6 Assignment and delegation clauses

In bilateral contracts both parties have obligations to perform and both parties receive rights to the other party's performance. For example, Golden Properties enters into a contract with Under-the-Sea Company in which Under-the-Sea agrees to design, build, and install a large saltwater aquarium to be placed in the lobby of a Golden Properties' building. In return, Golden Properties promises to pay Under-the-Sea for its services upon completion of the work. Golden Properties receives the right to Under-the-Sea's obligation to design, build, and install the aquarium. Under-the-Sea receives the right to Golden Properties' obligation to pay for the work upon completion. When drafting the contract, the parties must decide whether one or both parties should have the power to transfer their rights and obligations under the contract.

> ⚖ *A transfer of contract involves the transfer of rights and delegation of obligations under a contract.*

An **assignment clause** states whether the parties have the power to *assign* their respective *rights* under the contract to a third party. A **delegation clause** states whether the parties have the power to *delegate* their respective *obligations* under the contract to a third party. Although drafters commonly group assignment and delegation clauses into the same paragraph or section, the following subsections discuss them separately for clarity.

13.6.1 Assignment clause

After signing a contract a party might desire at a later time to assign its rights under that contract to a third party. Assigning contract rights is common in the commercial world and occurs for a number of business reasons, including the sale of assets, mergers, and the collection of money claims. Therefore, a contract might include an assignment clause that permits the parties to assign their rights under the contract. If the assignment clause gives the parties an unrestricted power to assign their rights, then the assigning party does not need to get the non-assigning party's approval or permission before making an assignment.

Assigning contract rights is accomplished by an assignment, in which the **assignor** (the party desiring to assign its rights) *clearly expresses* its *intent to make a present transfer* of its rights to the **assignee** (a third party). To be enforceable, the assignment must be supported by *consideration*. For instance, let's say that the contract between Golden Properties and Under-the-Sea permits the parties to assign their respective rights under the contract. After signing the contract, Golden Properties sells the office building to Shady Management and Under-the-Sea is notified of the assignment. Under-the-Sea must now perform its work for Shady Management.

U.S. common law favors the freedom to assign contract rights.[40] Therefore, assignments of contract rights are permitted unless

   (a) the assignment would
   – materially change the non-assigning party's performance obligation, or
   – materially increase the non-assigning party's burden or risk, or
   – materially lessen the likelihood that the non-assigning party would receive from the assignee performance of the assigned obligations, or
   – materially reduce the value of the assigned performance to the non-assigning party, or

---

40. *See* Shannon D. Kung, *The Reverse Triangular Loophole and Enforcing Anti-assignment Clauses*, 103 Nw. U. L. Rev. 1037, 1043 (2009).

> (b) the assignment is prohibited by statute or violates public policy, or
>
> (c) the contract includes an **anti-assignment clause** expressly prohibiting or restricting assignments.[41]

Whether a court will find an assignment unenforceable under the criteria of (a) or (b) will heavily depend on governing law and the facts of the case (e.g., the circumstances of the parties and the nature of the transaction). Such a discussion is beyond the scope of this book.[42] This section focuses on (c) and drafting an anti-assignment clause to limit or restrict the assignment of contract rights.

Although it is not uncommon to find assignment clauses giving one party or both parties unrestricted power to assign contract rights, a party might not want the other party to have this unrestricted power for the reasons listed in (a) above. Returning to the assignment of Golden Properties' rights in the aquarium contract to Shady Management, let's say that Golden Properties only assigned its interest in the contract and did not delegate its obligation to pay for Under-the-Sea's work. Under-the-Sea might be concerned that Golden Properties will be less motivated to pay it because Golden Properties will not be receiving the benefit of its work, the aquarium. The attorney for Under-the-Sea should have anticipated this possibility when negotiating the contract with Golden Properties and should have insisted on including an anti-assignment clause in the contract.

An anti-assignment clause can restrict one party's or both parties' power to assign rights. The clause could absolutely prohibit assignment, though the parties might find this too restrictive. Therefore, parties may settle on a clause that permits an assignment if specifically stated conditions are satisfied.

List of Drafting Guidelines

Considerations for drafting an anti-assignment clause include the following:

♦ Research governing law to determine whether there are any restrictions on anti-assignment clauses. For example, because the right to payment of money is so important to the U.S. credit economy, UCC § 9-406(d)[43] renders anti-assignment clauses unenforceable in the case of assignments for rights to payment in certain instances.[44]

---

41. Restatement (Second) of Contracts § 317(2) (1981).

42. *See* Tina L. Stark, "Assignment and Delegation," in *Negotiating and Drafting Contract Boilerplate, supra* n. 1, at 54-78 (providing a detailed discussion on assignment and delegation clauses, including historical background).

43. UCC § 9-406(d) (2010).

44. "It is . . . important to commerce that rights to payment be freely assignable; the modern credit economy would have a difficult time functioning if rights to payment could not

♦ Explicitly state the parties' intent to prohibit an assignment of rights. If the clause merely states, "The parties shall not assign this agreement," a U.S. court will likely interpret this very narrowly to prohibit only the delegation of their duties.[45] Instead, clearly state that the party or parties are prohibited from assigning its or their rights:

Neither party shall assign its rights under this agreement.

♦ Designate whether one or both parties are prohibited from assigning their rights. For instance, a party with stronger bargaining power might retain an unrestricted right to assign its rights while insisting on an anti-assignment clause that absolutely prohibits the weaker party from assigning its rights. If only one party is prohibited from making an assignment, state the restriction but also explicitly state the discretionary power of the other party to make an assignment (Exhibit 2).

Example 1—both parties:
Neither party shall assign its rights under this agreement.

Example 2—one party:
Under-the-Sea shall not assign its rights under this agreement. Golden Properties may assign its rights under this agreement.

♦ Under U.S. law a general prohibition against assigning rights (as shown in the previous Examples 1 and 2), will not necessarily prohibit an involuntary assignment arising by operation of law.[46] Therefore, drafters should state as precisely as possible what types of involuntary assignments, if any, are prohibited (e.g., merger, consolidation, dissolution or, if a party is a natural person, bankruptcy or death).

---

be assigned. A seller of goods would be reluctant to sell goods on credit if the seller could not discount the right to be paid to a financing institution." Bryan D. Hull, *Harmonization of Rules Governing Assignments of Right to Payment*, 54 SMU L. Rev. 473, 479 (2001).

45. *See* Restatement (Second) of Contracts § 322(1) & UCC § 2-210(4).

46. "Transfers by operation of law are generally considered involuntary transfers. They include court-ordered property transfers, bankruptcy-related transfers, and transfers to or from an executor or an administrator. Whether mergers and consolidations are transfers by operation of law is an open question. The cases reach inconsistent results." Stark, *supra* n. 44, at 42-43 (footnotes omitted).

> Neither party shall assign, voluntarily or involuntary, its rights under this agreement, whether by contract, merger, consolidation, dissolution, by operation of law, or other means.

◆ If a party has the power to make an assignment under certain conditions, state those conditions. Because public policy favors the freedom to make assignments, a U.S. court will construe the conditions as narrowly as possible. Therefore, you will want to state the conditions as clearly and precisely as possible.

*An **affiliate** means an entity that (1) controls another entity (e.g., subsidiary); (2) is controlled by another entity (e.g., parent company); or (3) is related to another entity (e.g., sibling) because both are controlled by a parent company.*

One of the simplest ways to guard against an unwanted assignment is to require the prior consent of the non-assigning party (Example 1 below). In this instance, the parties might consider whether additional standards for withholding consent should be included. You will find in some precedent contracts that sometimes a non-assigning party is given "absolute discretion" to reject the proposed assignment. Other times, a non-assigning party cannot "unreasonably withhold its consent." Because these qualifiers can lead to disputes over interpretation, consider carefully the ramifications before adding these qualifiers to a consent provision. Research the governing law to determine how courts have dealt with these issues. You may find that it is more prudent to exclude a qualifier from the consent provision.

Nevertheless, a party might insist on more detailed conditions beyond mere consent. For example, a party might foresee that it could assign its rights to an affiliate (e.g., Example 2 below). The exact conditions triggering a power to make an assignment will depend on the parties' negotiations in light of their particular circumstances and the nature of the transaction.

Example 1:
Without the prior written consent of the other party, neither party shall assign, voluntarily or involuntary, its rights under this agreement, whether by contract, merger, consolidation, dissolution, by operation of law, or other means.

Example 2:
Neither party shall assign, voluntarily or involuntary, its rights under this agreement, whether by contract, merger, consolidation,

Continued

> dissolution, by operation of law, or other means. Despite the preceding sentence, either party may affect an assignment to a wholly owned subsidiary of that party upon obtaining the prior written consent of the other party.

♦ If a party violates the anti-assignment clause, explicitly state the consequences of the violation. If the clause does not include this statement and a party violates the clause, then a court is likely to treat the assignment as a breach of an obligation. In this event, the non-assigning party might be awarded damages but still must perform the contract with the assignee. To ensure against the possibility of this outcome, consider explicitly stating the consequences. Two possible consequences might be voiding the assignment or terminating the contract.

  • *Voiding the assignment.* The anti-assignment clause could be drafted so that any *attempted* assignment in violation of the clause is void. Or, instead of automatically voiding the attempted assignment, the clause could provide that the non-assigning party has the discretionary power to void the assignment.

Example 1—automatically void:
Neither party shall assign, voluntarily or involuntary, its rights under this agreement, whether by contract, merger, consolidation, dissolution, by operation of law, or other means. Any attempted assignment in violation of this paragraph will be void for all purposes.

Example 2—discretionary power to void:
Neither party shall assign, voluntarily or involuntary, its rights under this agreement, whether by contract, merger, consolidation, dissolution, by operation of law, or other means. If a party attempts to assign its rights under this agreement in violation of this paragraph, the other party may deem the attempted assignment void for all purposes.

  • *Terminating the contract.* The clause could be drafted so that a violation of the anti-assignment restriction results in the immediate termination of the contract. Alternatively, the non-assigning party could be given the discretionary power to terminate the contract. In either instance, however, make clear that termination is in addition to any other legal rights and remedies available to the non-assigning party for the other party's breach.

> ### Example 1—*automatically terminate:*
> Neither party shall assign, voluntarily or involuntary, its rights under this agreement, whether by contract, merger, consolidation, dissolution, by operation of law, or other means. If a party attempts to assign its rights under this agreement in violation of this paragraph, this agreement will terminate. Termination of this agreement does not limit the non-assigning party's right to pursue other legal rights and remedies.
>
> ### Example 2—*discretionary power to terminate:*
> Neither party shall assign, voluntarily or involuntary, its rights under this agreement, whether by contract, merger, consolidation, dissolution, by operation of law, or other means. If a party attempts to assign its rights under this agreement in violation of this paragraph, the other party may terminate this agreement. Termination of this agreement does not limit the non-assigning party's right to pursue other legal rights and remedies.

13.6.2 Delegation clause

U.S. courts favor freely delegating obligations, unless the obligations involve services that are personal in nature or the contract explicitly prohibits delegation. As to the first exception, there is no simple, straightforward rule for what constitutes personal services. Outside of the more obvious examples (e.g., employment contracts, consulting contracts, or performance contracts involving famous entertainment artists or sports stars), it is difficult to predict whether obligations in a contract will be deemed to be personal services and thus non-delegable.[47] Therefore, if a party does not want the other party to delegate its power to perform to a third party, it should insist on including an anti-delegation clause in the contract. For example, Golden Properties, having seen Under-the-Sea's previous work and being impressed with the superior craftsmanship of their aquariums, wants Under-the-Sea to design and build the saltwater aquarium for its building. If the contract did not expressly prohibit Under-the-Sea's delegation, Under-the-Sea could delegate its performance obligations to an unknown or unskilled third party. Although Under-the-Sea still would remain liable for the third party's performance under the contract and any breach, Golden Properties wants the services of Under-the-Sea. Furthermore, it does not want to spend time litigating whether the contract was one for non-delegable personal services. Therefore, Golden Properties will insist on including an anti-delegation

---

47. *See generally* Larry A. Dimatteo, *Depersonalization of Personal Service Contracts: The Search for a Modern Approach to Assignability,* 27 Akron L. Rev. 407 (1994) (discussing the difficulty of determining whether services are personal).

The party delegating its performance obligations would be discharged of its obligations only if the non-delegating party enters into a contract with the delegate, called a novation. *Under a* **novation**, *the non-delegating party agrees to discharge the delegating party's obligation in consideration for the delegate undertaking the performance obligations.*

clause in the contract. A well-drafted Anti-delegation clause will make clear that Under-the-Sea cannot delegate its performance.

Many contracts neglect to mention explicitly whether the parties can delegate their obligations. As previously discussed (in section 13.6.1), if a contract merely states "the parties shall not assign this agreement," a U.S. court will likely treat this as a prohibition against delegation. While courts tend to disfavor anti-assignment clauses, they do not bear the same prejudice against anti-delegation clauses.

List of Drafting Guidelines

When drafting the delegation clause, consider the following.

♦ As previously mentioned, delegation clauses are often grouped with assignment clauses in contracts. However, this does not mean that both clauses must permit transfer (see Example 1), or that both clauses must prohibit a transfer (see Example 2), or that both clauses must even share the same restrictions on transfer (see Example 3). Variations will depend on the parties' negotiations (see Example 4). The possibilities are too numerous to mention here.

> *Example 1—permit unrestricted transfer:*
> The parties may assign their respective rights and delegate their respective performance of obligations under this agreement.
>
> *Example 2—absolutely prohibit transfer:*
> Neither party shall assign, voluntarily or involuntary, its rights under this agreement, whether by contract, merger, consolidation, dissolution, by operation of law, or other means. Neither party shall delegate its performance under this agreement. Any attempted assignment or delegation in violation of this paragraph will be void for all purposes.
>
> *Example 3—restricted transfer:*
> Without the prior written consent of the other party, neither party shall assign, voluntarily or involuntary, its rights under this agreement, whether by contract, merger, consolidation, dissolution, by operation of law, or other means. Without the prior written consent of the other party, neither party shall delegate its performance

Continued

under this agreement. Any attempted assignment or delegation in violation of this paragraph will be void for all purposes.

Example 4—a variation:
The parties may assign their respective rights under this agreement. Neither party shall delegate its performance under this agreement, without the prior written consent of the other party. Any attempted delegation in violation of this paragraph will be void for all purposes.

♦ Designate whether one or both parties are prohibited from delegating their performance.

Example 1—both parties:
Neither party shall delegate its performance under this agreement.

Example 2—one party:
Under-the-Sea shall not delegate its performance under this agreement. Golden Properties may delegate its performance under this agreement.

♦ If a party has the power to make a delegation under certain conditions, state those condition(s) as clearly and precisely as possible. See the discussion for creating conditions for assigning rights in section 13.6.1, which is also applicable to delegation of performance.

Example 1:
Without the prior written consent of the other party, neither party shall delegate its performance under this agreement.

Example 2:
Neither party shall delegate its performance under this agreement. Despite the preceding sentence, either party may effect a delegation to a wholly-owned subsidiary of that party upon obtaining the prior written consent of the other party.

♦ If a party violates the anti-delegation clause, explicitly state the consequences of the violation. See the discussion on stating consequences for violating an anti-assignment clause in section 13.6.1, which is also applicable here.

> ***Example 1—automatically void:***
> Neither party shall delegate its performance under this agreement. Any attempted delegation in violation of this paragraph will be void for all purposes.
>
> ***Example 2—discretionary power to void:***
> Neither party shall delegate its performance under this agreement. If a party attempts to delegate its performance under this agreement in violation of this paragraph, the other party may deem the attempted delegation void for all purposes.
>
> ***Example 3—automatically terminate:***
> Neither party shall delegate its performance under this agreement. If a party attempts to delegate its performance under this agreement in violation of this paragraph, this agreement will terminate. Termination of this agreement does not limit the non-delegating party's right to pursue other legal rights and remedies.
>
> ***Example 4—discretionary power to terminate:***
> Neither party shall delegate its performance under this agreement. If a party attempts to delegate its performance under this agreement in violation of this paragraph, the other party may terminate this agreement. Termination does not limit the non-delegating party's right to pursue other legal rights and remedies.

13.7 Successors and assigns clause

A *successors and assigns* clause is closely related to assignment and delegation clauses. Typical general language for this clause is as follows.

> This agreement is binding upon, and inures to the benefit of, the parties and their respective successors and assigns.

Two main purposes suggested for including a successors and assigns clause in a contract governed by U.S. law are

(1) to bind a transferring party's successors and assigns to the terms of the contract; and

(2) to restate the common law by binding the non-transferring party to perform its obligations in favor of the assignee.[48]

---

48. *See* Tina L. Stark, "Successors and Assigns," in *Negotiating and Drafting Contract Boilerplate, supra* n. 1, at 84-86 (identifying and discussing five purposes for a successors and assigns clause.)

However, at least one drafting scholar recommends omitting successors and assigns clauses from all contracts, reasoning in part that the clause "serves no useful purpose" and is "confusing."[49]

As to the purpose stated in (1) above, a contract containing a successors and assigns clause arguably cannot bind a third party to perform a contracting party's obligations because that third party is not a party to the contract. To bind a third party to perform a contract party's obligations, the third party must agree to do so *when it assumes the obligations*.[50] Regarding the purpose stated in (2) above, merely restating common law in this instance is arguably unnecessary: "If a party is permitted to assign its rights under a contract, it's obvious that the nonassigning party must perform in favor of the assignee—otherwise, being able to assign your rights would be of no value."[51]

The authors of this book agree with these arguments and thus recommend omitting successors and assigns clauses from U.S. contracts. Nevertheless, you might decide to include the clause in your draft if you believe it serves a valid purpose under the contract's governing law.

List of Drafting Guidelines

When drafting or deciding whether to include a successors and assigns clause, consider the following:

♦ If both parties are not permitted to assign their rights or delegate their obligations, then omit the successors and assigns clause from the contract. If you include the successors and assigns clause, it will conflict with the anti-assignment and anti-delegation clauses. U.S. public policy favors the freedom to assign rights and delegate obligations. Therefore, a U.S. court might give preference to the successors and assigns clause and find that the parties have the power to transfer their interests to third parties, despite the anti-assignment or anti-delegation clauses.

♦ If you include a successors and assigns clause, ensure that the successors and assigns clause does not conflict with the assignment or delegation clauses. When an assignment or delegation clause requires the satisfaction of certain stated conditions before a party can make an assignment or delegation, the successors and assigns clause should reflect these restrictions. In this event, insert the word *permitted* to modify the phrase *successors and assigns* in the successors and assigns clause. Also, in an abundance of caution,

---

49. Kenneth A. Adams, Adams Drafting Blog, *Getting Rid of the "Successors and Assigns" Provision*, http://www.adamsdrafting.com/2006/09/18/successors-and-assigns/ (Sept. 18, 2006) (responding and rejecting the purposes raised by Stark; *see supra* n. 48).
50. *Id.*
51. *Id.*

cross-reference to the assignment and delegation provisions to communicate the parties' intent that the successors and assigns clause is not to be used to determine the scope of the parties' power to make assignments or delegations.[52]

> This agreement is binding upon and inures to the benefit of the parties and their respective permitted successors and assigns. This provision does not address, directly or indirectly, whether the parties can assign their rights or delegate their obligations under this agreement. Sections xx and xx address these matters.

♦ The term *successors* usually refers to entities that, through consolidation or assumption of interest, have acquired the rights and assumed the obligations of the previous entity (the party to the contract containing the successors and assigns clause). *Successors* is not commonly applied to natural persons. If a natural person and an entity are the contracting parties, add "heirs, legal representatives, executors, and administrators" to the list of the successors and assigns clause.

> This agreement is binding upon and inures to the benefit of the parties and their respective heirs, legal representatives, executors, and [permitted] successors and assigns. This provision does not address, directly or indirectly, whether the parties can assign their rights or delegate their obligations under this agreement. Sections xx and xx address these matters.

If all parties are natural persons, then replace "successors" with "heirs, legal representatives, executors, administrators, and assigns."

> This agreement is binding upon and inures to the benefit of the parties and their respective heirs, legal representatives, executors, and [permitted] assigns. This provision does not address, directly or indirectly, whether the parties can assign their rights or delegate their obligations under this agreement. Sections xx and xx address these matters.

---

52. *See, generally, supra* n. 48, at 91-92.

13.8 Merger clause ·

In a merger clause (also called an *integration* clause or an *entire agreement* clause), the parties acknowledge that the written contract expresses their complete, exclusive, and final agreement and takes the place of all previous negotiations, communications, and agreements. The consequence of this statement isn't felt unless a dispute over the contract later arises. The intent of a merger clause is to bar a party in a contract dispute from admitting any oral statements or writings made prior to signing the contract and any oral statements made when signing the contract. Why would contracting parties want this? They are usually concerned about communications or drafts made during the sometimes hurried "give and take" of negotiations and last minute deal changes leading up to the final agreement. They might also be concerned about casual statements made when the contract is being signed. Because the written contract is the complete, exclusive testament to their final agreement, they do not want irrelevant information (anything predating the contract or oral statements when signing the contract) to contradict the contract.

A merger clause invokes the *parol evidence rule*, a common law rule recognized in the United States. Many other countries, however, do not recognize the rule.[53] Even though the parol evidence rule includes the word "evidence," it is not a rule of evidence. Rather, the parol evidence rule (PER) is a substantive rule used to interpret a written contract. Therefore, whether PER is applied will depend on the governing law of the contract. If a state law in the United States is the governing law of the contract, PER might be applied to limit the admissibility of some evidence.

Parol comes from the French word meaning *oral*, though PER affects both oral and written evidence. For the purposes of PER, **parol evidence** refers to oral statements or writings made prior to the signing of a contract, as well as oral statements made at the time the contract was signed. There are variations of PER. Generally in U.S. versions, PER applies in the following circumstances:

1. *Complete, exclusive, and final agreements.* If the written contract was intended by the parties to be and, in fact, is a complete, exclusive, and final expression of their agreement (a *fully integrated agreement*), then

---

53. *See, generally,* "CISG-AC Opinion no. 3, Parol Evidence Rule, Plain Meaning Rule, Contractual Merger Clause and the CISG," October 23, 2004, (Rapporteur: Professor Richard Hyland, Rutgers Law School, Camden, NJ, USA), 17 Pace Intl. L. Rev. 61, 66 (2005) (noting that France does not recognize the parol evidence rule in merchant contracts, and many other civil law jurisdictions have no parol evidence rule, citing Germany, Japan, and Scandinavian countries as examples).

parol evidence cannot be admitted to contradict, supplement, or explain anything in the contract. *The merger clause is intended to evidence the parties' intent that the contract is a fully integrated agreement. But, the mere presence of a merger clause in a contract does not necessarily guarantee that the court will find the contract fully integrated and apply PER.*

2. *Partially complete and final agreements.*

    a. *Disputed contract term is completely, exclusively, and finally expressed.* If the disputed contract term is completely, exclusively, and finally expressed in a partially integrated written contract, then parol evidence cannot be admitted to contradict, supplement, or explain the disputed term.

    b. *Disputed contract term is missing or incomplete.* If a disputed contract term is found to be missing, or is unclear or ambiguous, then parol evidence can be admitted to supplement or explain the term *to the extent the evidence is consistent with other terms in the contract.* But, even then, the admitted parol evidence will only be recognized as part of the contract *if the "consistent" evidence is found to be believable.*

While PER is intended to bar irrelevant evidence, its application can create harsh results, especially if a party acted dishonestly. Therefore, courts will not apply PER and will permit parol evidence to support a claim to invalidate a contract for reasons such as fraud, duress, and mistake.[54]

In the United States, merger clauses are customarily included in commercial contracts, and U.S. attorneys will likely expect and want a merger clause in international commercial agreements. U.S. courts will enforce a merger clause and apply the PER rule if the clause clearly states—and the court finds—that the contract is the complete, exclusive, and final expression of the parties' agreement.

The presence of a merger clause in a contract supports a showing that the parties intended to create a fully integrated contract, but the absence of a merger clause does not prevent a court from still applying PER. Even if a contract does not include a merger clause, a U.S. court may still apply PER if the conditions of PER are satisfied. PER is also recognized under the UCC.[55] Therefore, PER also applies to contracts for the sale of goods, unless the court finds the UCC supplanted by the CISG, which does not recognize PER.[56]

---

54. *See generally* Brian A. Blum, *Contracts Examples and Explanations* 347-383 (4th ed., Wolters Kluwer 2007), for a particularly well-articulated discussion of PER.

55. UCC § 2-202.

56. *See supra* n. 55, at 68-72.

List of Drafting Guidelines

When drafting a merger clause, consider the following:

♦ The governing law of the contract and the forum that will be deciding the issue. Ensure that the governing law recognizes PER and, if so, when PER will be applied. Be careful if you are using U.S. state contract law where the CISG might apply. (See the discussion in section 13.1.) If the CISG supplants state law, you might consider opting out of the entire CISG or at least expressly state that the parol evidence rule of the state will apply.

♦ As is the case with other contract provisions, there are no "magic words" that will guarantee the application of PER. Nevertheless, you should try to convey as clearly as possible that the parties intend for the contract to be a fully integrated agreement.

♦ If the parties have other agreements related to the same transaction, then consider specifically mentioning them in the merger clause as part of the complete, exclusive, and final agreement between the parties. Therefore, in a loan agreement, the borrower may also be signing a promissory note. Both contracts should reference the other document in the merger clause to clarify that neither one is superseded by the other.

The following is an example of a simple merger clause.

This agreement and all attached exhibits and schedules constitute

(a) the complete, exclusive, and final agreement between the parties, and
(b) supersede all prior proposals, negotiations, representations, warranties, commitments, agreements, or other communications, whether written or oral, between the parties

with respect to the subject matter of this agreement.

13.9 "No oral modification" and "no oral waiver" clauses

After a contract has been signed, the parties might want to add, cancel, or change the contract provisions. A "no oral modification" (NOM) clause provides that any modifications to the contract must be in writing. Be aware, however, that a party making an oral statement modifying a contract can be barred from invoking the NOM clause if the other party reasonably relied on the oral statement and acted to its detriment.[57] Also, U.S. courts generally find that parties can amend a NOM clause either by their conduct or by oral agreement. In these instances, a court's reasoning for finding a modification despite a NOM clause is based in the parties' freedom to contract, which includes changing their minds about the relationship even after signing the contract.

A modification usually requires the mutual consent of both contracting parties. But a waiver is often just *one party's* intent to depart from the terms of the contract. By giving a waiver, a party is either (1) surrendering its right to exercise remedies for the other party's breach or (2) excusing the nonoccurrence or delay of a condition precedent to performing its obligation.[58] A "no oral waiver" clause provides that waivers must be in writing. Unfortunately, similar to a NOM clause, a court can find a party waived a No Oral Waiver clause either through its conduct or through oral statements.

So why include NOM and no oral waiver clauses in a contract if the parties are able to amend or waive them? At the very least, these clauses provide an organized process for making changes. A party that has various departments and personnel dealing with the day-to-day performance of the contract can avoid confusion and discrepancies by requiring written records of any changes. Further, the NOM and No Oral Waiver clauses can specify who is authorized to make these changes. Designating authorized persons to make changes on behalf of a party gives the other party greater assurance that the changes are effective and can reduce the risk of a dispute arising from alleged changes made by non-designated agents. Finally, if a party can show that it always handled modifications and waivers by the procedures stated in the clauses, it could lend support to a defense against an alleged non-written change.

List of Drafting Guidelines

When drafting a NOM clause, consider the following:

♦ Expressly state that parties can modify the contract only in writing.

♦ Consider identifying the persons authorized to sign the modification on behalf of each party. If authorization by a group within the party's organization, such as a board of directors, is required, then state that the party will deliver a certified copy of the group's authorization to

---

57. Based on principles of fairness, estoppel theories of promissory estoppel or equitable estoppel are used by courts to enforce oral modifications despite the presence of a NOM clause in a contract. *See, generally,* Brian A. Haskel, "Amendment and Waiver," in *Negotiating and Drafting Contract Boilerplate, supra* n. 1, at 513-514.

58. E. Allan Farnsworth, *Contracts* § 8.5, at 561 (3d ed., Aspen 1998). *See also* 2 R. Anderson, Uniform Commercial Code § 2-209:7, at 319 (3d ed. 1982), *quoted in* Kerry L. Bundy & Scott H. Ikeda, "How Waiver, Modification and Estoppel May Modify Franchise Relationships," 30 Fran. L.J. 3, 4 (2010).

the other party as a condition precedent to giving effect to the amendment.

♦ Determine whether governing law imposes requirements or restrictions on the amendment process and incorporate any requirements or restrictions into the NOM clause. For example, Delaware statutory law[59] prohibits amendments to merger contracts after shareholders of a party have approved the original contract if the amendments adversely affect the value of the consideration received or otherwise adversely affect the shareholder's interests.[60]

The following is an example of a simple NOM clause.

> The parties may modify this agreement only if the modification is in writing and signed by the presidents of both parties.

List of Drafting Guidelines

When drafting a no oral waiver clause, consider the following.

♦ Expressly state that the waiver of any provision in the contract can only be made in a writing signed by the waiving party.

♦ Similar to modifications, consider identifying the persons authorized to sign the waiver on behalf of the waiving party.

♦ Limit application of the waiver to the present occurrence.

♦ Include a statement that the party's conduct or course of dealing will not constitute a waiver.[61]

The following is an example of a no oral waiver clause.

> The parties may waive a provision in this agreement only if the waiver is in writing and signed by the president of the party against whom the waiver is sought to be enforced. A waiver on any one occasion is not to be construed as a waiver of any right, remedy, or condition on any future occasion, unless expressly stated in the signed waiver. No failure or delay by any party (i) to exercise any right or remedy, or (ii) to require satisfaction of any condition,

Continued

---

59. Del. Code tit. 8, § 251(d).

60. *See supra* n. 59, at 530-531 (discussing the amendment process and providing suggested language for the NOM clause to reflect this process).

61. Related language in the example no oral waiver clause in this discussion is based on model language found in *supra* n. 59, at 530-532.

> and no course of dealing between the parties will operate as a
> waiver or estoppel of any right, remedy, or condition.

13.10 Severability clause

Sometimes, despite your best efforts to draft a clear and enforceable contract, changes in laws, regulations, or public policies can result in unenforceable provisions. When a provision is found to be unenforceable, the question
becomes whether the entire contract is void or whether the offending
provision can be severed from the contract, leaving the remaining provisions
in effect. In determining whether a provision is severable, U.S. courts will
weigh several factors, including the intent of the parties as expressly stated
in the contract, as well as the terms, nature and purpose of the contract.[62]
The purpose of a severability clause is to express the parties' intent as to what
should happen if a provision is found to be unenforceable.

List of Drafting Guidelines

When drafting a severability clause, consider the following:

◆ A statement deleting the offending provision or declaring the entire
  contract unenforceable. A severability clause typically expresses the
  parties' intent to delete the offending provision from the rest of the
  contract (as opposed to declaring the entire contract unenforceable)
  while keeping the remainder of the contract intact (Example 1).
  Alternatively, the parties could declare the entire contract automatically unenforceable (Example 2).

> *Example 1:*
> If any provision in this agreement is declared to be unenforceable
> by a court of competent jurisdiction, that provision is deemed sev-
> ered and the other provisions in this agreement will remain in
> effect.
>
> *Example 2:*
> If any provision in this agreement is declared to be unenforceable
> by a court of competent jurisdiction, then this entire agreement is
> unenforceable against either party.

---

62. *See, e.g., In re United Airlines,* 453 F.3d 463 (7th Cir. 2006); *Sonoma Falls Dev., LLC v.
Nevada Gold & Casinos, Inc.,* 272 F. Supp. 2d 919 (N.D. Cal. 2003); *Municipal Capital
Appreciation Partners, I, L.P. v. Page,* 181 F. Supp. 2d 379 (S.D.N.Y. 2002).

The problem with Example 1 is that it doesn't address what happens if the offending provision is an essential part of the contract or whether any attempt should be made to try to replace the offending provision. These issues are addressed in the following considerations.

♦ If the parties want to attempt to salvage or replace the offending provision, the severability clause should include a statement to this effect. Parties might want to negotiate a replacement provision, or they might want the court to attempt to salvage or replace the provision.

• *A court is given the power to salvage or replace the unenforceable provision.* The extent of a court's power to fix an unenforceable provision is mandated by state statute or common law. States differ in their approaches to dealing with the problem of a partially invalid contract. The three most common approaches are

(1) strike the entire clause, even if only part of that clause is invalid,

(2) delete the invalid words from the clause and enforce the rest to the extent it makes grammatical sense (commonly referred to as the *blue pencil doctrine*), or

(3) delete the invalid words and replace with reasonable terms under the circumstances (the *reasonable replacement approach*).[63]

If governing law allows a court to salvage the offending provision under either the blue pencil doctrine or the reasonable replacement approach, then the parties could include a statement that reflects the court's power to do this. The statement, however, must reflect governing law. For example, a severability clause cannot extend a court's power beyond what is mandated by law. Thus, a severability clause cannot give a court the power to carry out a reasonable replacement approach if it is in a jurisdiction that follows the blue pencil doctrine. The following language, for example, might be used in a jurisdiction that follows the reasonable replacement approach.

> If any provision in this agreement is declared to be unenforceable by a court of competent jurisdiction, that provision is deemed severed and the other provisions in this agreement will remain in effect. Notwithstanding the previous sentence, the court can reform the unenforceable provision to the minimum extent necessary to render the provision enforceable according to its original business purpose.

---

63. *See also* the discussion in Chapter 2 for the application of these approaches to a non-competition clause.

• *The parties negotiate a substitute provision.* As an alternative to asking a court to resolve the problem or as a first step before giving it to a court for resolution, the parties might want to attempt to negotiate a solution. Permitting the parties to negotiate an enforceable provision is a good option because it keeps the resolution in the control of the parties. However, if the parties are already involved in a legal dispute over the language, they might not be able to reach a satisfactory resolution on their own. Nevertheless, some parties prefer to include this provision as a first step toward resolution, with the second step being to give it to the court if the parties are unable to reach a satisfactory result. The following example expresses this intent. The statement regarding the court's power to resolve, in the event the parties cannot reach agreement, is drafted for a court in a jurisdiction that follows the reasonable replacement approach.

If any provision in this agreement is declared to be unenforceable by a court of competent jurisdiction, that provision is deemed severed and the other provisions in this agreement will remain in effect. Notwithstanding the previous sentence, the parties shall negotiate in good faith a substitute provision that to the extent possible is

   (1) enforceable, and

   (2) accomplishes the original business purpose of the unenforceable provision.

In the event the parties are unable to agree to a mutually satisfactory substitute provision, then the court can reform the invalid or unenforceable provision to the minimum extent necessary to render the provision enforceable according to its original business purpose.

♦ If the unenforceable provision is an *essential term*, the parties should consider whether the entire contract should be declared unenforceable. The problem here is that it could prove difficult to precisely define an essential provision. Imprecise wording creates fertile ground for litigation on this issue. The solution might be to specifically list the provisions that are essential. But problems could arise here, as well. While at the time of contracting the parties might readily identify some provisions that are essential to the contract, the essential nature of other provisions might not be apparent until the dispute actually arises. Thus, there's the risk of overlooking an essential provision. The parties need to weigh the strengths and weaknesses of each approach before deciding whether to reference essential provisions with more specificity. The following is an example that provides a little more guidance than merely stating *essential provisions* but does not go to the extreme of identifying particular provisions as *essential*. Language like this would be added, as appropriate, to the other provisions drafted in the severability clause.

> If the unenforceable provision is of such essential importance to the parties' agreement that the parties would not have contracted this agreement without those provisions, then this entire agreement is unenforceable against either party.

13.11 Counterparts clause

Parties, especially in cross-border contracts, are often not in the same location when signing a contract. Sometimes each party will sign a copy of the contract and deliver the signed contract to the other party with no party receiving a contract containing a page signed by all parties. It is common to include in U.S. contracts a *counterparts* clause in these circumstances. The clause permits each party to treat as a completely executed original contract the delivered copy executed by the other party.

List of Drafting Guidelines

When drafting a counterparts clause, consider including the following:

- State that each delivered counterpart signed by the other party will serve as a completed executed original.

- Clarify that all originals are the same instrument so that there is no question that the parties are bound to only one agreement.

- If permissible under the governing law, state that facsimile signature can serve as original signatures.

The following is an example of a counterparts clause.

> The parties may execute this agreement in two counterparts, each of which when executed and delivered to the other party will be deemed a completely executed original. All executed and delivered originals taken together will constitute a single agreement as if both parties had executed the same document. Signatures received by facsimile are deemed original signatures.

Exercises

▶ Exercise 13-1   Revise and draft a force majeure clause

Review the word list you prepared in Exercise 3-2. If you have not done Exercise 3-2, do so now.

Then, review the following force majeure clauses. Based on the discussion in this chapter, list the strengths and weaknesses of each provision.

Take one of the examples and revise, using clear and concise language and sentence structure.

Example 1:

> **24. Force Majeure.**
> (a) Neither Manufacturer nor Distributor shall be liable in damages, or shall be subject to termination of this Agreement by the other party, for any delay or default in performing any obligation hereunder if that delay or default is due to any cause beyond the reasonable control and without fault or negligence of that party; provided that, in order to excuse its delay or default hereunder, a party shall notify the other of the occurrence or the cause, specifying the nature and particulars thereof and the expected duration thereof and provided, further, that within fifteen (15) calendar days after the termination of such occurrence or cause, such party shall give notice to the other party specifying the date of termination thereof. All obligations of both parties shall return to being in full force and effect upon the termination of such occurrence or cause (including without limitation any payments which became due and payable hereunder prior to the termination of such occurrence or cause).
> (b) For the purposes of this Section 24, a "cause beyond the reasonable control" of a party shall include, without limiting the generality of the phrase, any act of God, act of any government or other authority or statutory undertaking, industrial dispute, fire, explosion, accident, power failure, flood, riot or war (declared or undeclared). [DA#8]

Example 2:

> 15.1 Force Majeure. Neither party will be liable for, or be considered to be in breach of or default under this Agreement on account of, any delay or failure to perform as required by this Agreement (other than for payments owed) as a result of any cause or condition beyond such party's reasonable control. [DA#36]

Example 3:

> 17.13 Force Majeure. Neither Party shall be liable for failure to perform or delay in performing any obligation under this Agreement, except the obligation to make payments when due, if such failure or delay is due to force majeure, including, but not limited to, war, embargo, riot, insurrection, sabotage or other civil unrest; fire, explosion, flood or other natural disaster; accident or breakdown

Continued

of machinery; unavailability of fuel, labor, containers, or transportation facilities; accidents of navigation, breakdown or damage of vessels or other conveyances for air, land or sea; other impediments or hindrances to transportation; strike or other labor disturbances; government restraints or any other cause beyond the control of the affected party; provided, however, that the Party so failing to perform shall (i) as soon as possible, inform the other Party of the occurrence of the circumstances preventing or delaying the performance of its obligations, and describe at a reasonable level of detail the circumstances causing such delay, and (ii) exert reasonable efforts to eliminate, cure or overcome any of such cases and to resume performance of its covenants with all possible speed. In such event, the non-performing Party will be excused from any further performance or observance of the obligation(s) so affected for as long as such circumstances prevail and such Party continues to use its best efforts to recommence performance or observance whenever and to whatever extent possible without delay. In the event that, by operation of law or governmental decree, it becomes illegal to market and sell a Product in the Territory, Distributor shall be relieved of its obligations under this Agreement (other than the obligation to make any payment due hereunder) only to the extent that they relate to such Product. Any Party so delayed in its performance will be under no liability for loss or damages suffered by the other Party thereby. Either Party may convene a meeting between the Parties to discuss the force majeure and its effect on any obligation under this Agreement. The Parties shall seek to modify the relevant provisions in order to accommodate the circumstances caused by the force majeure. If the Parties fail to agree on such modifications within thirty (30) calendar days after notice of the force majeure is delivered, either Party may terminate this Agreement by written notice to the other Party. Such termination shall be effective thirty (30) calendar days after the date of the written notice. [DA#27]

Example 4:

9.2 Force Majeure. Fires, floods, wars, acts of war, strikes, lockouts, labor disputes, accidents to machinery, delays or defaults of common carriers, orders, decrees or judgments of any court, or any other contingency beyond the control of the Company or the Distributor, whether related or unrelated, or similar or dissimilar to any of the foregoing, will be sufficient excuse for any resulting delay or failure in the performance by either party hereto of its respective obligations under the Agreement, but such performance will be excused only as long as the force majeure continues. [DA#29]

▶ **Exercise 13-2   Compare force majeure clauses**

Find force majeure clauses in the Consulting Agreement contracts collection on the website (www.aspenlawschool.com/books/Adams). Before you look up these clauses, think about potential force majeure situations in a consulting situation. Why might there be a need for force majeure clauses in consulting agreements?

▶ **Exercise 13-3   Questions**

1. Imagine several of the situations of a force majeure clause.
How might the phrase *prompt delivery* differ in meaning depending on the situation?

> Supplier shall, however, promptly make the delivery, at the agreed price, when any such cause or causes interfering with delivery shall have been removed. [DA#18]

2. Look at how the word *material* is used across several force majeure provisions. Do you see any problems with the expression *material covenant* in the provision below?

> However, if a force majeure event prevents a party's performance of a material covenant set forth herein, the other party can immediately terminate this Agreement. [DA#16]

3. What are the effects of the clause below, which follows a standard force majeure clause (referred to in this excerpt from DA#1 as *Article*)?

> The provisions of this Article shall not be applicable to any obligation involving the payment of money. [DA#1]

▶ **Exercise 13-4   Comparing and drafting notice provisions**

Compare the notice provisions below and compose a revised single version.

1. Which of the *effective* choices would you select for your rewrite: *effective on receipt* or *effective on dispatch*? Why?
2. Why don't the two versions include notice by email?

15.3 Notice. Notices or consents under this Agreement will be in writing and delivered personally or, if mailed, will be sent certified mail, return receipt requested, or by telex or facsimile or overnight express service, if addressed to the recipient's address set forth on the signature page of this Agreement, or in either case to such other address as may be established by notice to the other party. Notice will be effective only upon actual receipt. [DA#36]

1. Notice or Communication. Any notice or communication required or permitted hereunder (other than Administrative Notice) shall be in writing and shall be sent by registered mail, return receipt requested, postage prepaid and addressed to the addresses set forth below or to such changed address as any party entitled to notice shall have communicated in writing to the other party. Notices and communications to Company shall be sent to:

If to Go-Go:
   Go-Go Bike Company, Inc.
   1024 West Boulevard
   Oak Park, Illinois 60301 USA
   Attention: Legal Department

If to Tong:

   Tong Corp.
   10th Floor, 108
   Ming Sheng West Road
   Taipei, Taiwan
   Attention: Legal Department[64]

Notices and communications to Distributor shall be sent to address shown on first page of this Agreement. Any notices or communications to either party hereunder shall be deemed to have been given when deposited in the mail, addressed to the then current address of such party. [DA#17]

---

64. Taken from Figure 3-5 in Chapter 3.

Follow-up:

Go to contract DA#17 in the collection of distribution agreements on the website (www.aspenlawschool.com/books/Adams) and find the definition for *Administrative Notice*.

▶ **Exercise 13-5   Governing law provisions and forum selection clauses**

Below, you can see two governing law/forum selection clauses that specify the law of the state of California, one from a distribution contract and the other from a consulting contract.

List the differences between the two clauses.

---

12. Governing Law, Disagreements & Arbitration.
(a) This Agreement shall in all respects be interpreted, construed in accordance with and governed by the internal laws of the State of California, without regard to its conflict of law rules. The parties specifically exclude the application of the 1980 United Nations Convention on Contracts for the International Sale of Goods, if otherwise applicable. The place of making and the place of performance of this Agreement shall for all purposes be San Jose, California, regardless of the actual place of execution or performance. In the event of any litigation between the parties, the parties agree that the sole and exclusive venue and jurisdiction for any such action shall be in the state or federal courts situated in the County of Santa Clara, California. The parties agree that the above referenced courts shall have personal and exclusive jurisdiction over the parties for any dispute arising out of this Agreement that is not covered by the arbitration provisions set forth herein below. [DA#28]

Governing Law: This Consulting Agreement is to be construed and enforced according to the laws of the State of California. This Consulting Agreement shall not be construed more strictly against one party than the other, merely by virtue of the fact that it may have been prepared by counsel for one of the parties, it being recognized that both Company and Consultant have contributed substantially and materially to the negotiation and preparation of this Consulting Agreement.

Venue: Venue in any action arising from this Consulting Agreement shall be in Orange County, California. [CA#21]

▶ **Exercise 13-6   Questions**

1. In the clause below, would the insertion of a comma before *which* change the meaning of the governing law clause? Explain your answer.

> Governing Law. This Agreement (and any other documents referred
> to herein) shall in all respects be interpreted, enforced and gov-
> erned by and under the laws of the United States and the State of
> California applicable to instruments, persons and transactions
> which have legal contacts and relationships solely within the
> State of California. [DA#38]

2. In the clause below, would it be enough to designate the law of the
   United States in a cross-border agreement? Explain your answer.

> GENERAL PROVISIONS This Agreement shall be governed by and
> construed under the laws of the United States of America. The
> parties intend to exclude the application of the United Nations Con-
> vention on Contracts for the International Sale of Goods to this
> Agreement and this Agreement shall not be subject to the terms
> thereof. [DA#37]

▶ **Exercise 13-7   Drafting "choice of language" clauses**

Analyze the choice of language clauses below and draft a more concise
single version. For each clause, identify anything that would be more appropriate to include in other provisions of the contract, rather than in the choice
of language clause.

> This Agreement, which is in the English language only (which shall
> be controlling), shall be governed in all respects by the laws of the
> State of Utah, U.S.A. (excluding principles of conflicts of law), as if
> this Agreement were executed in and to be wholly performed in the
> State of Utah. In construing this Agreement, none of the parties
> hereto shall have any term or provision construed against such
> party solely by reason of such party having drafted the same. The
> United Nations Convention on Contracts for the International Sale
> of Goods shall not apply to this Agreement. [DA# 7]

> This Agreement shall be made in the English language, which lan-
> guage shall be controlling in all respects, and all versions hereof in
> any language shall not be binding upon the Parties. All communi-
> cations and notices to be made pursuant to this Agreement, includ-
> ing all Attachments and related documentation, shall be in the
> English language. [DA#10]

Language. This Agreement shall be construed and interpreted in English, and any translation hereof to a language other than English shall be for convenience only. [DA#16]

ENGLISH LANGUAGE CONTROLS. This Agreement is entered into in the English language and in the event it is ever translated into another language and there is a dispute as to the meaning or interpretation of this Agreement as a result of the translation, the original English language version shall control. [DA#22]

Headings and Language—Headings and captions are for convenience only and are not to be used in the interpretation of this Agreement. The official text of this Agreement shall be the English language, and such English text shall be controlling in all respects, notwithstanding any translation hereof required under the laws or regulations of any other country. The parties undertake to translation hereof required under the laws or regulations of any other country. The parties undertake to use the English language in respect of all documents and communications contemplated hereby, except where another language must be used under the laws and regulations of another country. In any such case, a certified English translation shall be supplied to the other party by the party using such document or making such communication. [DA#25]

Follow-up:

Look up various Arbitration clauses throughout the three contract collections and find examples that describe which language should be used in the arbitration.

▶ **Exercise 13-8 Questions**

1. How does the placement of the adverb *only* change the meaning of the sentence?

Version 1:
The English language version shall **only** be used in the interpretation of the contract terms.

Version 2:
Only the English language version shall be used in the interpretation of the contract terms.

Continued

> **Version 3:**
> The English language version shall be used **only** in the interpretation of the contract terms.

2. What does the use of the pronoun *that* in this version of a clause imply?

> The Agreement **that** is in English shall be interpreted in accordance with the commonly understood meaning of the words and phrases hereof in the United States of America . . . . [DA#8]

▶ **Exercise 13-9   Comparing anti-assignment clauses**
Compare the difference in phrasing across all three assignment clauses.

	Who can do what?	Exception 1	Exception 2
	Neither Party may assign this Agreement or any rights hereunder . . . [DA#24]	. . . except upon prior written consent of the other Party, which consent may be withheld in such other Party's sole discretion. [DA#24]	Notwithstanding the foregoing, either Party may assign its rights and obligations to an Affiliate of such Party, although no such assignment shall relieve the Party of its primary responsibility for performance hereunder. [DA#24]
	Neither party may assign any of its rights or delegate any of its obligations under this Agreement . . . [DA#29]	. . . without the prior written consent of the other, in its sole discretion . . . [DA#29]	
	Neither party shall assign its rights nor delegate the performance of its duties or other obligations under this Agreement including any claims arising out of or connected with this Agreement . . . [DA#1]	. . . without the prior written consent of the other party. [DA#1]	

Continued

	Who can do what?	Exception 1	Exception 2
	This Agreement and the rights hereunder are not transferable or assignable by a party . . . .[DA#25]	. . . without the prior written consent of the other party. [DA#25]	. . . except for rights to payment and except to a person or entity who acquires all or sub-stantially all of the assets or business of Supplier, whether by sale, merger or otherwise. [DA#25]

Additional information:

	This Agreement shall be binding upon, and inure to the benefit of, the permitted assigns and successors of the Parties hereto. [DA# 24]	
	assign . . . and any attempt to do so will be void and will be a material breach of this Agreement. [DA#29]	

▶ **Exercise 13-10   Questions**

1. Is there a difference in meaning between *may assign* and *shall assign*? Explain your answer.
2. Does the expression *this Agreement or any rights hereunder* or *This Agreement and the rights hereunder* differ substantially from the expression *rights or . . . obligations under this Agreement*? Explain your answer.
3. What is the difference in the use of *assign, transfer,* and *delegate*?
4. What is the meaning of the word *otherwise* in the clause *whether by sale, merger or otherwise* in DA#25?
5. What is the difference between *void* and *voidable* in the following clause from DA#29?

> . . . and any attempt to do so will be void and will be a material breach of this Agreement.

Follow-up:

Go to contracts DA#1, DA#25, and DA#29 and see if you can find a clause similar to the following clause found in DA#24: *This Agreement shall be binding upon, and inure to the benefit of, the permitted assigns and successors of the Parties hereto.*

▶ **Exercise 13-11   Drafting severability clauses**

Compare the phrasing of the following five severability clauses across their individual components. Explain the difference in word choice across every sub-category.

	CA#9	CA#16	CA#11	CA#6	CA#12
If what	any paragraph, subparagraph, or provision of this Agreement or the application of such paragraph, subparagraph, or provision	any provision of this Consulting Agreement	any provision of this Agreement	any term, provision, covenant, or condition of this Agreement	any portion of this Consulting Agreement
Is held to be invalid	is held to be invalid	is found to be unenforceable	is found to be invalid or unenforceable	is held to be invalid, void, or unenforceable	is void or deemed to be unenforceable for any reason
By whom	by a court of competent jurisdiction	by an arbitrator or court of competent jurisdiction	under judicial decree or decision	by a court of competent jurisdiction	
What	the remainder of the Agreement, and the application of such paragraph, subparagraph, or provision to persons or circumstances other than those with respect to which it is held invalid	such provision	the remainder	the rest of this Agreement	the unenforceable portion
Shall happen	shall not be affected and shall be deemed modified to the extent necessary to allow enforceability of the provision as so limited, it being intended that the parties shall receive the benefits contemplated in this Consulting Agreement to the fullest extent permitted by law	shall be deemed modified to the extent necessary to allow enforceability of the provision as so limited, it being intended that the parties shall receive the benefits contemplated in this Consulting Agreement to the fullest extent permitted by law	will remain valid and enforceable according to its terms	shall remain in full force and effect	will be deemed severed from the remaining portions of this Consulting Agreement, which will otherwise remain in full force
	CA#9	CA#16	CA#11	CA#6	CA#12

▶ **Exercise 13-12 Analyze and rephrase**

The following clause contains two sentences, one that is 111 words and the other that is 35 words.

1. In the first sentence, decide which distinct topics the sentence covers and then split it up into shorter units of meaning.

> *Severability*
>
> The invalidity of any one or more of the words, phrases, sentences, clauses, provisions, sections or articles contained in this Agreement shall not affect the enforceability of the remaining portions of this Agreement or any part thereof, all of which are inserted conditionally on their being valid in law, and, in the event that any one or more of the words, phrases, sentences, clauses, provisions, sections or articles contained in this Agreement shall be declared invalid, this Agreement shall be construed as if such invalid word or words, phrase or phrases, sentence or sentences, clause or clauses, provision or provisions, section or sections or article or articles had not been inserted. If such invalidity is caused by length of time or size of area, or both, the otherwise invalid provision will be considered to be reduced to a period or area which would cure such invalidity. [CA#7]

2. Analyze the meaning of the following sentence:

> If such invalidity is caused by length of time or size of area, or both, the otherwise invalid provision will be considered to be reduced to a period or area which would cure such invalidity. [CA#7]

   a. What do you think the drafter meant by *invalidity caused by length of time or size of area*?
   b. Can you reduce a provision to a time period or an area?

▶ **Exercise 13-13 Drafting waiver clauses**

Look at the following four waiver clauses and decide whether the waiver clauses in the consulting contract examples are different from those in the distribution contract examples, and, if so, in what respect.

Then, compose one model waiver clause if it could be used in both types of contracts.

> Waiver. Any waiver of the provisions of this Consulting Agreement or of a party's rights or remedies under this Consulting Agreement

Continued

must be in writing to be effective. Failure, neglect, or delay by a party to enforce the provisions of this Consulting Agreement or its rights or remedies at any time, will not be construed as a waiver of such party's rights under this Consulting Agreement and will not in any way affect the validity of the whole or any part of this Consulting Agreement or prejudice such party's right to take subsequent action. No exercise or enforcement by either party of any right or remedy under this Consulting Agreement will preclude the enforcement by such party of any other right or remedy under this Consulting Agreement or that such party is entitled by law to enforce. [CA#18]

11.9 No Waiver. No failure by either Consultant or ABC to insist upon the strict performance by the other of any covenant, agreement, term or condition of this Agreement or to exercise the right or remedy consequent upon a breach thereof shall constitute a waiver of any such breach or of any such covenant, agreement, term or condition. No waiver of any breach shall affect or alter this Agreement, but each and every covenant, condition, agreement and term of this Agreement shall continue in full force and effect with respect to any other then existing or subsequent breach. [CA#6]

B. Waiver:
Failure by either party at any time to require performance by the other party or to claim a breach of any term of this Agreement will not be construed as a waiver of any right under this Agreement, will not affect any subsequent breach, will not affect the effectiveness of this Agreement or any part thereof, and will not prejudice either party as regards any subsequent action. [DA#18]

Waiver
16.04 The failure of either Party hereto at any time to require performance by the other Party of any provision of this Agreement shall not affect the right of such Party to require future performance of that provision. Except as otherwise provided herein, any waiver by either Party of any breach of any provision of this Agreement must be in writing to be effective and shall not be construed as a waiver of any continuing or succeeding breach of such provision or a waiver of any other right under this Agreement. [DA#24]

▶ **Exercise 13-14   Drafting counterpart clauses**

Review the counterpart provisions below and draft a model counterpart clause.

Are there any points in the provisions below, you would not include in a counterpart clause?

> This Agreement can be executed in identical duplicate copies. The parties will execute at least two identical original copies of this Agreement. Each identical counterpart shall be deemed an original, but all of which together will constitute one and the same instrument. [DA#5]

> This Agreement can be signed in two counterparts each of which will be deemed to be an original, but which together will form a single Agreement as if both parties had executed the same document. [DA#10]

> This Agreement can be executed in multiple counterparts, any one of which will be deemed an original, but all of which will constitute one and the same instrument. [DA#11]

> The Section and other headings contained in this Agreement are for reference purposes only and shall not in any way affect the meaning and interpretation of this Agreement. This Agreement may be executed in counterpart, each of which shall be deemed an original, but both of which together shall constitute one and the same instrument. The parties agree that facsimile signatures of the parties shall be binding. [DA#7]

> Counterparts. This Agreement can be executed in any number of counterparts. When each Party has signed and delivered to all other Parties at least one such counterpart, each of the counterparts will constitute one and the same instrument. [DA#12]

▶ **Exercise 13-15   Questions**

1. Try to find synonyms for the word *execute*, the way it is used in counterpart provisions. Then, look up the word *execute* in a legal dictionary and determine whether your suggested synonym(s) could replace *execute* as that word is used in the counterparts provision.
2. Look at how the word *original* is used in Exercise 13-14. Can you find synonyms in other examples, either in the preceding exercise or in contracts from the companion website (www.aspenlawschool.com/books/Adams)?

▶ **Exercise 13-16   Add to your vocabulary list**

Add at least ten new words to your vocabulary list from the "Contract Database" file on the companion website. Use the model from section 1.4 in Chapter 1 for guidance. Modify your old lists if you have new information regarding a word.

▶ **Exercise 13-17   Pegasus/Azteca deal—drafting the miscellaneous provisions**

Using your draft of the provisions from the Pegasus/Azteca deal in Exercise 9-17 in Chapter 9 and the term sheet found in the materials section of Chapter 10 on the companion website (which provides additional agreed terms for this deal), do the following:

1. Identify the agreed terms that are miscellaneous provisions.
2. For each identified term that is a miscellaneous provision.
   a. Identify the type of provision (see Chapter 7) that best expresses the agreed term.
   b. Draft the agreed term into contract provisions applying the concepts discussed in this chapter and in Chapters 4, 6, 8, and 9.
   c. Determine the order in which these provisions should be presented in the contract.

The End of the Contract

14.1 Drafting the concluding statement

The *concluding statement* formally ends the substantive provisions in the body of the contract and transitions the reader to the signature blocks. A simple statement can be sufficient, such as "Agreed" or "Agreed and signed by the parties on the date stated in the introduction." However, a more explanatory concluding statement might be necessary in any or all of the following circumstances:

(1) If the date of the contract is not stated in the introductory statement.
(2) If the contracting parties are signing the contract on different dates.
(3) If performance under the contract (the contract's **effective date**) begins on a date different from the date stated in the introductory statement or the date(s) when the contracting parties sign the contract.

Including multiple dates in a contract can lead to confusion as to which date is the contract date and which date is the contract's effective date. The concluding statement can be a good place to clarify all this. The following is a list of scenarios to consider when drafting a concluding statement.

♦ The contract date is the same as that stated in the introductory statement and the parties are signing on that date.

> The parties have signed this agreement on the date stated in the introductory statement.

♦ The contract date and the contract's effective date are when the last party signs the contract.

> The date of this agreement and the effective date of this agreement are the date the last party signed, as designated by the date adjacent to that party's signature.

♦ The contract date is the one stated in the introductory statement and the parties are signing on that date, but the effective date is another date expressly stated in the body of the agreement.

> The parties have signed this agreement on the date stated in the introductory statement, but the effective date of this agreement is the date stated in Section xx.

♦ The contract date is when the last party signs the contract, but the effective date is another date.

> The effective date of this agreement is the date stated in Section xx, and the date of this agreement is the date the last party signed, as designated by the date adjacent to that party's signature.

14.2 Signature blocks

The format of the signature line varies according to whether the signatory is a natural person or an entity. For a natural person, the name of the person (the same name used in the introductory statement) appears under the signature line:

> _____
> Karl J. Bauer

For signatories that are corporations or limited liability entities, the entity's full name (the same name used in the introductory statement) is inserted as a heading above the signature line. The signature line is prefaced by the word *By* to signify that the individual signing on behalf of the entity is acting in an official capacity as an agent for the entity. If the name and title of the individual is known, then this information should be typed underneath the signature line; otherwise, leave this information blank so it can be filled in at the time of signing.

> **Example for corporation**
>
> ABC Corporation, Inc.
> By: _____
>   Name:
>   Title:
>
> Hand Allied Services Co., Inc.
> By: _____
>   Name:
>   Title:

If the parties are signing on different dates, then a blank line for the date should appear next to each party's signature line.

> **Example for corporation, different dates**
>
> ABC Corporation, Inc.
> By: _____   _____
>   James Smith   Date
>   President
>
> Hand Allied Services, Co., Inc.
> By: _____   _____
>   Marie Hand   Date
>   President

14.3 Seals

In the United States, the requirement of a seal has been widely abolished, and where it is still in effect it is often limited to specific types of transactions.[1] You should check the law governing the contract to determine whether seals are still recognized. If seals are recognized, determine which documents must include a seal and the procedure that will satisfy the seal requirement. Traditionally, seals consisted of melted wax dripped onto the document and

---

1. *See, generally,* Richard A. Lord, *Williston on Contracts* § 2:17 (4th ed. 2012) (available at Westlaw, WILLSTN-CN § 2:17), for a table on the status of seals in each state, including any statutes of limitations and statutory citations.

impressed with the authenticating person's symbol or mark. In some states, the seal requirement has been simplified over time to consist merely of authenticating person's embossed mark or symbol on the document by merely typing the word *seal* on the document.[2]

At one time in the United States a contract under seal created an irrebuttable presumption of consideration. This is no longer the case. Now the contract must have an exchange of bargained-for promises or performance, both of which must have economic value, to satisfy the consideration requirement for an enforceable contract. In those states that still recognize seals, a document signed under seal might have a lengthier statute of limitations than a contract signed without a seal.[3]

14.4 Attachments

All schedules and exhibits referenced in the contract provisions must be attached to the back of the contract. **Schedules** typically contain information considered an integral part of the agreed terms of contract. Information placed in schedules might include (1) information subject to frequent changes, such as price lists; (2) lengthy, technical information, such as a long list of product models and stock numbers; or (3) confidential information that the parties might not want to share with an audience beyond those who need to know.

Exhibits usually contain information deemed not to be an integral part of the agreed terms but nevertheless relevant to the contract. For example, other related contracts (such as a promissory note attached to a loan agreement), forms, illustrations, and maps are examples of information that might be attached as an exhibit to a contract.

Schedules should be identified separately from exhibits. For example, if there are two schedules attached to a contract and three exhibits, the contract provisions will reference the schedules as "Schedule 1" and "Schedule 2" in the contract provisions, and the provisions will reference the exhibits as "Exhibit 1," "Exhibit 2," and "Exhibit 3." The previous examples provide a numerical sequence, though they could just as easily be given an alphabetical

---

2. *See Whittington v. Dragon Group L.L.C.*, 991 A.2d 1, 14 (Del. Super. 2009) (court found that the word *seal* typed next to an individual's signature is sufficient to create a sealed instrument, though).

3. *See, e.g., State* ex rel. *Sec. of Dept. of Transp. v. Regency Group, Inc.*, 598 A.2d 1123 (Del. Super. 1991) (court found that contracts under seal are not controlled by a 3-year statute of limitations mandated by state statute but are subject to the common law 20-year statute of limitations); *Osprey Portfolio, LLC v. Izett*, 32 A.2d 793, 798 (Pa. Super. 2011) (citing 42 Pa. Consol. Stat. Ann. § 5529(b)(1)) (court found that a guaranty, signed with the word *SEAL* printed next to the signature, was an instrument under seal and thus governed by a 20-year statute of limitations, as opposed to a 4-year statute of limitations for instruments not under seal).

sequence: "Schedule A" and "Schedule B"; "Exhibit A," "Exhibit B," and "Exhibit C." References to schedules and exhibits in the contract provisions can be underlined or placed in bold type to facilitate locating where they are mentioned in the contract.

> Distributor shall notify Manufacturer of orders of the Product by completing a written purchase order in the form attached as **Exhibit 3**. The current prices and minimum order quantities for each model of the Produce is shown in the attached **Schedule 5**.

Exercises

▶ **Exercise 14-1   Pegasus/Azteca deal—drafting the end of the contract**

Review your draft of the contract between Pegasus Snowboards Inc. and Deportes Azteca, Ltda., which you created during the course of the exercises in the preceding chapters. Draft the concluding statement and signature blocks.

Glossary of Terms

Acceleration clause: A contract **provision** that provides, upon an **event of default**, all sums payable by the **defaulting party** will or can become immediately due.

Acknowledgement: A **declaration** by a **contracting party** recognizing that stated facts, usually provided by another contracting party, are correct.

Active voice: A grammatical construction where the one performing the action of the verb is the subject of the sentence.

ADR: *See* **alternative dispute resolution.**

ADR institution: An established organization offering **ADR** services for **arbitration, mediation,** and other ADR processes; offered services might include providing model procedural rules, model ADR clauses for contracts, facilities, and lists of persons registered to serve as **arbitrators, conciliators,** or **mediators.**

ADR provisions: Contract **provisions** stating alternative ways for the parties to resolve disputes other than through formal litigation in the courts, such as through **informal negotiations, mediation,** and **arbitration.**

Ad hoc mediation: A mediation process where disputing parties create and use their own process rules or adapt an ADR institution's mediation rules to suit their particular needs and goals.

Affiliate: An entity that controls another entity (e.g., subsidiary), that is controlled by another entity (e.g., parent company), or that is related to another entity (e.g., sibling) because both are controlled by a parent company.

Agreed term: An aspect of the **contracting parties'** anticipated contractual relationship that the parties have negotiated and upon which the parties have reached an agreement.

Alternative dispute resolution (ADR): A means for resolving disputes other than through formal litigation in the courts (e.g., **informal negotiations; mediation; arbitration**).

Ambiguity: An uncertainty of meaning or intention created when a word, phrase, or **provision** is capable of two or more reasonable but contradictory meanings. *See also* **semantic ambiguity; syntactic ambiguity;** or **contextual ambiguity.**

Amendment clause: A contract **provision** that states the method for amending the contract. *See also* **no oral modification clause.**

Anti-amendment clause: *See* **no oral modification clause.**

Anti-assignment clause: A contract **provision** that prohibits or restricts one or more of the **contracting parties** from transferring its **rights** under the contract to **third parties.** *See also* **assignment clause.**

Anti-delegation clause: A contract **provision** that prohibits or restricts one or more of the **contracting parties** from delegating its **obligations** under the contract to **third parties.** *See also* **delegation clause.**

Anti-waiver clause: *See* **no oral waiver clause.**

Arbitral award: A decision rendered by an **arbitrator** that settles the parties' dispute. The decision can be binding or non-binding on the disputing parties; *see* **binding arbitration** and **non-binding arbitration.**

Arbitration: An ADR method where the disputing parties present their respective positions (sometimes through a hearing where they provide evidence) to **arbitrators**, who will render a decision for resolving the dispute.

Arbitrator: An impartial third party who presides over an **arbitration** and renders a decision for resolving the dispute. Also referred to as a **neutral**.

Assignee: The party in an **assignment** who is receiving property or **rights** from the **assignor**.

Assignment: The transfer of **rights** or property from an **assignor** to an **assignee**.

Assignment clause: A contract **provision** that states whether one or more of the **contracting parties** has the power to transfer its **rights** under the contract to **third parties**. *See also* **anti-assignment clause**.

Assignor: The party in an **assignment** who is transferring its property or **rights** under a contract to a **third party** (commonly referred to as the **assignee**).

Attachments: Documents, lists, maps, and other information that are **exhibits** or **schedules** attached to the back of a contract.

Background: *See* **recitals**.

Basket: In an **indemnification**, a **provision** providing for the **indemnitor's** responsibility for certain losses if the losses exceed a stated amount.

Beginning of a contract: The first part of a contract, typically containing the title of the contract, the **introductory statement**, **recitals**, and **transitional clause**.

Binding arbitration: Disputing parties are required to abide by the **arbitral award** rendered by the **arbitrator(s)**.

Blue-line: The act of striking out unreasonable terms of a contract **provision**. *See also* **blue pencil doctrine**.

Blue pencil doctrine: A principle observed by some U.S. courts that supports deleting unreasonable words of a contract **provision** if those words are grammatically separable from the rest of the provision, and enforcing the remaining words in the provision.

Boilerplate provisions: *See* **miscellaneous provisions**.

Breach: Failure by a **promisor** to perform its **obligation**.

Bring-down provision: A contract **provision** requiring that a **representing party** restate a **representation** made at an earlier date.

Canons of contract construction: Principles of contract interpretation that courts may use to help interpret contract language (e.g., *contra proferentem*; *ejusdem generis*; *noscitur a sociis*).

Cap: In an **indemnification**, limits an **indemnitor's** responsibility to losses under a certain stated amount.

Choice of language clause: A contract **provision** that identifies the language(s) used for the contract and which language will be controlling in the event of a discrepancy or dispute.

CISG: *See* **Convention on Contracts for the International Sales of Goods**.

Circular definition: A statement providing the meaning of a **defined term** that uses the defined term as part of the definitional statement; therefore, it usually does not provide an adequate explanation of the defined term's meaning. (For example, "'liabilities' means 'Distributor's liabilities.'")

Clause: In contracts often used to refer to a particular type of contract provision (e.g., **severability clause**; **non-compete clause**); in grammar used to refer to a sentence construction that contains a subject and a verb (*see also* **dependent clause** and **independent clause**).

Closing: A meeting where the **contracting parties** sign documents and, if relevant, the business deal is funded. If the deal involves a sale of property, the seller will transfer ownership of property to the buyer in exchange for the buyer's payment of the purchase price.

Closing deliveries: The items for which a **contracting party** will be responsible to bring to the **closing**.

Closing provision: A contract **provision** addressing aspects of a **closing**, including time, place, date, and **closing deliveries**.

Collateral: Property or goods pledged or given to **guarantee** the **performance** of an **obligation**.

Conciliation: A non-binding **ADR** method where the disputing parties seek to resolve their differences through mutual collaboration and problem solving with a **conciliator**.

Conciliator: An objective **third party** who advises and guides disputing parties toward resolving their dispute in a **conciliation** and may make proposals to settle the dispute. Also referred to as a **neutral**.

Concluding statement: Signals the end of the **middle of the contract** and provides a transition to the **signature blocks**.

Condition: A possible future occurrence that, if it occurs, will result in a consequence that is either a **condition precedent** or a **condition subsequent**.

Condition precedent: A possible future occurrence that, if it occurs, will result in a consequence that creates an **obligation**, a **right**, a **discretionary power**, or a situation.

Condition subsequent: A possible future occurrence that, if it occurs, will result in a consequence that terminates an **obligation**, a **right**, a **discretionary power**, or a situation.

Confidentiality clause: A contract **provision** that restricts a **contracting party** from disclosing certain private information about another party, unless explicit exceptions apply.

Consequential damages: Indirect losses resulting from an **event of default**.

Consideration: An exchange of promises or performance bargained for by the **contracting parties**.

Contextual ambiguity: A situation created when two or more provisions in a contract conflict with each other.

Contextual definition: A definition of a defined term that is inserted as part of a sentence where the defined term is first applied. *See also* **embedded definition**.

Contra proferentem: A **canon of construction**; ambiguous words or phrases are construed against the drafter.

Contract term: The duration of a contract.

Contracting party: An individual or entity signing the contract.

Convention on Contracts for the International Sale of Goods (CISG): A treaty to which the United States and other countries are signatories, governing the cross-border sale of commercial goods; the CISG is law in all fifty states of the United States and, except for limited circumstances, will supersede any state-adopted **UCC** rules when a transaction involves the international sale of goods.

Core provisions: Contract **provisions** that are not **exit provisions**, **alternative dispute resolution provisions**, or **miscellaneous provisions**, and that state specific aspects of the **contracting parties'** contractual relationship.

Counterparts clause: A contract **provision** that addresses the circumstance when the **contracting parties** sign the contract at different times and places, including whether a delivered contract signed by a party can be taken together with other copies signed and delivered by other parties to constitute a completed executed original.

Coupled synonym: Two words with the same meaning used together to express a thought. Coupled synonyms create a **redundancy** and thus should be avoided in contract drafting.

Covenant: *See* **obligation**.

Covenant not to compete: *See* **non-competition clause**.

Cure: To correct or fix a problem that, if left uncorrected or unfixed, will cause an **event of default**.

Damages: A monetary sum that a **promisee** is entitled to receive for a **promisor's** failure to **perform** its **obligation**.

Deal: As used in transactional work, an agreement between two or more parties, to transact business for their mutual benefit.

Declaration: A formal statement expressly stating that the facts referenced in the statement are true (e.g., **representation**; **acknowledgement**).

Defaulting party: A **contracting party** that is responsible for or creates a circumstance that results in a **potential event of default** or an **event of default**.

Defined term: A word or phrase that is given a unique meaning in a contract. A definition is provided for the word or phrase the first time it is mentioned in the contract. Throughout the contract, the first letter of each word in the defined term is capitalized. *See also* **one-shot definition**; **circular definition**; **embedded definition**; **contextual definition**; and **definition sentence**.

Definition section: A section or part of the contract listing all the **defined terms** used in the contract along with their respective definitions.

Definition sentence: A statement providing the definition of a **defined term** that is either (i) inserted as a separate sentence in the section of the contract where the

defined term is first applied (*see also* **embedded definition**) or (ii) inserted as a sentence where the **defined term** is listed in the **definition section** of the contract.

Delegate *(noun)*: An individual or entity assuming the **obligations** of a **delegating party**.

Delegate *(verb)*: To designate another to perform on the **delegating party's** behalf

Delegating party: The party delegating its **obligations** under a contract to a **third party** (commonly referred to as a **delegate**).

Delegation clause: A contract **provision** that states whether the **contracting parties**, or any of them, have the power to delegate their respective **obligations** under the contract to **third parties**. *See also* **anti-delegation clause**.

Dependent clause: A sentence with a subject and a verb that cannot stand by itself. It needs an **independent clause** for grammatical and logical completion.

Disclaimer of warranty: A contract **provision** that limits or repudiates a **promisor's** liability for breaching its **express warranty** or **implied warranty**.

Discretionary power: As used in this book, a contract **provision** that gives one or more of the **contracting parties** the freedom of choice to act or to refrain from acting.

Draft: In transactional work, either (1) a noun meaning either (i) a suggested version of a document, or (ii) a written order by one party instructing another party to pay money from an account to a third party; or (2) a verb meaning to write a suggested version of a document.

Drafter: A person who writes a version of a contract.

Drop-dead date: A date by which the **closing** must occur or the transaction contemplated by the contract is terminated.

Due diligence: As used in transactional work, conducting an investigation of a target company, property, or security to evaluate it for purposes of whether to move forward with acquiring it.

Effective date: The date when the contract **provisions** go into operation.

***Ejusdem generis*:** A **canon of construction**; general words following specifically listed words include only those items similar in nature to the listed words. (For example, if a contract provision referenced the distribution of corn, melon, beans, and peas, then *produce* would not include eggs because this is produced by an animal, not a plant.)

Embedded definition: A definition of a **defined term** that is either (i) inserted as part of a sentence where the defined term is first applied (**contextual definition**) or (ii) inserted as a separate sentence in the section of the contract where the term is first applied (**definition sentence**).

End of the contract: Found after the **middle of the contract**, this part of the contract is comprised of the **concluding statement**, **signature blocks**, and, if any, **attachments**.

Endgame provisions: *See* **exit provisions**.

Enjoin: To prohibit by an **injunction**.

Entire agreement clause: *See* **merger clause**.

Enumeration: As used in contract drafting, a format for listing items for purposes of large-scale organization and small-scale organization.

Escrow: An arrangement in which a neutral **third party** holds money, documents, or property in trust and delivers the items to a designated party upon the occurrence of an event or satisfaction of a condition.

Event of default: An occurrence that gives rise to the **non-defaulting party's** right to seek **remedies** from the **defaulting party**.

Exception: A situation excluded from a contract **provision**.

Exhibit: Information attached to the back of the contract that is not deemed to be an integral part of the contract provisions but nevertheless is relevant to the contract, such as promissory notes, forms, illustrations, and maps.

Exit provisions: Contract **provisions** addressing when a contract ends prematurely as well as the parties' obligations and rights when the contract ends prematurely or naturally. Also called **endgame provisions**.

Expiration: The ending of a **contract term** as anticipated and hoped for by the parties. *See also* **natural ending**; **termination**.

Express warranty: A **warranty** explicitly stated in the contract.

FAA: *See* **Federal Arbitration Act**.

Federal Arbitration Act (FAA): U.S. (federal) codified law governing arbitration in contract disputes arising from interstate commerce.

FOB: An abbreviation for *free on board* or *freight on board.* FOB addresses the **contracting parties'** duties relating to the shipment and delivery of goods, including which party pays for the shipping costs, method of delivery, payment, and liability, as well as designating the point at which responsibility for the goods is transferred to another party. FOB rules vary and depend on the governing law.

Force majeure clause: A contract **provision** that excuses a **contracting party's** inability to **perform** certain **obligations** when nonperformance is due to circumstances beyond the party's control and are usually unforeseeable.

Forum non conveniens: A principle that permits a court to decline exercising jurisdiction over a case, even though the court has personal jurisdiction over the parties and subject matter jurisdiction over the claim, if it determines that another court is a more appropriate forum.

Forum selection clause: A contract **provision** that designates the court or courts where disputes will be decided.

Fraudulent misrepresentation: An untrue **representation** made by a **representing party** who knows the statement is untrue or makes the statement in reckless disregard of whether it is true.

Fully integrated agreement: As it relates to the **parol evidence rule**, a written contract that is a complete, exclusive, and final expression of the **contracting parties'** agreement.

General provisions: *See* **miscellaneous provisions**.

Good faith: In contract drafting, a **contracting party's** honest conduct and fair dealing with the other **contracting parties** in keeping with the standards of its trade.

Governing law clause: A contract **provision** stipulating the rules that will be used for interpreting the contract and filling in gaps left by the contract provisions.

Grace period: In **potential events of default**, a span of time during which a **defaulting party** has the opportunity to **cure** a problem that, if left uncorrected or unfixed, will cause an **event of default**.

Guarantee: A promise that a contract, action, or other matter will be carried out as stated.

Guaranty: A written document providing that an individual or entity promises to pay or otherwise perform another's **obligation** in the event that **obligor** fails to do so; the document serves to **guarantee** the **performance** of another's obligation.

Holding party: For purposes of this book, a party providing private information that is subject to a **confidentiality clause**.

Housekeeping provisions: *See* **miscellaneous provisions**.

Implied warranty: A **warranty** that is imposed by the law governing the contract, even though no explicit language in the contract provides for the warranty (e.g., an implied warranty of merchantability; implied warranty of fitness for a particular purpose).

Incidental damages: Losses incurred when dealing with a **breach**.

INCOTERMS®: A collection of definitions and rules, published by the International Chamber of Commerce, particularly addressing the international transport and delivery of goods.

Indemnification: A contract **provision** or standalone agreement requiring the **indemnitor** to pay for certain losses or claims of the **indemnitee** and, in some instances, defend the **indemnitee** against certain actions brought by third parties.

Indemnify: To reimburse the **indemnitee** for certain **damages** sustained by it.

Indemnitee: The party protected from losses or claims under an **indemnification**.

Indemnitor: The party undertaking the duty of **indemnification**.

Independent clause: A complete sentence that includes a subject and a verb; in contrast to a **dependent clause**, it can stand alone and needs no other clause for completion.

Informal negotiations: The disputing parties attempt to resolve their dispute through direct negotiations without using a neutral third party to help facilitate or oversee the negotiations.

Injunction: A court order directing or prohibiting an action.

Innocent misrepresentation: An untrue **representation** made by a **representing party** who had no duty to ascertain the truth of the **representation**.

Integration clause: *See* **merger clause**.

Introductory statement: Often the first paragraph of a contract that introduces the **contracting parties** and sometimes states the date of the contract.

Joint venture: A for-profit business enterprise conducted by a group of people, entities, or both; it is of limited duration and is created for a specific purpose.

Knowledge qualifier: A word or phrase that limits a **representation** to the **representing party's** awareness of the facts.

Legalese: Vocabulary used in the legal profession that sounds lawyerly but provides no legally enforceable power. Legalese can confuse or make meanings unclear, and so legalese should be omitted from the contract and replaced with simple vocabulary that communicates the meaning more clearly and precisely.

Limitation on damages clause: A contract **provision** that limits **damages** that can be recovered for a **breach**.

Liquidated damage clause: A contract **provision** that sets in advance a **damage** amount that will be paid by a **defaulting party** upon an **event of default**.

Materiality qualifier: A word or phrase in a **representation** that reduces the risk of the **representing party** (e.g., material; material adverse effect).

Mediation: An ADR method where the disputing parties seek to resolve their differences through mutual collaboration and problem solving with a **mediator**.

Mediator: An impartial **third party** who advises and guides disputing parties toward resolving the dispute in **mediation**. Also referred to as a **neutral**.

Merger clause: A contract **provision** stating that the written contract expresses the **contracting parties'** complete, exclusive, and final agreement, taking the place of all previous negotiations, communications, and agreements. The aim of the clause is to invoke the **parol evidence rule**, which would bar a party in a contract dispute from admitting any oral statement or writings made prior to signing the contract and any oral statements made when signing the contract. Also commonly referred to as an **entire agreement clause** or an **integration clause**.

Middle of the contract: Found between the **beginning of the contract** and the **end of the contract**, this part of the contract is comprised of **core provisions, exit provisions, dispute resolution provisions,** and **miscellaneous provisions**.

Miscellaneous provisions: Found at the end of the **middle of the contract,** these provisions address matters not covered elsewhere in the contract, including administration, enforcement, interpretation, and execution of the contract. Also commonly referred to as **boilerplate provisions, general provisions, housekeeping provisions,** or **standard provisions**.

Misrepresentation: An untrue **representation**. *See also* **fraudulent misrepresentation; innocent misrepresentation;** and **negligent misrepresentation**.

Monetary provision: A contract **provision** that addresses aspects of payment for services rendered or for property received.

Natural ending: The ending of a **contract term** as anticipated and hoped for by the parties.

Negligent misrepresentation: An untrue **representation** made by a **representing party** who fails in its duty to use reasonable care to ascertain and communicate the truth of the statement.

Neutral: An impartial third party who either (1) advises disputing parties and helps facilitate a resolution to the dispute (*see* **mediator** and **conciliator**) or (2) presides over an **arbitration** and renders a decision for resolving the dispute (*see* **arbitrator**).

New York Convention: The 1958 Convention on the Recognition of Enforcement of Foreign Arbitral Awards, with at least 146 signatory countries, provides for a signatory's recognition and enforcement of foreign arbitral awards with only limited exceptions.

NOM: *See* **no oral modification clause**.

No oral modification (NOM) clause: A contract **provision** stating that any amendments to the contract must be in writing. Also commonly referred to as an **anti-amendment clause**. *See also* **modification clause**.

No oral waiver clause: A contract **provision** stating that any **waiver** must be in writing. Also commonly referred to as an **anti-waiver clause**. *See also* **waiver clause**.

Nominalization: The act of converting a noun, adjective, or adverb into a noun as part of a longer phrase (e.g., turning the verb "to agree" into a noun in the phrase "making an agreement").

Non-binding arbitration: Disputing parties are not required to abide by the **arbitral award** rendered by the **arbitrator(s)**.

Non-competition clause: A contract **provision** restraining a **contracting party** from competing with another party's business. Also referred to as a *covenant not to compete*.

Non-defaulting party: A contracting party who receives the right to exercise remedies from the **defaulting party** upon an **event of default**.

Noscitur a sociis: A **canon of construction**; the meaning of a word or phrase may be known from the words surrounding it. (For example, in a lease for office space, the landlord has promised to keep all floors, stairs and hallways free of obstruction, then a floor used exclusively for storage is not included because stairs and hallways refer to passageways.)

Notice provision: A contract **provision** that establishes a method for the **contracting parties** to communicate with each other during the **contract term** and stipulates when the communication is deemed received.

Novation: An agreement where a party to a contract agrees to discharge a **delegating party's** obligations under the contract in consideration for a **delegate** undertaking performance of the **delegating party's obligations**.

Obligation: A **promise** made by one or more of the **contracting parties** giving rise to a duty in that party or parties to take action or to refrain from taking action. Also referred to as a **covenant**.

Obligee: *See* **promisee**.

Obligor: *See* **promisor**.

One-shot definition: When a **defined term** is used only once in a contract.

Operative phrase: As used in this book, a particular group of words reserved for and consistently used in a contract to express a particular type of contract **provision**. Using an operative phrase can help clarify the **contracting parties'** intent. (For example, this book's recommended use of *except as otherwise provided* or *notwithstanding anything to the contrary* as two examples of phrases that can express an exception.)

Operative word: As used in this book, a particular word reserved for and consistently used in a contract to express a particular type of contract **provision**. Using an operative word can help clarify the **contracting parties'** intent. (For example, this book's recommended use of *shall* whenever stating an **obligation** or this book's recommended use of *may* whenever stating a **discretionary power**.)

PER: *See* **Parol evidence rule**.

Parol evidence: Oral statements or writings made prior to the **contracting parties'** signing of the contract, and oral statements made at the time of the parties sign the contract.

Parol evidence rule (PER): A common law rule recognized in the United States. For a **fully integrated agreement**, **parol evidence** cannot be admitted to contradict, supplement, or explain anything in a written contract. For a **partially integrated agreement**, parol evidence (i) cannot be admitted to contradict, supplement, or explain a **term** that is completely, exclusively, and finally expressed; but (ii) can be admitted to supplement or explain a **term** that is not completely, exclusively, and finally expressed to the extent the evidence is consistent with other terms in the contract. If parol evidence is admitted under item (ii) in the previous sentence, the evidence will only be recognized as part of the contract if it is found believable.

Parri passu: Latin, meaning "on equal footing." Those in an identified group are treated with equal rights and without priority over others in the same group. (For example, in a loan arrangement, two or more lenders are in *pari passu* if they share equal **rights** to a pro rata share to payments and equal priority regarding **collateral**.)

Partially integrated agreement: As it relates to the **parole evidence rule**, a written contract containing some **provisions** that are the complete, exclusive, and final expression of the **contracting parties'** agreement, but other provisions are incomplete or **agreed terms** are missing.

Passive voice: A grammatical construction where the one receiving the action of the verb is the subject of the sentence.

Perform: To act or to refrain from acting.

Performance: The act of carrying out an action or the act of refraining from taking an action.

Performative: As used in this book, a contract **provision** stating actions taking place simultaneously with the **contracting parties'** signing of the contract. *See also* **primary performative.**

Potential event of default: A circumstance that is not deemed serious enough to create an immediate **event of default.** The event of default occurs only if certain conditions are satisfied. These conditions vary, though they usually include written notice to the **defaulting party** of the **non-defaulting party's** intent to end the contract and exercise other **remedies.** Sometimes this notice will give the defaulting party a **grace period** to **cure** the problem.

Precedent: As used in contract drafting, a model form contract or a contract drafted for another transaction used as a starting point for drafting the present contract.

Premature ending: An ending to a contract prior to the completion of the **contract term** through the **contracting parties'** mutual consent, due to the actions of a **contracting party** (e.g., **breach**; **misrepresentation**), or by operation of law (e.g., business declared illegal; death; legal incapacity).

Primary obligations: As used in this book, **obligations** establishing the **consideration** for the contract.

Primary performative: As used in this book, a **performative** inserted at or near the beginning of the **core provisions** that expresses the essence of the **contracting parties' consideration** for the contract.

Procedural statement: As used in this book, a contract **provision** that manages or facilitates the contract's administration.

Promise: As used in this book, a statement that creates a duty in the **contracting party** to **perform** as stated.

Promisee: An individual or entity entitled to **performance** of an **obligation.** Also referred to as an **obligee.**

Promisor: An individual or entity undertaking a duty to carry out a **performance.** Also referred to as an **obligor.**

Provision: In contract drafting, a sentence, paragraph, section, or subsection of a contract that addresses an aspect of the **contracting parties'** contractual relationship.

Punitive damages: Damages awarded to the prevailing party in a legal action, in addition to actual damages, that are designed to punish the wrongdoer for its reckless or malicious conduct and to discourage future wrongful conduct.

Reasonable replacement approach: A principle observed by some U.S. courts that condones deleting invalid words in a contract **provision** and replacing them with reasonable **terms** under the circumstances.

Recitals: A series of fact statements found between the **introductory statement** and **transitional clause** that might include a statement of the **contracting parties'** intentions for entering into the contract, important historical background relating to the business deal, or a statement of the contract's intended purpose. Also referred to as **background.**

Redundancy: Needless repetition. *See* **coupled synonym.**

Remedial provision: A contract **provision** stating a **remedy.**

Remedy: As used in contracts, a means of providing relief to a **promisee** for a **promisor's** failure to **perform** an **obligation.** (For example, **specific performance** or **damages.**)

Representation: As used in this book, a contract **provision** that is a statement of fact (past or present, or both) made by a **contracting party** with the intent to induce another party to enter into the contract.

Representing party: As used in this book, a **contracting party** that makes a **representation.**

Rescission: A **remedy** permitting a **contracting party** to avoid or undo the contract; rescission comes with **restitution.**

Restatement of the Law of Contracts: A series of contract rules that are not binding on any court but can serve as a basis for making common law. There are two series of these Restatements, the first treatise was published in 1929 and a second edition, called the Restatement (Second) of the Law of Contracts, was published in 1979. Both Restatements were prepared by the American Law Institute, an organization of lawyers, law professors, and judges. The rules are intended to provide general principles of contract law, which state courts widely use to create common law.

Restitution: A **remedy** requiring the return of any property received by **contracting parties** under the contract or, if this is not possible, the monetary value of the property.

Right: The entitlement to a **promisor's performance** of an **obligation**.

Schedule: Information considered an integral part of the contract but is attached to the back of the contract, as opposed to inserting the information in a contract **provision**, usually because it is (i) information subject to frequent changes, such as price lists; (ii) lengthy, technical information, such as a long list of product models and stock numbers; or (iii) confidential information that the **contracting parties** might not want to share with an audience beyond those who need to know.

Seal: Still used in some jurisdictions to authenticate a document or a contracting party's signature; a symbol or mark traditionally consisting of melted wax dripped onto a contract and impressed with the authenticating person's symbol or mark, but more recently simplified in some jurisdictions to merely an embossed mark or symbol of the authenticating person or the typed word *seal* next to the signature.

Semantic ambiguity: A situation created when a symbol or word is capable of two or more reasonable but contradictory meanings.

Severability clause: A contract **provision** addressing what should happen if a provision in the contract is found unenforceable.

Specific performance: A **remedy** ordered by a court that requires a **promisor** to perform its **obligation**.

Signature blocks: Found after the **concluding statement**, this section presents the name of the parties and signature lines for each contracting party; under certain circumstances, it includes a date line adjacent to each signature line for that party to complete upon signing.

Standard provisions: *See* **miscellaneous provisions**.

Statute of frauds: A common law rule recognized in the United States mandating that certain contracts are unenforceable unless recorded in a signed writing.

Statute of limitations: A law that imposes a time limit for suing on a claim.

Successors and assigns clause: A contract **provision** that aims (i) to bind a transferring party's successors and **assignees** to the provisions of the contract, and (ii) to restate the common law by binding the non-transferring party to perform its obligations in favor of the **assignees**.

Survival clause: A contract **provision** that addresses the continuation of **representations** or **obligations** beyond **closing** or a contract's **termination**.

Syntactic ambiguity: A situation created when the relationship between words and phrases in a sentence gives rise to two or more reasonable but contradictory meanings.

Tabulation: A formatting technique that sets off **enumerated** items from the surrounding text by placing it in a separate, indented block.

Term: In contract drafting, *term* can refer to (i) a word or phrase (e.g., **defined term**); (ii) an important requirement or condition of the parties' agreement (*see also* **agreed term**; **terms of agreement**), or (iii) the duration of a contract (*see also* **contract term**).

Terms of agreement: *See* **agreed term**.

Termination: The ending of a contract, including a **natural ending** (also referred to as an **expiration**) or **premature** ending.

Third party: In contract drafting, an individual or entity who is not one of the **contracting parties**.

Tipping basket: In an **indemnification**, the **indemnitor** will be responsible for all losses if losses exceed a stated amount.

Transitional clause: A short statement that signals the end of the **recitals** and the beginning of the **middle of the contract**.

UCC: *See* **Uniform Commercial Code.**

UNCITRAL: The United Nations Commission on International Trade Law.

UNIDROIT: *Institut International Pour L'Unification du Droit Privé* (International Institute for the Unification of Private Law). It is an organization, with over 63 "Member States" worldwide (including the United States), with an aim "to study needs and methods for modernising, harmonising and co-ordinating private and in particular commercial law as between States and groups of States and to formulate uniform law instruments, principles and rules to achieve those objectives." *UNIDROIT: An Overview*, http://www.unidroit.org/dynasite.cfm?dsmid=103284 (accessed Dec. 15, 1012).

UNIDROIT Principles of International Commercial Law: A model set of contract rules for all types of international transactions, drafted by a group of international experts.

Uniform Commercial Code (UCC): A series of rules, drafted by lawyers and legal scholars, governing different types of business transactions; for example, Article 2 of the UCC focuses on rules for transactions involving the sale of goods. Every state in the United States has adopted some variation of the UCC as law.

Uniform Trade Secrets Act (UTSA): A set of rules governing trade secrets that defines trade secrets, designates what constitutes misappropriation of trade secrets, and provides **remedies** for the misappropriation of trade secrets. Forty-seven states and the District of Columbia have adopted the UTSA, each with some modifications.

UTSA: *See* **Uniform Trade Secrets Act.**

Vagueness: A situation where a word or phrase creates a measure of uncertainty but does not create an **ambiguity**.

Verbose: Using too many words to communicate a thought.

Waiver: A **contracting party's** (i) relinquishment of its election to claim damages for another party's breach, or (ii) excuse of a delay or excuse of a non-occurrence of a **condition precedent** to **performance.**

Waiver clause: A contract **provision** stating the effect of a **waiver** and the process for waiving. *See also* **no oral waiver provision.**

Waiving: The act of giving a **waiver.**

Warranty: A **promise**, express or implied, made by a **contracting party** that the subject of the **promise** is as stated and will continue to remain so. *See also* **express warranty** and **implied warranty.**

Zero-based drafting: Drafting provisions without the aid of **precedent**. Also commonly called drafting "from scratch."

Index